German Universities
Past and Future

POLICIES AND INSTITUTIONS
Germany, Europe, and Transatlantic Relations

Published in Association with The American Institute for Contemporary German Studies (AICGS), Washington, D.C.
General Editor: **Carl Lankowski**, Research Director of the AICGS

Advisory Board:
Christopher Allen, University of Georgia
Leslie Adelson, Cornell University
David Audretsch, Wissenschaftszentrum, Berlin
David Calleo, SAIS, Johns Hopkins University
Marion Deshmukh, George Mason University
Claudia Dziobek, International Monetary Fund
Barry Eichengreen, University of California at Berkeley
Claudia Koonz, Duke University
Andrei Markovits, University of California at Santa Cruz
Wolfgang Reinicke, The Brookings Institution
Angela Stent, Georgetown University

Titles in Preparation
GERMAN PARTIES IN TRANSITION
Edited by **Christopher S. Allen**
1998   ISBN 1-57181-127-3

GERMANY IN THE SHAPING OF THE NEW EUROPE
Edited by **Michael Kreile** and **Carl Lankowski**
1998   ISBN 1-57181-120-6

EUROPEANIZING SECURITY?
NATO and an Integrating Europe
Edited by **Carl Lankowski** and **Simon Serfaty**
1999   ISBN 1-57181-129-X

GERMAN UNIVERSITIES PAST AND FUTURE

Crisis or Renewal?

Edited by

Mitchell G. Ash
The University of Iowa

Berghahn Books
Providence • Oxford

First published in 1997 by
Berghahn Books

Editorial offices:
165 Taber Avenue, Providence, RI 02906, USA
3, NewTec Place, Magdalen Road, Oxford, OX4 1RE, UK

© The American Institute for Contemporary German Studies 1997

Library of Congress Cataloging-in-Publication Data

```
German universities past and future : crisis or renewal? / edited by
Mitchell G. Ash.
      p.   cm. -- (Policy and institutions)
   Revised versions of papers and invited commentaries, as well as
selections from the discussion, of a conference held at the School
of Advanced International Studies of the Johns Hopkins University,
November 1995, and sponsored by the Harry and Helen Gray Humanities
Program of the American Institute for Contemporary German Studies.
   Includes bibliographical references (p.  ) and index.
   ISBN 1-57181-070-6 (alk. paper)
   1. Universities and colleges--Germany--History--Congresses.
2. Education, Higher--Aims and objectives--Germany--Congresses.
3. Education, Higher--Political aspects--Germany--Congresses.
4. Humboldt, Wilhelm, Freiherr von, 1767-1835--Congresses.   I. Ash,
Mitchell G.   II. American Institute for Contemporary German Studies.
III. Series.
LA728.G473   1997
378.43--dc21
                                                        96-52552
                                                            CIP
```

British Library Cataloguing in Publication Data

A catalogue record for this book is available
from the British Library.

Printed in the United States on acid-free paper.

CONTENTS

Contents

INTRODUCTION

⬭

Mitchell G. Ash

In the late 1980s, commentators generally agreed that West German universities were in a state of crisis. Widely diagnosed symptoms of that crisis included lack of resources to respond to growing numbers of students, inadequate maintenance or expansion of buildings and equipment, overburdened senior faculty, insufficient positions for qualified younger scholars, and, last but not least, a widespread sense of malaise due to the absence of a generally accepted sense of purpose. During the first few years after unification, talk of "renewal" took center stage; however, the term was and continues to be applied mainly to the restructuring of universities in East Germany – a restructuring carried out largely in the image of the very West German system that had been agreed to be in crisis a short time before. After such a turn of events, one might expect views of universities throughout Germany to become more optimistic. Instead, the crisis discussion has resumed. The titles of recent popular books and newspaper articles – "The Uncontemporary University"; "Can the University Still Be Saved?"; "Rotten to the Core?" – make this point clearly enough.[1] How can or

1. J. Mittlestraß, *Die unzeitgemäße Universität* (Frankfurt a.M., 1994); M. Daxner, *Ist die Universität noch zu retten?* (Reinbek bei Hamburg, 1996); P. Glotz, *Im Kern verrottet? Fünf vor zwölf an Deutschlands Universitäten* (Stuttgart, 1996). See also: W. Hoffmann, "Die Elite hat abgewirtschaftet. Hochschule: Knappe Finanzen, Studentenschwemme und egoistische Professoren ruinieren das Prunkstück des deutschen Bildungssystems," *Die Zeit*, Vol. 50, No. 13 (24 March 1995): 34; "'Überfüllt und Kaputt,'" *Der Spiegel*, 42/1995, 58-66. For

should German universities be reformed to deal with the challenges of a new century; will the needed changes be possible? Answering these questions will have significant implications for the vitality of cultural institutions in the new Germany.

Unified Germany is also constructing a new identity, an effort in which reconsiderations of Germany's past are playing a significant role. For German universities, too, images from the past are central to current efforts to establish new or to reformulate older institutional structures, and are particularly prominent in ongoing discussions of the meaning and purpose of higher education. To gain perspectives for the future, it is therefore appropriate to take the long view that historical research can offer. It is also necessary to broaden the institutional and policy-oriented perspectives ordinarily associated with discussion of higher education and focus as well on broader questions of cultural identity in this field and the way such identity is expressed or embodied in discourse. In order to accomplish these tasks, American and German historians of the German universities came together in November of 1995 with leading academics and state officials currently responsible for making policy in German and American higher education at a conference held at the School of Advanced International Studies of The Johns Hopkins University, and sponsored by the Harry and Helen Gray Humanities Program of the American Institute for Contemporary German Studies in Washington, D.C. This volume brings together revised versions of the papers and invited commentaries presented at that conference, along with selections from remarks made during the discussion.

The central issue addressed in this volume can be formulated in two German words: *Mythos Humboldt*. That phrase is difficult to translate into English; "Humboldt as myth," might be a reasonable, if awkward, equivalent. The important point is that the phrase incorporates two meanings of the word "myth." When writers speak of myths and legends in history, they generally refer to statements that may be widely believed, but do not stand up to historical investigation. There is, however, another meaning of the term "myth" familiar from cultural anthropology. In this sense myths are the stories people tell

---

a more optimistic view, see N. Grunenberg, "Und der Zukunft zugewandt: Studenten in Deutschland – Sie haben Spaß am Studium und planen pragmatisch ihre Karriere," *Die Zeit*, Vol. 50, No. 53 (27 October 1995): 1. For further references see the selected bibliography at the end of this volume.

themselves to make their history and culture meaningful. Acceptance of such mythical tales, or at least participation in the discourse they establish, thus defines membership in that culture. Denial of those myths or refusal to accept the terms of discourse they constitute implicitly subverts that membership or puts it into question.

The contributors to this volume employ the term *Mythos Humboldt* in both of these senses. The authors in Part One ask, for example, whether the ideal of the modern German research university, formulated in the early nineteenth century and later summarized evocatively in the slogans "freedom of teaching and learning" and "unity of teaching and research," was actually the sole creation of its reputed author, Wilhelm von Humboldt. More importantly, they also ask whether and for how long that ideal corresponded to any institutional reality in Germany. Their answer is that by the twentieth century at the latest the ideal advanced by Humboldt and others and the institutional realities of German universities had drifted far apart from one another. The emergence of the mass university in West Germany since the 1960s widened the gap still further.

Nonetheless, the name of Humboldt and the freedoms of teaching, learning, and research that the name symbolizes are still evoked with great frequency and evident sincerity in German debates about universities, even when – or perhaps precisely because – the speakers are fully aware that these symbols no longer have much connection with contemporary academic life. Do Humboldtian ideals bear any relation to reality in unified Germany? If they do not, one must then address the second, deeper meaning of the term "myth" just described and ask: why have Humboldtian ideals nonetheless retained their power for so long, and why do they retain their power today? That is not only a topic for historians, but also a question about the nature of cultural politics in unified Germany.

The purpose of this volume is therefore to address both the past and the future of German universities. That aim is achieved here in three ways:

- by confronting current university leaders and policy makers from Germany with some of the historical realities behind the rhetorical shibboleths about the grand heritage of the German research university commonly employed at academic celebrations;
- by confronting historians of German universities with some of the complex realities of current and future academic policy making in the new Germany; and

- by bringing both groups together with American academic leaders, because the founders of the American research university drew much of their inspiration from the Humboldtian ideal, and because in America, too, questions are being asked about the mission and future of the university as a cultural institution.

The volume is divided into two parts, which respectively address the modern history and the future tasks of German universities. Part One provides historical background for discussion of the current situation by analysing continuity and change in the roles of universities in German society and culture in the nineteenth and twentieth centuries, including the impact of unification. Prussian reformers such as Wilhelm von Humboldt, Friedrich Daniel Schleiermacher, and others envisioned a university in which the unity of teaching and research, along with the freedom of teaching and learning, would together produce a scholarly and scientific elite equal to the challenges of the modern world. At the turn of the century, when Imperial Germany's economic power and scientific prestige reached its height, the model attributed to Humboldt was widely admired and imitated, not least in the United States. And yet, that system had already become something quite different from what it had been in Humboldt's day. In the Nazi era, Humboldtian ideals were undermined and ultimately discredited by political manipulation and by the behavior of German academics themselves. In the postwar years, their successors carefully reconstructed the myth in West Germany, only to see it undermined more deeply than ever by the emergence of the mass university in the 1960s. Has the persistent appeal of *Mythos Humboldt* as the guiding ideal for the mission of German universities become an obstacle to recasting the terms of the discussion in order to better reflect contemporary realities?

Part Two considers the present and future roles of universities in the new Germany, and of German universities in a changing international situation. How relevant are contemporary German universities to the political, economic, social, and cultural life of the Federal Republic? What is, and what should be, the mission of universities in contemporary Germany today and in the future? Should they be primarily centers of research and higher learning, or training grounds for specialized occupations; can these purposes still be combined, as they have been until now? Can German universities achieve more control over their own administrative and financial affairs, and play a cultural leadership role today and in the future; or will they only react to political, social, and cultural change? Will German universities regain the role they allegedly once had, of forming and transmitting cultural values? Or will they, like American universities, become centers of social and cultural conflict?

Part One
Mythos Humboldt:
Universities in Nineteenth- and Twentieth-Century Germany

German universites face many of the same pressures and problems that also confront their sister institutions in other highly developed nations; yet there are aspects of their situation that are directly attributable to Germany's particular history. The contributions in Part One offer historical overviews of those aspects of higher education that are important for the contemporary issues outlined above.

In his chapter on German universities before 1945, Rüdiger vom Bruch analyzes the conception of the research university pioneered in Prussia by Humboldt, Schleiermacher, and others at the beginning of the nineteenth century and the "long farewell from Humboldt" that followed. As he argues, by the turn of the twentieth century it had become clear that the ideals and policies of the German university reformers were in deep tension with two fundamental trends – the emergence of a modern system of specialized, large-scale scientific research on the one hand, and the parallel growth of professional society based on a system of advanced academic qualifications on the other. In response, Prussian state officials such as Friedrich Althoff and prominent academics such as Adolf von Harnack created – or rather recreated – the modern research university between 1890 and 1914. In doing so, Harnack, at least, invoked the ideals propagated by Humboldt and others a century earlier. But the system of educational and scientific institutions he, Althoff, and others established resembles the one now in place in Germany far more than the one Humboldt had in mind.

Humboldtian ideals and imagery nonetheless persisted. In the Weimar era, vom Bruch argues, Humboldtian rhetoric became central to academics' increasingly vociferous calls for a meaningful worldview in the face of the disintegration they associated with modernity. Thus, one reason for the persistence of *Mythos Humboldt* is that it justified

German professors' standing as cultural leaders. As vom Bruch shows, organizational changes in funding for research saved the German higher educational and scientific system from financial disaster in the early 1920s, but this did not assure that German academics would have any inner commitment to the new democracy. Under Nazism, both the purported cultural leadership role of German academics and the freedom of university teaching and research suffered extreme set-backs, due not only to political attacks and indoctrination from without but also to passive acceptance of or active collaboration with Nazism by academics themselves.

The next two chapters on German universities from 1945 to 1989, one focusing on West Germany and one on East Germany, consider the changing socio-cultural standing and political roles of German universities in the postwar period. Writing about West Germany, Konrad Jarausch shows how leading academics such as Karl Jaspers tried to restore and simultaneously renew Humboldtian ideals, in order to help universities recover from the damage sustained under Nazism. Some innovations in academic self-governance resulted; for example, the Free University of Berlin, founded with American support, gave students a greater role in academic governance than they had had in the past. But in the end, renewed invocations of *Mythos Humboldt* in the Adenauer era constituted an alibi justifying the corporate privileges of professors who devoted more time to continuing past research programs than to innovation.

As Jarausch shows, the true break in both the social and political roles of universities in West Germany came in the 1960s. The massive expansion of that period was initially supported by a consensus encompassing the entire societal spectrum; conservative technocratic modernizers sought to increase the number and quality of trained professionals, while liberals advocated social opening and the right to an education for all. After the student revolts of the late 1960s, that consensus evaporated. From the late 1970s onward, massive underfunding set in, brought about in part by erroneous demographic projections. By the 1980s, *Mythos Humboldt*, however inspiring it may have been in earlier times, had become hopelessly dysfunctional, helping to block or inhibit the imagination required for reform.

In his chapter on universities in East Germany, John Connelly argues that "Humboldt" – the new name given the University of Berlin in 1949 – became a symbol of "socialist humanism" coopted by the Socialist Unity Party in order to mask the deliberate reversal of the very ideals allegedly embodied by that name. In the GDR, the unity and freedom of teaching and research were displaced by growing standardization of higher education in a centrally planned economy and insistence on the ideological primacy of Marxism-Leninism, especially in the social sciences and humanities. Connelly compares the situation in East Germany not with West Germany, as is commonly done, but rather with policies and structures elsewhere in the Soviet bloc. By this standard, he argues, the GDR produced the most thoroughly "Stalinist" higher education system. The 1960s saw major efforts at higher education reform in the GDR; however, these had purposes and results quite different from the reform efforts in the FRG during the same period. Thus, Connelly concludes, there was a growing sense of stagnation and crisis in both East and West German higher education in the 1980s, but for very different reasons in the two states.

Part One concludes with my own paper discussing the process and impact of unification in German higher education. The chapter begins with the irony mentioned above – that a West German higher education system widely agreed to be in deep crisis was imported largely unchanged into the new German states after 1989. This would appear at first to support a "colonialist" interpretation of the unification process as a whole; the irony deepens with the realization that the predominant term for this process is "renewal." However, I argue that the picture in higher education is more mixed than either the "colonization" or the "renewal" perspectives would suggest. West German legal and institutional frameworks were indeed implemented in the new states, with only slight modifications and high social costs. But this vast structural change did not lead to a complete takeover by West Germans in all disciplines. My conclusion briefly considers the role of federal-state tensions and the confusion of science policy and social policy in this transformation, whether and why opportunities for innovation in both East and West were grasped or missed, as well as the prospects for a new academic-political culture in unified Germany.

In his response to this paper, Gunnar Berg, rector of the Martin Luther University in Halle from 1992 to 1996, focuses on areas in which universities in the new German states, particularly his own university, have tried to open up avenues for innovation while going through extensive and often painful personnel reductions and institutional restructuring.

Part Two
The Present Situation and Outlooks for the Future

The contributions in Part Two present analyses of the current and projections for the future situation of the German universities, along with comparisons of the situation in Germany with that of universities in the United States. Though each of the four chapters focuses on a different policy question, the term *Mythos Humboldt* provides a unifying thread.

In his chapter, Peter Lundgreen confronts the Humboldtian myth with the complex realities of current German university life and policy making. Given the long-standing conflict, already mentioned, between basic research and higher learning versus professional training, Lundgreen asks, what meaning can the vaunted unity and freedom of teaching and research that have historically been and remain constitutive for discussion of the German universities still have? Lundgreen maintains that the ideal still has meaning for the minority of students training for academic or research careers, but little significance for the vast majority of university students. Nonetheless, current proposals to separate occupation-oriented basic education from more advanced preparation for a scholarly career still face resistance.

In research, Lundgreen argues, the major danger is the very non-Humboldtian fiction that all German universities are equal. This misapplication of academic collegiality has resulted in egalitarian distribution of research funds within and among universities that has retarded innovation and can no longer be sustained financially. Efforts by professional training institutions (*Fachhochschulen*) to gain university status only compound the problem. In university governance, Lundgreen argues, the Humboldtian ideal found and still finds expression in the notion of academic self-administration – the election of university governing bodies with professorial majorities, and of deans, rectors or presidents from among the faculty. Given the size and complexity of modern higher education institutions, this form of academic self-governance has long been inadequate. The only hope for the future in times of scarcity, Lundgreen concludes, is to professionalize university administration, and to give administrators both the autonomy and the authority to make faculties accept that there will be losers as well as winners. In response to Lundgreen's presentation, Daniel Fallon argues that the task for the future should not be to decide between a single- or a two-stage model for higher education, but to reinterpret Humboldtian core values in a way that will satisfy the public's interest in producing both high quality research and well-trained professionals. Needed in both American and German state universities, he maintains, is not leadership training for all, but training for sophisticated participation in a service-oriented economy and a knowledge-based society. The result will be functional differentiation not *within* universities, but rather *among* many different *kinds* of higher education institutions. Fallon provocatively suggests that the number of research universities will not rise but decline in both Germany and the United States, because public authorities are likely to support only a limited number of such institutions.

In his chapter, Rainer Künzel contributes to the currently intensifying debate on political control and funding of German universities. One of the secrets of the success of the German universities in the past was the fact that the autonomy of state governments in cultural affairs *(Kulturhoheit der Länder)* assured the existence and support of multiple centers of academic excellence. This principle was retained and reinforced in the early Federal Republic, while the Higher Education Framework Law *(Hochschulrahmengesetz)* of 1976 reflected a perceived need for common standards in areas such as university governance. In the current era of scarcity, however, the cultural autonomy of the *Länder* is becoming a straitjacket; tight financial and administrative regulation by state ministries extends to curriculum planning, naming of professors, regulating admissions, and decisions on number and kinds of staff in addition to tight budgetary control. Such bureaucratic control only exacerbates the crisis caused by underfunding.

Neither bureaucratic control nor underfunding is new in German university history. Indeed, it could be argued that, apart from two relatively prosperous periods from 1890 to 1914 and the 1960s and 1970s, German universities have always been financially squeezed. Nonetheless, the structural issues posed are real enough. Künzel therefore asks: Will universities devote time to defending existing programs and budgets that might better be spent on reform; and will they finally receive the planning autonomy that they need from their *Länder* governments in order to have the flexibility they will need to deal with fiscal stringency? He acknowledges that granting universities financial and administrative autonomy may well become an invitation to manage scarcity, but argues that moving in this direction is the best way to respond creatively to the need for increased competition among universities while modifying its potentially negative effects through planning and quality control. Künzel agrees with Peter Lund-green that professionalization of university administration is desirable, but suggests that it is likely to be implemented differently from the American system, given existing structures mandating codetermina-tion of policy by faculty, staff, and students *(Gruppenuniversität)*.

One route taken by American universities appears closed in Ger-many. Because German universities continue to be seen as a public service and higher education as a public good, and also because Ger-man tax law makes it extremely difficult for private citizens to support state enterprises, the prospects of private universities appear practi-cally nil, though new cooperative arrangements between existing uni-versities and private firms may help on the margins. Seen in historical perspective, this is ironic; for it was precisely the mixture of state and private industry funding that made German universities and basic research so productive under the German Empire.

In his response to Professor Künzel, C. Peter Magrath considers the ideal and reality of academic freedom and institutional autonomy in contemporary American research universities. After painting a vivid portrait of the current American scene, including reduced levels of state and federal funding, and growing linkages to private donors and enterprises, Magrath discusses some of the varied strategies university administrators are developing in response to this challenge. Despite increasingly strained finances, as well as an increasing tendency to regard higher education as a private good and students as customers, Magrath maintains that American scientists have contined to avoid interference with basic research, and that a sense of public purpose continues to be shared by privately and publicly supported universities in the United States.

In her chapter, Evelies Mayer, former minister of education in the state of Hesse, discusses her own experiences and frustrations as a higher education reformer, and the implications of those experiences for the more general question, "whom do German universities now serve?" In her view, the West German reform era of the 1960s and 1970s was a disaster, not because the political commitment to reform went too far, but because it did not go far enough. The universities were opened to more and different kinds of students, but were neither adequately financed nor administratively restructured for the task. In her account of Hesse's recent experience with reform, Mayer reports that all participants, students as well as faculty, questioned the validity of the Humboldtian myth and particularly rejected the unity of teaching and research; but at the same time they cited Humboldt in support of arguments for university autonomy and against ministerial "intrusions." Mayer remains optimistic about the possibilities of reform from within, but doubts that this can happen in a period of severe funding cuts.

Turning to the question "whom do universities now serve," Mayer suggests that in their own ways, teachers and students appear to be getting what they want out of higher education institutions; but their purposes appear to be diverging rather than converging. Faculty cope with the mass university by reducing preparation and counseling time. Students complain of poor teaching and distant professors, but have a pragmatic orientation toward their studies and appear confident that they can continue to combine pursuit of personal interests and higher social status. In any case, university life is less important to the new type of student living off campus and combining work, study, and in some cases family. Mayer's remarks raise the question of whether it is possible or even necessary to agree upon a single mission for institutions that perform multiple roles for such diverse client groups. Implicitly, they also point to the changing, increasingly fragmented inner framework of German universities. Given the political conflicts that often rage within and around them, it appears clear that German universities, especially the larger ones, are hardly to be characterized as communities.

In his comment on Professor Mayer's paper, Steven Muller outlines basic differences in the legal status and constitutional structures of German and American universities. He then presents his views on the ways that the new communications technologies will radically change both the future clientele and the modes of operation of the modern university. The concept of community gets an original twist here; Muller argues that over time, a global community now being created by new information technologies will increasingly substitute for the seemingly more intimate community of teachers and learners.

Finally, Hans-Joachim Meyer, the last education minister of the GDR and currently minister for science and art in Saxony, addresses the role of universities in contemporary German political culture. After providing a broad overview of the historical role of universities, students, and professors, in German history, Meyer surveys the fundamental changes in German political culture that began in the 1960s from an East German perspective. In his view, 1968 was a watershed in both West and East Germany, albeit in very different ways.

In West Germany, the 1968ers made long-term contributions to liberalizing German society and making it less elitist and nationalist. But the excesses of the student revolt also had the effect of alienating universities from society and removing them from their formerly central role in German political culture – an alienation symbolized by lack of funding and decaying facilities. In addition, Meyer argues that by opting for a leftist utopian dream that had already become a bitter reality in the East, the student rebels contributed to undermining German identity and left West Germany "gloriously unprepared for German unity." The intellectual contribution of West German universities to unification, aside from the reorganization of their East German counterparts, has been miniscule, and university governance is hardly a model of democracy.

In East Germany, Meyer argues, 1968 was also a turning point, because it was only then, during the so-called Third Higher Education Reform, that the universities came under immediate and nearly complete SED party control. The result was that the role of East German academics in German unification was even less prominent than that of West German academics. In contemporary East German universities, Meyer sees countervailing trends; impulses to introduce more democratic self-government are counterbalanced by a return to traditional academic forms, for example the use of robes and hoods at convocations. Public respect for universities and their products appears to be returning in the new German states, Meyer concludes, but "universities still have a long way to go before they will again by regarded as centers of intellectual life" in Germany as a whole. Both West and East Germans need to acquire different sorts of what Meyer calls "competence" for dealing with an entirely new situation. West Germans need understanding, patience, and self-reflection, while East Germans need to learn how to use the tools of democracy and the legal state.

Conclusion: Open Questions

The contributions in this volume provide a comprehensive overview of the historical development of modern German universities and of their prospects for the future. Many questions remain open.

When the rhetoric of the Humboldtian university is evoked to support the idea of a more elite university, or when claims are made that universities should become more practically useful, are we hearing statements of individual client groups, each of which is presenting its needs as a candidate for the purpose of the university as a whole? Has the role of universities as regional economic factors – both as employers themselves and as providers of professional training – become more important than their international reputations for research and scholarship?

In the past, Germany dealt with the problems of such multiple roles and clienteles mainly by creating new research and training institutions, ranging from the technical and pedagogical academies of the 19th and early 20th centuries to the specialized professional training institutions *(Fachhochschulen)* founded in the Federal Republic since the 1970s. The high level of specialization and the decoupling of occupational training from general education and basic research that have been characteristic of these institutions were even more extreme in the GDR. Is the current controversy over efforts to raise the status of *Fachhochschulen* nothing more than a replay of the status and role conflicts that occurred between universities and technical academies at the end of the nineteenth century? More important, is it enough to create and support new institutions while leaving the old ones essentially unchanged? How can cooperation of universities and academics with industry be improved and programs of study streamlined, as currently demanded by policy makers, while maintaining the integrity and quality of basic research?

The social opening of higher education to children of groupings outside the traditional educated elites, and also to women of all classes, occurred, albeit to differing extents and for different reasons, in both West and East Germany. Has that trend made the universities potential scenes for social conflict? In what ways are images of the American situation, for example portrayals of the "political correctness" debate, playing a role in German discussions? Given that German universities were once centers of anti-Semitic, nationalistic and xenophobic attitudes and the resurgence of such attitudes in German society since unification, what is the situation of foreign students in Germany today? Does the recent drop in the number of foreign students coming to study in Germany have anything to do with this issue, or is it attributable primarily to German universities' growing reputation for mediocrity?

Given the past behavior of German academics in political crises, the peculiarities and self-blockages of academic governance, and the present political apathy of so many German students, in what sense if any can it be said that universities provide training in democratic citizenship? Has the defensiveness of professors in the face of calls for student evaluation of teaching reinforced student cynicism on this score?

The tension, not to say the blatant contradiction, between the propagated ideal of the Humboldtian university and the reality of the mass university, especially in West Germany, continues apace. Comparisons to the American situation today seem quite apposite, and they are being made all the time in discussions of the situation in Germany. But those comparisons are often based on false premises, in particular the premise that the American elite universities are in any way comparable with the German universities. The real counterparts are probably places like the University of Michigan at Ann Arbor or even Ohio State in Columbus. Is the tendency to evoke Harvard in such comparisons, particularly visible in conservative German commentators, understandable only in light of the social function of *Mythos Humboldt* as an alibi for the status consciousness of German professoriate, or does it have other roots?

For none of the questions that are addressed in this volume is there any single, easy answer. By combining historical, cultural, and policy studies, the volume may help to broaden the informational and analytical base for both historical and policy studies, contribute new perspectives, and thus help show the way toward gaining a better grasp of the possibilities of and constraints on German higher education now and in the future.

Part One

∞

MYTHOS HUMBOLDT: UNIVERSITIES IN NINETENNTH- AND TWENTIETH-CENTURY GERMANY

Chapter One

A SLOW FAREWELL TO HUMBOLDT?

Stages in the History of German Universities, 1810–1945

~

Rüdiger vom Bruch

The title of my essay contains a topic and expresses a thesis. I wish to assess the stages of the history of twentieth-century German universities in light of the question of whether and to what degree these stages represent an irreversible departure from the model created by Wilhelm von Humboldt, a model that is generally viewed as the foundation of the modern German research university and the worldwide reputation it had achieved by the late nineteenth century. Thus, I shall ask, first, just what this Humboldt university was. I shall then survey from this vantage point the lines of its development in the twentieth century; and finally I will ask what the findings mean for contemporary debates on the idea of the university in Humboldt's sense.

Let me take as a starting point the threefold division of German university history proposed by the Giessen historian Peter Moraw in 1981, which has found great resonance in scholarly circles.[1]

---

1. P. Moraw, "Aspekte und Dimensionen älterer deutscher Universitäts-geschichte," in *Academia Gissensis. Beiträge zur älteren Gießener Universitäts-geschichte*, eds. P. Moraw and V. Press (Marburg, 1982), 1-43.

According to Moraw, we have a preclassical phase stretching from the mid-fourteenth century to 1800; dating from the early nineteenth century there followed a classical phase based upon the new idea of the university; and finally a postclassical phase began in the 1960s and 1970s. There are good reasons for this threefold division, the most important being that with its help Moraw links several perspectives, including institutional changes and intellectual and scientific innovation, as well as changes in the environment of the university. There is no doubt that the modern German university is indebted to the concepts and reforms of the early nineteenth century. Nor is there any doubt that the social character and institutional parameters of this research university entered a state of permanent crisis in the wake of the politically motivated explosion in the size of the student body after about 1960, with the announcement of democratically motivated educational opportunity, and finally with the student movement of 1968. Since then the university has been characterized by continuous new waves of reform and changes in government, without any long-term, effective, or convincing conceptualization. However, owing to the emergence of certain structural changes in the complex organization of the German university, Moraw also finds it necessary to introduce an intermediate, high-classical phase dating from around 1870.

My thesis is that this intermediate phase was of crucial importance, and that at this time and increasingly by 1900 the German university system, then rising to world renown, had, in spite of its successes in teaching and research, already begun to distance itself structurally from the premises of the Humboldt university. Not only did the German universities of 1900 differ markedly from those predating the reforms of the early nineteenth century, but they had also greatly distanced themselves from the conceptual foundations of the new university founded in Berlin in 1810. The situation of the German university today is closer to that of 1900 than to that of 1810. Our problems are rooted to a large degree in the time around 1900, and the questions we ask about the conceptual preconditions of the Humboldt university are related in many ways to the questions asked in 1900.

Am I here relativizing the deep break of the 1960s and 1970s? All of us are aware of the dramatic increase in enrollments since

1960 and of the problems associated with it. Curiously enough, however, at the beginning of that structural change in the traditional German university system, in 1960, a memorandum appeared that insisted on the principles of the old Humboldt university. And no less curiously, as we shall see, important structural changes after 1900 were also justified in an equally important memorandum by referring back to Humboldt.

In its first report on the expansion of institutions of higher education, the West German Science Council *(Wissenschaftsrat)* emphasized in 1960 that its task was not "the development of a single system of reform for higher education in Germany." Instead, the Council desired to retain the founding principles of German higher education. The Council described these principles as, first, the organization of higher education as a "community of scholars with equal rights"; second, the unity of research and teaching, that is, the view that the purpose of higher education is not solely the dissemination of knowledge; and third, the linkage of specialized training and general, humanist education.[2] As we all know, in the years that followed not just one system, but rather many, often contradictory systems were developed.

Following the traumatic experiences of the National Socialist period, German universities in the early Federal Republic appealed to earlier traditions. Symptomatic in this regard is a statement made in 1992 by the legal historian and former president of the West German Rectors' Conference, Helmut Coing, that after 1945 one wanted to reproduce the circumstances of the Weimar Republic. "There existed no inclination to embark on basic reform of higher education involving either a change in its constitution or its pedagogical methods over and against the Weimar period."[3] As early as 1946 Karl Jaspers had written his essay, "The Idea of the University," in the same spirit.[4] A few years later, and with similar

2. Wissenschaftsrat, 1960, 1962, cf. *Dokumente zur Gründung neuer Hochschulen,* ed. R. Neuhaus (Wiesbaden, 1968), 5.
3. H. Coing, "Der Wiederaufbau und die Rolle der Wissenschaft," in *Wissenschaftsgeschichte seit 1900,* ed. H. Coing et al. (Frankfurt am Main, 1992), 87. Cf. K. H. Jarausch, "The Humboldt Syndrome: West German Universities 1945-1989- An Academic *Sonderweg?*" in this volume.
4. K. Jaspers, *Die Idee der Universität* (Berlin, 1923, new ed. Berlin, and Heidelberg 1946).

intent, Ernst Anrich published the founding documents of the modern German university, dating to the first decade of the nineteenth century.[5]

In all of these cases, the intended point of reference was the Humboldt university, and this shaped reality. We must therefore ask: How was the Humboldt university perceived, what was deemed to be worthy of support, which lines of structural opposition were pushed aside? Was the university in late Imperial Germany and in the Weimar Republic still the university of Humboldt? In the contribution by Coing one sentence gives pause for thought: "Hence, the goal was to recreate the German university in the form which it had assumed in the Weimar period. At that time it was still shaped essentially by the ideas of Wilhelm von Humboldt and Althoff and also still enjoyed a good international reputation."[6]

Wilhelm von Humboldt and Friedrich Althoff, who was responsible for higher education policy in Prussia from 1882 to 1907, certainly count among the most prominent figures in German scientific and education policy in the nineteenth and twentieth centuries. But do they contradict one another? Althoff, under whose auspices the term *Wissenschaftspolitik*, best translated as science policy, was developed, created a state-directed system of industrial functionalization of higher education and focused research competence outside the universities. Humboldt's model of scientific self-regulation as a condition of individual cultivation can hardly be reconciled with this program of societally efficient promotion of research. The relationship between science and the state, to address this point first, had changed significantly for both.

With the single exception of academic appointment policy, whereby the neutral state had to counteract the patronage of a familial university by ensuring scientific accomplishment, Humboldt had considered the state a danger to the effort of acquiring autonomous scientific knowledge. In the Althoff era the state was supposed to protect the university from special interest groups challenging free academic research. Thus, Humboldt demanded

5. E. Anrich, *Die Idee der deutschen Universität. Die fünf Grundschriften aus der Zeit ihrer Neubegründung durch klassischen Idealismus und romantischen Realismus* (Darmstadt, 1956).
6. Coing, "Wiederaufbau", 88.

for higher education "the most active and strongest vitality," distant from everything even remotely similar to school-like practice. Only then could it be of use to the common weal, to the state, and to society. Humboldt added that the state "must always remain conscious of the fact that it neither does nor can affect this, and that, instead, it is detrimental to this goal as soon as it tries to assert its influence, and that things would work infinitely better without the state."[7]

The Althoff era was shaped by different concepts. In a letter to a colleague, the Protestant theologian, influential promoter of higher education, and conceptual founder and first president of the Kaiser Wilhelm Society for the Advancement of Science, Adolf Harnack, wrote around 1910: "With regard to [the relationship between] the state and science, one primary concern appears to me to be important for our age and for the future, namely, that science will certainly fall victim to capitalism and its raw interests if the state does not retain control of it."[8] The Kaiser Wilhelm Society would "direct capital under the auspices of the state and of the academy into a pure bed. One can truly say that, as regards science, our state is pure." The theologian Harnack found himself in agreement here with the most important state official for educational affairs, Friedrich Althoff, just as a century earlier the theologian Friedrich Daniel Ernst Schleiermacher, whose importance for the founding of the Berlin university has long been underestimated, had been in agreement with the preeminent state official, Wilhelm von Humboldt.

The state as an honest broker or as a directing agent? In considering such distinctions in the relationship between the university and the state around 1810 and 1910, we touch on an important issue concerning the conception of the Berlin university that arose between the devastating defeat of Prussia by Napoleon in 1806 and the establishment of the university in October of 1810. The "Humboldt University" concept is not immediately identical to the struc-

7. W. v. Humboldt, "Über die innere und äußere Organisation der höheren wissenschaftlichen Anstalten in Berlin," 1809/10, in *Idee und Wirklichkeit einer Universität. Dokumente zur Geschichte der Friedrich-Wilhelms-Universität zu Berlin*, ed. W. Weischedel (Berlin, 1960), 194.
8. A. von Zahn-Harnack, *Adolf von Harnack* (Berlin, 1936), 423.

tural characteristics of Peter Moraw's "classical German university." These characteristics can be condensed into two elements: first, the entry of research into the university in the form of research based teaching; second, the simultaneous emergence of a system of modern, methodologically exact specialized fields, each with its specific disciplinary matrix. If we understand the classical German university in these terms, irrespective of the continuous debates over the crisis of the university that have accompanied and enlivened recent academic history, then a farewell to Humboldt dating to about 1910 will be difficult to pin down and can be doubted justifiably today. If, on the other hand, we examine the central tenets of the so-called Humboldt university itself, then things appear differently. That this examination is relevant is evidenced not least in the founding principles of the German university cited earlier from the report of the Science Council in 1960 – the community of scholars with equal rights, the union of research and teaching in place of the simple dissemination of knowledge, and the linkage of specialized training and general, humanist education.

This extends beyond the two elementary criteria of the modern German university just named and points to the very Humboldt university that I must now introduce in order to be able to discuss the problem of a farewell to Humboldt. Crucial in this context is Humboldt's memorandum of 1809/10, only rediscovered around 1900, entitled "On the Internal and External Organization of Institutions of Higher Education in Berlin."[9] The memorandum is important, even though the contemporary idea of the new German university actually represents a conglomeration of the very heterogeneous, yet mutually stimulating conceptions of many individuals. I wish to lay out four aspects of Humboldt's memorandum. The first is the liberal idea of demarcation vis-a-vis the activity of the state that I have already considered. Second is the crucial transition from the well-worn concept of the *universitas litterarum* to a philosophically grounded idea of the unity of the sciences. All reformers presumed this idea, referring to Immanuel Kant's late work of 1798 on the "Dispute of the Faculties." According to Kant,

9. Cf. Humboldt, "Über die innere und äußere Organisation" (cit. n. 7), also published in *Gelegentliche Gedanken über Universitäten*, ed. E. Müller (Leipzig, 1990), 273-83.

because church and state norms dominated the three faculties (theology, law, and medicine), it was necessary that "to ensure a general learned education there should exist a further faculty that, with respect to its teachings, was independent of the government, a faculty that had no orders to give but that was free to judge everything relevant to the interests of science, i.e., relevant to the truth."[10] As opposed to the three professionally oriented faculties, the philosophical faculty was to be "free in its judgments" and to enjoy extensive autonomy.

It is not my intention here to enter into a debate on the mutual interaction between this epistemological position and the approximately contemporary success of the Philosophical Faculty, which long included the natural sciences. I do wish, however, to stress that, again simultaneously and under the direct influence of Kantian philosophy, outdated legal learning (Rechtsgelehrtheit) was transformed to a legal science (Rechtswissenschaft), and that the emergence of a disciplinary matrix in the modern natural sciences did not take place in Germany until the period between about 1760 and 1850, in constant interaction with experimentation and philosophical assumptions, especially those drawn from the romantic philosophy of Schelling. Thus, the founding of the *universitas litterarum* in conjunction with the *scientia scientiarum* and the specific lines of reasoning and questions drawn from general philosophic principles constitute the second pillar of the Humboldt university.

A third aspect is designated by the new middle-class concept of education (Bildung). This concept was given added force by Goethe's idea of an individual, organic self-development, which over the course of the nineteenth century was then politically instrumentalized and socialized as part of a strategy of social demarcation of formal educational rights. But as an idea depicting not what actually existed but rather what should exist, Humboldt's concept of education as an opportunity for the development of one's personality through science continued to resonate. In the interaction of an idealistically grounded doctrine of science and a neohumanistically formed concept of education, the Humboldt university evolved its truly innovative force.

10. I. Kant, "Der Streit der Fakultäten," in *Sämtliche Werke*, ed. K. Vorländer, Vol. 5 (Leipzig, 1912), 57f., 66f.

Of course, and this is my fourth point, this required that science be resituated away from the tradition of encyclopedic knowledge and toward the principle of research. Nowhere is this better illustrated than in this famous and often cited passage from Humboldt's memorandum: "In the organization of institutions of higher education everything depends upon retaining the principle that knowledge must be considered as something not yet wholly discovered and never entirely discoverable, and that it must incessantly be sought as such."[11] In view of this designation, which frees science of all immediate practical considerations, science must be institutionally situated in a continuous and reliable status of autonomy. The responsibility of the state to ensure this is not the same as nor can it be reduced to the state's legitimate interest in recruiting well-qualified personnel. This is precisely what the phrase "solitude and freedom" *(Einsamkeit und Freiheit)*, later popularized by sociologist Helmut Schelsky, means.[12] Thus, it seems to me, we have located the four essential premises of the Humboldt university. However, we must supplement these premises by three further important boundary conditions.

On the initiative of Schleiermacher, the new philosophical justification of the *universitas litterarum* was joined with the basic corporate-legal and institutional pattern of the old German university as a composite institution with a rectorial constitution and self-recruitment of faculty. Furthermore, research gravitated from the academies of science to the universities. As a result, the model of the special occupationally oriented school, which emanated powerfully from France but was also favored in Germany, was promptly dispatched and the old, run-down model of the "university" was given new life. In the reformed Prussian variation, this model served as a paradigm for university reform not only in German-speaking culture, but in many other states as well. We should bear in mind, however, that the chance to transform the designation of the German university from a utilitarian to an idealistic institution was made possible by a singular and energetically exploited window of opportunity. That window of opportunity was Humboldt's short

11. Humboldt, cf. n. 9, 274f.
12. H. Schelsky, *Einsamkeit und Freiheit. Idee und Gestalt der deutschen Universität und ihrer Reformen* (Reinbek, 1963).

tenure of less than a year as section chief in the Prussian ministry. Before and after Humboldt the Prussian ministry of education was dominated by figures such as Massow, von Beyme, and Schuckmann, all of whom, like the King himself, supported utilitarianism; this should have resulted, but did not result, in a policy favoring the special school model for professional training.[13]

The second important boundary condition for the creation of the Humboldt university was the administrative and institutional norms for educational certification established in Prussia around 1810. Examples include: the functional demarcation between the Gymnasium and higher education by the Abitur, and also between university study and the profession by the doctorate degree; a now-systematized mode of qualification for the civil service with standardized, double state examinations; and the Habilitation as a requisite second doctorate for admission to university teaching, which had been nominally recognized in the eighteenth century, but was now formalized. Also important, however, was the expansive introduction of seminars in the humanities as the institutional realization of the principle of research-based teaching, soon accompanied by comparably conceived institutional laboratories in the natural sciences.[14]

Finally, the third boundary condition concerns the newly founded universitas magistrorum et scholarium anchored alongside the new universitas litterarum. The new scientific ethos in the faculty corresponded in the late eighteenth and early nineteenth century with a new, diligent seriousness of the students, as recent work on the socialization of young educated ranks in Germany around 1800 has demonstrated. In place of traditional carefree attitudes and at times juvenile behavior, there emerged in orders, regional groupings, and early student associations a tendency toward initi-

13. Cf. U. Muhlack, "Die Universitäten im Zeichen von Neuhumanismus und Idealismus: Berlin," in Beiträge zu Problemen deutscher Universitätsgründungen der frühen Neuzeit, eds. P. Baumgart and N. Hammerstein (Nendeln, 1978), 299-340.
14. Cf. P. Lundgreen, "Zur Konstituierung des 'Bildungsbürgertums': Berufs- und Bildungsauslese der Akademiker in Preußen," in Bildungsbürgertum im 19. Jahrhundert, vol. 1, eds. W. Conze and J. Kocka (Stuttgart, 1985), 79-108; R. S. Turner, "Universitäten," in Handbuch der deutschen Bildungsgeschichte, vol. 3, eds. K.-E. Jeismann and P. Lundgreen (München, 1987), 221-49.

ation into a future civic and professional ethos. Scientific work as a precondition of future professional responsibility challenged in remarkable ways the trusted patterns of student freedom as a libertine phase between school and profession.[15] This ends our survey of the Humboldt university as a powerful idea that at least in part was transformed into reality. There is little doubt that over the course of the nineteenth century many aspects of this Humboldt university only slowly assumed concrete form. Compared to the idea, the reality of the university was the subject of constant and legitimate criticism, and all four fundamental principles were burdened by difficult and often lazy compromises. The ideal of the Humboldt university was never wholly consistent with the real German university of the nineteenth century, not even in Berlin. Nevertheless, that real university drew its dynamism from the ideal construction.

There are good reasons to question whether this was the case in the twentieth century as well. The increasing student enrollments already described, and the new quality of contemporary complaints about a questionable structural change of the classic German university, give pause for thought. For historians today, however, these points in themselves cannot serve as arguments for diagnosing a qualitative transformation and depicting it as a slow farewell to Humboldt.

First, I would like to emphasize that just when the basic parameters of the conceptual foundation of the Humboldt university had been irreversibly shaken, at the turn of the century, they became known and were put into service as an alibi for a presumably tradition-oriented rounding-off of this Humboldt university. This is precisely what justifies speaking of the myth of the Humboldt university. In his research for a biography of Wilhelm von Humboldt shortly before 1900, Bruno Gebhardt discovered the memorandum of 1809/10, and Adolf Harnack employed this source in his justifi-

---

15. Cf. W. Hardtwig, "Sozialverhalten und Wertwandel der jugendlichen Bildungsschicht im Übergang zur bürgerlichen Gesellschaft (17.-19. Jahrhundert)," *Vierteljahrschrift für Sozial- und Wirtschaftsgeschichte* 73 (1986): 305-35; W. Hardtwig, "Krise der Universität, studentische Reformbewegung (1759-1819) und die Sozialisation der jugendlichen deutschen Bildungsschicht," *Geschichte und Gesellschaft* 11 (1985): 155-76.

cation of the Kaiser Wilhelm Society as a research organization independent of the universities.[16] Harnack instrumentalized Humboldt's reference to supporting institutions next to the university and the academies of science in order to argue that the idea of research outside the universities lay in Humboldt's conception itself. In fact, however, Harnack's argument was hardly compatible with Humboldt's theoretical concepts. What then did the unity of the sciences mean around 1900, if research was becoming increasingly specialized outside of a *scientia scientiarum*? The linkage of teaching and research was also being broken apart. Research at technical universities as well as universities was becoming increasingly oriented toward the demands of practice; and teaching, in part in the universities and more so in the competing new types of higher education such as commercial schools, moved toward the training needs of the special school model. The linkage of teaching and research was already viewed in some technological and natural sciences as a hindrance to the efficient promotion of research.

In view of the new needs for qualified personnel in an industrialized society, a heretofore important but unstable relationship between scientific claims to autonomy and state recruitment needs appeared to require modification. Until the 1880s, the doctorate had been the standard first degree in the German universities. From the 1880s onward a new type of training and examination, the diploma, was created, first at technical universities and later in chemistry programs. The diploma exam was the result of negotiations between professional associations, the state, and the universities and had serious repercussions for the organization of teaching and studies. Around 1900 it was supplemented by a commercial teaching diploma at commercial schools, and in 1923 it was introduced in departments of economics at universities nationwide.

The need for a highly specialized division of research labor, especially in medicine and the natural sciences, also encouraged hier-

---

16. *Wilhelm von Humboldts Politische Denkschriften*, vol. 1: 1802-1810, ed. B. Gebhardt (Berlin, 1903), 250-60; A. Harnack, *Gedanken über die Notwendigkeit einer neuen Organisation zur Förderung der Wissenschaften in Deutschland*, Berlin, 21 May 1910; cf. *Forschung im Spannungsfeld von Politik und Wissenschaft. Geschichte und Struktur der Kaiser-Wilhelm/Max-Planck-Gesellschaft*, eds. R. Vierhaus and B. vom Brocke, 21f., 27-30.

archically organized and institutionally based research, which contrasted with the corporate principle of collegiality within the academic faculties, and which was increasingly perceived to be in contradiction to Humboldt's idea of a "learned republic." Similar tendencies became visible in the long-term research projects of the academies of sciences, for which the historian of antiquity, Theodor Mommsen, in 1890, first coined the expression *Grossforschung*, that is, large-scale research that could not be accomplished by a single individual, but had to be directed by one.[17] Worthy of note, finally, are two further new types of research: industrial research, practiced early and extensively in Germany as part of the development of key modern technologies; and state-sponsored research, which expanded rapidly in late Imperial Germany. Both of these new types of research offered young university researchers new career and research opportunities.[18] In these circumstances, could the cultivation of the personality possibly serve in any way as a point of orientation for higher education?

At German universities themselves such transformation processes in the Humboldt university were carefully registered and, naturally, hotly debated. This was illustrated at the meetings of German educators called *Hochschullehrertage* in 1911, in the debate on university and extra-university research institutes as well as in debates surrounding the opening of universities with strong or predominant ties to local communities, such as in Frankfurt am Main, Hamburg, Cologne, and Dresden. Should the conditions be created for the flexible support of research by partially removing research facilities from the universities – which would guarantee the Humboldt university's sense of identity, as Harnack believed? Or should at least research institutes in the humanities be moved inside the universities, as the Leipzig cultural historian Karl Lamprecht argued? What were the opportunities and dangers involved in the different concepts for the founding of universities focusing

17. *Sitzungsberichte der Königlich Preußischen Akademie der Wissenschaften zu Berlin* (Berlin, 1890), 792.
18. P. Erker, "Die Verwissenschaftlichung der Industrie. Zur Geschichte der Industrieforschung in den europäischen und amerikanischen Elektrokonzernen 1890-1933," *Zeitschrift für Unternehmensgeschichte* 35 (1990): 73-94; *Staatliche Forschung in Deutschland 1870-1980*, eds. P. Lundgreen et al. (Frankfurt am Main, 1986).

either on a thoroughly statist education policy with centrally organized and directed priorities, or on communal and regional initiatives moving research to the fringe of industrial centers, and to what degree did both endanger solitude and freedom? These were all contentious issues.[19] But the debates of the *Hochschullehrertag*, known in public as the "professor's union," as well as the recently edited protocols of the meetings of the *Hochschulreferenten*, the officials responsible for higher education in the states of the German Empire, both illustrate, upon critical reflection, just how and why the measures were adopted that would change the constitutional form and idea of the outdated German university.[20]

Finally, what was the social composition of this university, of this *universitas magistrorum et scholarium* that had been revivified in 1800? Here again we observe deep changes around 1900. For students around 1800, I mentioned a new civic and professional work ethic that supported and characterized the reform concepts. Of course this also existed around 1900, even though by this time most student associations had solidified around their own subcultures and around expectations of professional patronage. More important, however, as contemporaries noticed and as recent research has more strongly emphasized, were nationalist and especially anti-semitic currents in leading student associations. Also more important were calls for autonomy from circles close to the youth movement, that drove a wedge between a hunger for experience unique to that generation and the teaching and research community.[21]

But we can also observe significant erosion of the Humboldt ideal with respect to teachers. As expectations of upward mobility proved ever more often to be dead ends, and as structural problems put off the long awaited call to a chair for many instructors,

19. Cf. R. vom Bruch, "Wissenschaftspolitik, Kulturpolitik, Weltpolitik. Hochschule und Forschungsinstitute auf dem Deutschen Hochschullehrertag in Dresden 1911," in *Transformation des Historismus. Wissenschaftsorganisationen und Bildungspolitik vor dem Ersten Weltkrieg. Interpretationen und Dokumente*, ed. H. W. Blanke (Waltrop, 1994), 32-63.

20. *Hochschulpolitik im Föderalismus. Die Protokolle der Hochschulreferenten der deutschen Bundesstaaten und Österreichs 1898 bis 1918*, eds. B. vom Brocke and P. Krüger (Berlin, 1994).

21. K. H. Jarausch, *Students, Society and Politics in Imperial Germany: The Rise of Academic Illiberalism* (Princeton, 1982).

sociopolitically inspired professional organizations emerged. The goal of a full chair became a utopian dream for the majority; the attractive reward of scientific asceticism seemed obsolete in the eyes of most scientists. The trend of the day was toward a social safety net for intermediate posts, for widows and for orphans; non-tenured faculty sought to expand their corporate legal opportunities. Karl Lamprecht spoke appropriately of the small social question within the realm of the university.[22] Corporate autonomy was threatened not only by internal social problems, but also by challenges from without and as a result of the contradictions between academic integrity and sociopolitical claims. Professional, political, and bureaucratic interests hobbled the "ideal union of free intellects" of which Fichte had once written.

Although the premises of the research university had long been anchored in the confessionally diverse cultural regions of Germany, in northern Germany and less so in the south they were considered proof of the superiority of the Protestant university. It is not by chance that following the so-called *Kulturkampf* of the 1870s several cultural shockwaves shook higher education, including the 1901 debate between Theodor Mommsen and the Munich political economist Lujo Brentano on the issue of "objectivity" *(Voraussetzungslosigkeit)*. The debate was sparked by the call of the young historian Martin Spahn to the chair in Catholic history in Strassburg, whereupon the Goerres society and Count Hertling responded in the so-called parity debate.[23]

While it was difficult for a Catholic to be called to chair in northern Germany, it was nearly impossible for a Jewish scholar. The few exceptions could be quickly recounted. Political lines of division were even more rigid. Pacifist convictions led to broken careers, as in the case of Ludwig Quidde in 1893, or to tumultuous actions, as in the case of respected scholars such as Friedrich Wilhelm Foerster in the First World War. Socialists remained entirely excluded from university teaching positions, as demonstated by the so-called *lex Arons*, the case of the removal of

---

22. K. Lamprecht, *Rektoratserinnerungen*, ed. A. Köhler (Gotha, 1917), 70; cf. R. vom Bruch, "Universitätsreform als soziale Bewegung," *Geschichte und Gesellschaft* 10 (1984): 80.

23. C. Weber, *Der "Fall Spahn" (1901)* (Rome, 1980).

the social democratic physicist Leo Arons from his position as a lecturer in Berlin.[24] It is also worth noting, however, that at the beginning of the century women entered the university as regular students and, in exceptional cases, as university teachers for the first time, although this occurred in the face of much opposition.

In admitting women the state was clearly not heeding the demands of the German women's movement, but rather the sociopolitical pressure created by the schooling of girls in the upper-middle classes and the demand for female doctors and social workers in the wake of obligatory health insurance and above all the expansion of community social services. To be both a woman and a Jew proved to be an extremely high career risk, as illustrated by the examples of the historian Hedwig Hintze and the physicist and chemist Lise Meitner, who managed to obtain a position at Otto Hahn's Kaiser Wilhelm Institute for Chemistry, but not a teaching post.

Finally, the contradictions between the international community of scholars and the patriotic sense of duty were two sides of the same coin in this imperialist age. The First World War has accurately been characterized as a war of intellects and of words.[25] This was certainly not only true of the German empire – the international exclusion of German scientists after the war, a consequence of the call to arms signed by many German professors early in the war, was no less debilitating for reputations, working conditions, and intellectual openness than the political polarization of German university teachers during the war itself, that cast a long shadow across the Weimar Republic.

The third issue I mentioned concerns the strictures of state bureaucracy, which brings us back to the so-called "Althoff system." There existed at least two "Althoff systems." One was the systematic effort to determine, with the help of trusted academic consultants, the most promising younger scientists in every discipline – a quality control mechanism that, though widely criticized

---

24. D. Fricke, "Der Fall Leo Arons," *Zeitschrift für Geschichtswissenschaft* 8 (1960): 1069-1107.
25. *Der Krieg der Geister,* ed. H. Kellermann (Dresden, 1915), Cincinnatus, *Der Krieg der Worte* (Stuttgart, 1916); cf. R. vom Bruch, "Krieg und Frieden," in *Bereit zum Krieg,* eds. J. Dülffer and K. Holl (Göttingen, 1986): 75, 90.

by many as being harmful to the Humboldt university, produced exceptionally efficient results in science policy.[26] On the other hand, there were serious interventions in the freedom of teaching as well as the "almighty" Althoff's highly disrespectful treatment of professors, whom he generally viewed as being spineless. It was this second Althoff system that Max Weber forthrightly criticized in 1908, although he blamed Althoff's personality less than the structural problems of state bureaucracies, which oversaw not only the system of higher education, but also the teachers working there.[27] In 1907 Werner Sombart had written in the same vein, arguing that the Althoff system was not the cause, but rather the result of state bureaucracy.[28]

If we summarize the processes surveyed so far, then much speaks for Max Weber's sharp judgment in his Munich lecture in 1917, "Science as a Vocation." There, in a conclusion that is certainly a product of his own biography, but is also verified by historical analysis, Weber remarked: "Inside and out, the old constitution of the university has become a fiction."[29] Thus, the Humboldt university, much hailed in this age, proved to be a myth, albeit a powerful one. It was a myth that not so much described reality, as provided an ideal blueprint for correcting it. However, if with Peter Moraw we reduce the Humboldt university to its character as a research university, then Weber's verdict is incorrect, in spite of structural changes in Imperial Germany. This university had a level of performance rarely seen before, even in the humanities, despite complaints about the supposed preference given to research in the natural sciences. Three examples will make this point. Early in the century American research organizations exerted pressure to change the composition of the Nobel prize committee, because German

26. *Wissenschaftsgeschichte und Wissenschaftspolitik im Industriezeitalter. Das "System Althoff" in historischer Perspektive*, ed. B. vom Brocke (Hildesheim, 1991).
27. R. vom Bruch, "Max Webers Kritik am 'System Althoff' in universitätsgeschichtlicher Perspektive," *Berliner Journal für Soziologie*, vol. 5, no. 3 (1995): 313-26.
28. W. Sombart, "Althoff," *Neue Freie Presse*, Vienna, No. 15427, 4 August 1907; cf. B. vom Brocke, "Hochschul- und Wissenschaftspolitik in Preußen und im Deutschen Kaiserreich, 1882-1907: das 'System Althoff'," in *Bildungspolitik in Preußen zur Zeit des Kaiserreichs*, ed. P. Baumgart (Stuttgart, 1980): 13f.
29. *Max Weber-Gesamtausgabe*, vol. I/17 (Tübingen, 1992): 75.

scholars predominated among the prize winners. Secondly, subscriptions to German scientific journals by foreign libraries spoke for themselves. And thirdly, in many fields German was the leading international language of science, although this did not prevent German professors from acquiring good foreign language skills.

A wholly different picture first emerged not with the political upheaval of 1933, but in the interwar years. The model of the German research university, long held to be superior, was now threatened in Germany itself. After 1920, following its "worldwide influence," one now spoke only of the "distress of German science."[30] I have already mentioned the isolation of German scholars from their foreign colleagues owing to their political engagement in the First World War. In the context of inflation and rising costs following the war, German university and nonuniversity research threatened to lose touch with international science and scholarship. German scholars remained almost completely excluded from international congresses for years; recent foreign literature could not be acquired because of the shortage of currency reserves. The German market for journals and books languished, long-term projects stagnated, and much needed instruments in laboratories and institutes were not to be had.

In this situation I judge the changes of 1920 to be very important. I mean the founding of three organizations: the Emergency Association (Notgemeinschaft) as a precursor to the German Research Association, the Donor Alliance (Stifterverband) for German Science, and the industrially oriented Helmholtz Society.[31] In the beginning there was pure emergency, a mending of gaps. The initiative for further-reaching changes came from the Alliance of German Academies, from research libraries, and from some states. The most important trio influencing scientific policy was composed of the president of the Kaiser Wilhelm Gesellschaft, Adolf von Harnack, the chemist Fritz Haber, and Althoff's successor, Friedrich Schmitt-Ott. In spite of their sympathies with the pro-

30. E.g., G. Schreiber, Die Not der Wissenschaft und der geistigen Arbeiter (Leipzig, 1923).
31. Cf. U. Marsch, Notgemeinschaft der Deutschen Wissenschaft. Gründung und frühe Geschichte 1920-1925 (Frankfurt am Main, 1994); W. Schulze, Der Stifterverband für die Deutsche Wissenschaft, 1920-1995 (Berlin, 1995).

jects of the academies in the humanities and with the needs of libraries, they quickly realized that, after an initial phase of closing gaps, it was necessary to develop a program of priorities for the future, because only the productive vigor of science could help the defeated German empire regain international stature. In technology and the natural sciences prospects for regaining that stature appeared promising. Though today's current phrase, *Wirtschafts- und Wissenschaftsstandort Deutschland*, was not used, the debate revolved around similar issues.

As recent research has shown, the ingenious scientist and policy maker Fritz Haber was especially influential. It was his initiatives that resulted in the Emergency Association's program of priorities and, after 1923, its promotion of young scholars.[32] The funds of the Donor Alliance and the contributions of the Rockefeller Foundation were designed primarily for basic research, whereas the activities of the Helmholtz Society were a cause for concern because they syphoned off money from industry for practice-oriented research. A very similar constellation of forces arose again in 1949/50 in a debate over the new Frauenhofer Society and its relationship to the German Research Association, the Donor Alliance, and the Max Planck Society.

Taken together, we can say that the changes of 1920 saved the German research university. But the emphasis had shifted, I believe with long-term consequences, in favor of research outside the universities in the Kaiser Wilhelm Institutes and to the disadvantage of the humanities. The great proclamations of an Age of Natural Science by Werner von Siemens and Rudolf Virchow had prompted an aggressive epistemological counterattack by Wilhelm Dilthey, Heinrich Rickert, and Max Weber. The intellectual battle raged on in the Weimar period, without really reaching a final decision.[33] However, in the emergency situation of the early

32. Marsch, *Notgemeinschaft*; D. Stoltzenberg, *Fritz Haber. Chemiker, Nobelpreisträger, Deutscher, Jude* (Weinheim, 1994).

33. Cf. P. Lundgreen, "Differentiation in German Higher Education," in *The Transformation of Higher Learning 1860-1930* (Stuttgart, 1983), 149-79; R. vom Bruch, "Vom Bildungsgelehrten zum wissenschaftlichen Fachmenschentum. Zum Selbstverständnis deutscher Hochschullehrer im 19. und 20. Jahrhundert," in *Von der Arbeiterbewegung zum modernen Sozialstaat*, eds. J. Kocka, H.-J. Puhle, K. Tenfelde (München, New Providence, London, Paris, 1994), 582-600.

Weimar Republic, research policy initiatives and directives set a one-sided, long-term, and irreversible course.

In 1924 the prominent Prussian minister and authority on cultural affairs, Carl Heinrich Becker, affirmed the German university's position as a "fortress protecting the grail of pure science."[34] The task lay not in praising it, but in further developing it. As they emerged from the authoritarian state, Becker assigned to the old universities an orienting function in the new, democratic, multiparty state. His "Thoughts on the Reform of Higher Education" in 1919 and his promotion of chairs in sociology created heated controversy.[35] But did this policy ask more of universities than they were able to deliver? Did the claim to provide social and political orientation presume binding value criteria? Indeed, did it presume the "total world view" of which Eduard Spranger had spoken in 1912?[36] Could the goal of the Humboldt university be more than the cultivation of the individual personality in a cosmos of possible norms? And could even that goal be traced back in any way to Wilhelm von Humboldt? To this day, these questions remain the subject of ongoing debate.

The history of the German university in the Weimar Republic was overshadowed by an inherited and for the age typically acrimonious polarization of worldviews. In his book, *The Decline of the German Mandarins*, Fritz Ringer has characterized this polarization, in a slightly reductive manner, as a dispute between orthodox and modernist mandarins.[37] Yet there is no doubt that the history of triple deprivation recently emphasized by Dieter Langewiesche dominated consciousness in German universities. Meant here are the long term cultural dispossession of the German educated class's common intellectual property, the political dispossession of the lost war in 1918, and the material dispossession resulting from high rates of inflation up to 1923. All of these decisively reduced the willingness of the educated elites to

34. C. H. Becker, *Vom Wesen der deutschen Universität* (Leipzig, 1925): 7.
35. C. H. Becker, *Gedanken zur Hochschulreform* (Leipzig, 1919); idem., *Kulturpolitische Aufgaben des Reiches* (Leipzig, 1919).
36. E. Spranger, *Wandlungen im Wesen der Universität seit 100 Jahren* (Leipzig, 1913): 35.
37. F. K. Ringer, *The Decline of the German Mandarins. The German Academic Community, 1890-1933* (Cambridge, MA, 1969).

provide loyal support to the Weimar Republic, in spite of its indisputable policy achievements.[38]

It is well known that susceptibility to National Socialist ideology and its promises of redemption was far greater and well established in the student body than among professors. This was evident in the student body as early as 1930, in Tübingen earlier than in Heidelberg, at the technical academy in Berlin earlier and more virulently than at the University of Berlin. Much research has been conducted on this issue.[39] We should bear in mind, however, that a large portion of the student body in the Weimar period appeared to be more outgoing and in need of orientation than many previous generations. Moreover, their relationship to the university and to scientific study was based on different social circumstances. Family support in covering the costs of education, one of the central characteristics of the classical German university, occurred only rarely in the Weimar period. Far more typical, and contrary to the glorification of happy fraternity life in popular films of the day, was the working student. Of course the extraordinary situation of 1923 did not last. At that time, during the semester breaks 94 percent of all students, and as many as 46 percent of students during the semester, were forced to work either because of economic necessity or as "acts of moral self-qualification."[40] In the future, the historiography of universities should pay greater attention to this aspect, and to the history of students in general.

Space does not permit me to delve further into the impact of the National Socialist dictatorship. The degree to which scholarly excellence at German universities was bled to death by the dismissals and expulsions is well known, although the humanities,

38. D. Langewiesche, "Die Eberhard-Karls-Universität Tübingen in der Weimarer Republik. Krisenerfahrungen und Distanz zur Demokratie an deutschen Universitäten," *Zeitschrift für Württembergische Landesgeschichte* 51 (1992): 345-81.

39. Cf. H. Titze, "Hochschulen," in *Handbuch der deutschen Bildungsgeschichte*, vol. 5: 1918-1945, eds. D. Langewiesche and H.-E. Tenorth (München, 1989), 209-40; M. Gehler, "Neuere Literatur zur Geschichte der Universitäten, Wissenschaften, Studenten und Korporationen in Deutschland und Österreich unter besonderer Berücksichtigung der Jahre 1918-1945," *Archiv für Sozialgeschichte* 34 (1994): 300-32.

40. Langewiesche, "Universität Tübingen," 352ff.; M. H. Kater, *Studentenschaft und Rechtsradikalismus in Deutschland 1918-1933* (Hamburg, 1975).

the social sciences, natural sciences, and medicine were affected, in that order, to different but increasing degrees.[41] I mention also the terms *Gleichschaltung* and *Führeruniversität*. Of course after 1934 there existed new realms in which scientific research and teaching could be pursued relatively unhampered. Specific disciplines, such as psychology and business science, even advanced their professional development under the National Socialists, although this has only recently been admitted. Nevertheless, there is no question about the final result: the negative policies and practices of the brown rulers concerning higher education severely damaged the German university, its reputation, and its self-understanding, even if alternative National Socialist models, such as Alfred Rosenberg's Elite Schools, failed entirely.[42]

But is consideration of structural changes enough? Does it suffice to weigh the political and ideological deformations of institutions and the voluntary subjection and accommodation of persons against residues of relative normality, against specific phases of professionalization, and against the resistance of individual academics? The problem lies at a deeper level. Peter Moraw's prosopographic and structural approach indicates that there was a transition in the 1960s from the classical phase of the modern German research university to the postclassical phase of a crisis-ridden mass university. But if we link this modern research university to the principles of the idea of the Humboldt university, even though these ideals never described reality but were instead a constant challenge to their own realization, then this idea was discredited definitively between 1933 and 1945, and the classical phase ended not in the 1960s but rather in the 1930s. Academic self-discipline as a precondition to the development of the personality, as Wilhelm von Humboldt under-

41. For specifics, see the literature cited in the "Introduction" to *Forced Migration and Scientific Change: German-Speaking Scholars and Scientists after 1933*, eds. M. G. Ash and A. Söllner (New York, 1996).
42. *Erziehung und Schulung im Dritten Reich*, 2 vols., ed. M. Heinemann (Stuttgart, 1980); *Die Universität Göttingen unter dem Nationalsozialismus*, eds. H. Becker et al. (Munich, 1987); *Hochschulalltag im 'Dritten Reich'. Die Hamburger Universität*, eds. E. Krause, L. Huber, and H. Fischer (Berlin, 1991); P. Chroust, *Giessener Universität und Faschismus. Studenten und Hochschullehrer 1918-1945* (Münster and New York, 1994); *Die Freiburger Universitaet in der Zeit des Nationalsozialismus*, eds. E. John, B. Martin, and H. Ott (Freiburg, 1991).

stood it, proved to be an ideological and illusory construct in the face of the trials and challenges of Nazism.

Open investigative curiosity, independent of the ideology and the utilitarian directives of the state, contradicted not only National Socialist doctrines, but also the preexisting individual dispositions of a majority of German academics. The idea of the Humboldt university had always fed on a myth of the personal moral responsibility of academic work – a myth that was largely accepted in society and to which academics appealed. National Socialism not only destroyed the German university as a self-administering corporate body and as an independent research community with a functioning system of rules; it also drove the social and moral codes of group conduct ad absurdum – codes of conduct that were often proclaimed, increasingly fragile, yet still virulent in terms of external and self-perception. In late Imperial Germany the question of "solitude and freedom" had been posed again in light of structural developments; in the Weimar Republic the stage was set for new initiatives in scientific policy; but in the National Socialist period the model of solitude and freedom was renounced.

It is against this backdrop that we must understand postwar efforts to return to Imperial Germany and Weimar through the myth of the Humboldt university, the emphatic confession of Jaspers in 1945, and Coing's review in 1992. But from a historical perspective we must recognize a slow farewell to Humboldt in the twentieth century and not lament its passing. The myth is ill suited for nostalgic glorification, but recalling the foundations of the Humboldt university can lead to new initiatives going beyond continuous academic reflection.

Two things appear to be necessary. First, it is important to realize that supposedly historically motivated programmatic statements are useless for conceptualizing reform if they reveal themselves to be perhaps politically understandable, but historically questionable constructions. Helmut Schelsky's well-known book entitled "Solitude and Freedom" (*Einsamkeit und Freiheit*), published in 1963, can serve as an example. The book, the theses of which were recently sharpened by Michael Zoeller at a conference of the Konrad-Adenauer-Stiftung in Kassel,[43] demonstrated the capacity of

---

43. Kassel conference, September 15-17, 1995, Zöller comments to my paper.

the German research university to distance itself from its intellectual fathers and thereby lay the groundwork for the legitimacy of the reform concepts in higher education of the 1960s. Schelsky's argument is that the modern German research university developed so successfully not because, but in spite of the concepts of its founding fathers. They were concerned, in Schelsky's view, not with independent scientific research, but rather with an efficient Prussian university, that was useful to the state. Furthermore, Schelsky claimed to observe an ideologically constructed, curiously formulated, and in the long term ominous continuity stretching from Fichte to Hegel and rooted in Swabian pietism. Finally, Humboldt's memorandum of 1809/10 is characterized by very imprecise formulations regarding actual organizational needs.

Such accusations cannot be verified in the sources. The state-centered and utilitarian intentions of von Beyme and Schuckmann stand in stark contrast to Humboldt's program in education and science. Furthermore – this has received too little attention in the literature – Humboldt's conception was decisively influenced by Schleiermacher's memorandum of 1808, "Timely Thoughts," the only memorandum, by the way, that was not requested by von Beyme himself, but rather written at Schleiermacher's own initiative.[44] In essential ways, the Humboldt university is a Kant-Schleiermacher university, characterized by philosophical roots and sober pragmatism.

Let us mention four arguments for this claim here. In conscious opposition to the state-centered model of special schools, Schleiermacher emphasized the corporate autonomy of the full university in accordance with old European assumptions. This is precisely what Humboldt, in opposition to the models of Fichte and others, based his design on. Humboldt also adopted from Schleiermacher the seminar as the organizational basis of the research university. Schleiermacher also exerted strong influence on the actual constitutional form of the new Berlin university, helping to formulate the early statutes of 1810 and participating in the difficult process leading to the statutes of 1817, whereby he placed great importance on

44. F. D. E. Schleiermacher, *Gelegentliche Gedanken über Universitäten im deutschen Sinne. Nebst einem Anhang über eine neu zu errichtende* (1808).

the section concerning the role of students in a disciplinary state and legal order. Finally, Schleiermacher, rooted as he was in the Silesian brotherhood, had nothing to do with the Swabian pietism enveloping Fichte and Hegel in Tübingen.

Schelsky's polemical remarks directed at Fichte's program of a national training institution are certainly convincing, but his "inferred plan" of 1807 left no traces beyond those of Schleiermacher in Humboldt's memorandum, the language of that differs pleasingly from the style of Fichte.[45] Above all, however, Humboldt sanctioned no official mandate for a state university in accordance with the views of the king. Rather, the memorandum sought to develop a concept of reform for the ailing academy of science in Berlin. Against the backdrop of the prior research monopoly of the academies, Humboldt's project took into consideration the organization of upper-level schools, the demarcation of general education in the Gymnasium, and research-oriented teaching at the universities. The academy, the university, and what Harnack later called the "lifeless institutes," that served in a technical support capacity and that Humboldt wanted to see placed entirely under the supervision of the state, together constituted the facilities for upper-level research.

These findings should be taken into account when reference is made to the Humboldt university in contemporary debates on the reform of higher education. There appear to be many myths of the Humboldt university, depending on one's current needs. A takeover strategy in order to legitimate new changes, such as Harnack carried off in 1910, seems to be just as problematic as the demarcation strategies of 1963 and 1995; none of them can stand up to critical historical reconstruction.

In disputes over value judgments the historian cannot reach a decision based on his expertise. He can, however, place the findings of his profession at the disposal of collective memory. How and in what context was the Humboldt university conceived at the beginning of the nineteenth century, and what historical conditions shaped it in the early decades of our century? At issue here is

---

45. J. G. Fichte, *Deduzirter Plan einer zu Berlin zu errichtenden höhern Lehranstalt, die in gehöriger Verbindung mit einer Akademie der Wissenschaften stehe* (1807).

not whether this question and its answer are important or even desirable for the contemporary debate. A historical perspective could, however, also arrive at the conclusion that the idea of the modern university according to the conceptions of Schleiermacher and Humboldt may today be better preserved in the North American than in the German system of higher education. But this would open an entirely new debate.

DISCUSSION

STEVEN MULLER: This has been a very good and rich presentation. I do not want to do it an injustice by just picking at a little piece of it, but I would like to make two observations and request your response. It was very interesting to hear you talk about Humboldt's devotion to the liberal ideas of the limits on the state, and it does seem to me that throughout what you have been saying, one of the tensions that continues is the relationship between the state and the university. That makes it possible to look at something to which you alluded but which you did not look at in detail. Why is it that a university that lived with the *Mythos Humboldt* did not react more strongly between 1933 and 1945 to what was clearly an elimination of some of the freedoms to which the institution was dedicated? This also raises ongoing questions about intellectual freedom and the role of public authority.

The other point that I was interested in was this. One of your three pillars of Humboldt's thought is the concept of education as the self-development of organic individuals, the opportunity to develop a personality. This could be still subsumed in German under *Bildung*, a word for which English has no equivalent, although we do talk about character formation and personal development in higher education in this country. It seems to me that the tension between the notion of individual development expressed in the concept of *Bildung*, and the role of the university of responding to the needs of industry and other social needs, is also a constant. I do not even want to disagree with your title, "A Slow Farewell to Humboldt," and your conclusion. But it does seem to me that these fundamental tensions, at least these two, continue to be unresolved on the university scene worldwide, and particularly in the Federal Republic.

MITCHELL ASH: The last question could nicely be summarized with two German words that are very difficult to translate into English,

Bildung versus *Ausbildung*, education as the cultivation of person-ality versus training for occupations.

HANS-JOACHIM MEYER: I would like to raise the following point. You spoke about Humboldt's concept of academic freedom. Don't you think that it is necessary to distinguish between individual academic freedom and academic freedom as a corporate concept, that is, academic autonomy? My impression is that these distinc-tions are often not made. Referring to a lawsuit we just had in North Rhine-Westphalia, in which policy changes initiated by the state were challenged by university representatives as breaches of academic freedom, it seems to be a very topical problem. Of course, you know that Humboldt did not think very much of the ability of scientists and scholars to govern themselves. He was strongly against the self-constitution of faculties. In a letter to his wife, he compared scientists to a group of comedians. In his words, it is much more difficult to have scientists, send a group of come-dians. And, as I think you noted, it was Schleiermacher who introduced all of these elements of academic autonomy; for exam-ple, the slate of three candidates for a professorship, or the con-cept that the Academic Senate should comprise all of the professors of universities. That is, he really did not consider acad-emic autonomy as corporate responsibility. In my view, this is really the basic structural problem of the German university and has been up to this time.

Although it is of course correct to maintain and to underline that it was Humboldt who strongly emphasized that the state should not interfere into research and teaching, he emphasized the responsibility of the state to provide the structure and conditions for doing teaching and research. I remember that, for example, his idea was to set up a (state) deputation for education affairs, and there was no question in his mind that it was he who appointed the members of this deputation and its director. There was absolutely no idea of having elections.

Relating to your question, Dr. Muller, possibly it is this differ-ence – really, this conflict or even a contrast – between an indi-vidual concept of academic freedom and the fact that there is practically no corporate concept of academic autonomy that explains why German university professors at the time of the Weimar Republic did not see that there were dangers for democracy. In fact, most of them were strictly against democracy.

The other thing I would like to raise is this: Is it not necessary when discussing Humboldt's ideas to distinguish between system-related structures and process-related structures? This could be the modern version of Humboldt's idea, that what we need in academic life are process-oriented structures, not system-oriented structures. That could lead to a way out of our present dilemma.

FRANK TROMMLER: I would like to put this discussion into an American context and especially the context of current American discussions on the academy. That term is used in an interesting way in the United States. For Europeans the academy means an Academy of Science, a place where no teaching is done. But in America the term is still used at the moment as a general designation for academic institutions. What I have noticed is that this word is used to some extent almost idealistically, creating a bit of an inner connection with the myth of Humboldt because we belong to this set of institutions. I find that the way in which the term "academy" is used in many contemporary discussions indicates that a change is occurring now in view of multiculturalism. What I propose in my comment is to build a bridge from the mythical use of Humboldt to the myth of the academy, because what I notice now is that one cannot just talk about the academy. One would have to speak in the United States of the old academy versus the new academy that is taking shape in the American university system.

What I would like to come back to is Max Weber, someone who criticized the contemporary myth of Humboldt, by noting that it was used as an alibi to maintain the status of the German mandarinate in the early twentieth century. This is what I would like to ask: Can you find more in Weber; did he advocate a change towards a new university system?

RÜDIGER VOM BRUCH: These were not so much questions about, as further developments of, my presentation. The most important question raised, which I discuss at the end of my paper, is this: In reflecting on the foundations of the Humboldt university today, is a thorough institutional renewal needed, for which the American university might be a better model than a German system that appeals symbolically to Humboldt but in reality is far removed from Humboldt?

A second, related topic raised by the discussants is *Bildung* versus *Ausbildung*. This is a central theme in the history of the modern German university. I mentioned that everything about the *Spezialschulmodell* around 1800 seemed to be moving toward what we would today call the *Fachhochschule* – specialized training institutions for specific professions – and not toward the university as we know it today. I believe that this is relevant for contemporary discussion in Germany. This is why I cited the Science Council's 1960 paper. We must realize what *Bildung* means and does not mean today. We must reflect on the fact that in German history *Bildung* often did not mean the formation of personality, as it did for Humboldt, but rather the formation of a worldview, of *Weltanschauung*. That was the aim of the "German mandarins." Is that identical with Humboldt's conception of personality? A total *Weltanschauung*, such as Eduard Spranger demanded in the 1920s, is this something that can be traced back to Humboldt? I am very skeptical about that.

Another important issue is *Bildung* as *Freiheit* – the concept of academic freedom applied to academics as a corporate group. It is correct that Humboldt did not go into much detail on this issue, but he did say one thing. The state should only interfere with academic self-government in one area – in appointments policy – in order to work against the old *Familienuniversität*, i.e., nepotism; but otherwise the state was to stay out of university affairs. The fundamentals of this doctrine were developed by Schleiermacher, not Humboldt. In this sense the classical German university was not a Humboldt, but rather a Kant-Schleiermacher university.

On Dr. Muller's question about the role of the universities in the Nazi period, and on the question raised by Minister Meyer, whether there are reasons why German professors did not see the dangers to democracy in the Weimar era, I will speak only briefly. On the Nazi era I can only refer you to my written remarks. But here again, as in the Weimar era, the issue is *Bildung* as *Weltan-*

schauung rather than personality formation. Fundamental for understanding the political behavior of professors in the Weimar and Nazi periods is what I call the threefold dispossession process – economic, social, and cultural losses in the professoriate's standing after 1918.

Chapter Two

THE HUMBOLDT SYNDROME

West German Universities, 1945–1989 – An Academic *Sonderweg*?

∽

Konrad H. Jarausch

In the postwar period, the West German university system was both highly successful and deeply troubled. External representations such as Hansgert Peisert's 1990 survey exude a self-congratulatory tone that contrasts sharply with the laments of many students and professors who are actually having to confront its problems.[1] Compared with the disastrous conditions of much East German academe, the retrospective satisfaction of the Federal Republic in the superior functioning of its own system is all too understandable. But the validation of its institutions and practices, offered by their transfer to the East, covers up a high degree of frustration with its own shortcomings during the second half of the 1980s.[2] Although the reform debate has been silenced by the demands of unification, on the eve of that caesura Western higher education had itself reached a stage of latent crisis.

1. H. Peisert and G. Framheim, *Higher Education in the Federal Republic of Germany* (Bonn, 1990), 4ff.
2. K. H. Jarausch, "Creative Destruction: The Transformation of the East German University System," forthcoming in *United Germany in a United Europe: Chance and Challenges*, ed. R. Hoffmann (New York, 1997).

Remote from such preoccupations, official university rhetoric seems to owe more to inspirations from a distant past than to the challenges of the present. Especially at important occasions such as founding anniversaries, academic speeches like to pay tribute to a neohumanist vision, most forcefully articulated by Wilhelm von Humboldt during the Prussian reform era. This classically-based imperative of general cultivation (*allgemeine Menschenbildung*) had inspired generations of intellectuals in Central Europe to liberate themselves from practical restraints and strive for aesthetic self-perfection. This conception proved so alluring that even after the achievement of its practical aims, neohumanist rhetoric continued to function as a kind of founding discourse that has guided the self-understanding of German higher education and constrained its institutional development.[3]

In contrast to such theory, West German practice prided itself on the modernity and efficiency of its research. Especially the Max Planck Institutes in the sciences have regained a worldwide reputation, certified by their share of Nobel prizes, and the facilities of many technical institutes tend to be first rate. In cross-national comparisons, Federal Republic indicators occupy a middle ground in terms of size of age cohort in postsecondary training (around 30%), proportion of women studying (about 2/5), differentiation of institutional types, diversification of subject matter, and the like.[4] Representatives of German scholarship are therefore highly visible in international congresses, usually constituting the largest and most innovative contingent after the Americans.

Perhaps a transatlantic perspective can make an observer more sensitive to this discrepancy between rhetoric and reality. Most colleagues who work within the FRG system have to make their peace with its contradictions so as to get the best out of the sometimes frustrating circumstances. But to someone like myself who is both an outsider and an insider as well as a historian of higher education,

3. F. Paulsen, *Die Geschichte des gelehrten Unterrichts auf den deutschen Schulen und Universitäten vom Ausgang des Mittelalters bis zur Gegenwart* (Berlin, 1920), 2 vols.; R. vom Bruch, "A Slow Farewell to Humboldt? Stages in the History of German Universities in the 20th Century, 1810-1945," in this volume.
4. H. Peisert and G. Framheim, *Systems of Higher Education in the Federal Republic of Germany* (New York, 1978).

the distance between the self-representation and the actual functioning of German institutions seems astounding, raising the question of what the implications of such a lag in consciousness might be.[5] Though I have not done much archival work on postwar universities, this topic has dominated countless conversations during research leaves in Bonn, Koblenz, and Berlin as well as teaching stints at universities in Saarbrücken, Göttingen, and Leipzig.

The purpose of the following remarks is therefore to take a closer look at the effect of the Humboldtian discourse on the postwar development of the West German university system. In order to combine a chronological approach with a topical perspective, this reflection will proceed in four sequential, but partly overlapping stages, centered on distinctive problematics. In exploring their tension, this paper will both analyze the normative debates about university goals as well as structures and survey higher education enrollments, practices, and politics, taking as one indicator the shifting preoccupations of the pronouncements on *Hochschulreform*. Instead of passing general judgments, the analytical challenge is to uncover the peculiar mixture of strengths and weaknesses that characterized the German universities in the second half of the twentieth century.[6]

Restoration

Owing to the physical and psychological damage left by the Third Reich, the first priority in 1945 was simply the reopening of academic institutions. Most teaching had ceased in the summer semester of 1944, many buildings, laboratories, and collections lay in ruins, and the student body as well as the professoriate was dispersed. To provide a perspective for the future, allied education

---

5. K. H. Jarausch, "Amerikanische und deutsche Bildungskarrieren im Vergleich – Einige Vorüberlegungen," in *Vermittlung fremder Kultur. Theorie – Didaktik – Praxis*, eds. A. Wolff and W. Rug (Bonn, 1988).

6. In keeping with the reflective character of this essay, the notes are not intended to be exhaustive but rather try to suggest further reading. Cf. D. Goldschmidt, U. Teichler and W.-D. Webler, eds., *Forschungsgegenstand Hochschule. Überblick und Trendbericht* (Frankfurt, 1984).

officers and some untarnished academics began to work on resuming some semblance of instruction during the winter semester of 1945/6.[7] Under these extreme conditions, the very restoration of scholarly lecturing and writing seemed like a triumph over racist destruction. While some prominent Nazis among the faculty were purged and discredited SS members barred from studying, most academics desperately longed to return to some kind of normalcy that they usually defined as a blend of the best of imperial and Weimar legacies.[8]

Instead of leading to a renewal, the postwar chaos prompted a return to Humboldtian rhetoric as an uncompromised tradition. But a century and a half after its inception, this once inspiring vision had rigidified into a ruling discourse that glossed over basic contradictions with pat formulas: the incantation of academic freedom and autonomy (Einsamkeit und Freiheit) conflicted with the need for state support; the stress on universalism of subjects and philosophical perspective clashed with scientific specialization; the emphasis on individual aesthetic cultivation, called Bildung, contrasted with the needs of systematic scholarship, as Wissenschaft is best rendered; and the imperative of linking teaching and research (Einheit von Lehre und Forschung) was proving ever more difficult to realize.[9] By reviving the rhetoric of self-cultivation, the universities also returned to the problems of elitism, arrogance, and apoliticism.

In spite of this neotraditional self-image, higher education practice was forced to modernize piecemeal. Because Nazi restrictions and the war had dammed up demand for academic training, enrollments doubled quickly to over 100,000 students. As a result of armament programs, many scientific and technological subjects as

---

7. J. F. Tent, Mission on the Rhine: Reeducation and Denazification in American-Occupied Germany (Chicago, 1982). Cf. M. Heinemann, ed., Umerziehung und Wiederaufbau. Die Bildungspolitik der Besatzungsmächte in Deutschland und Österreich (Stuttgart, 1981).

8. M. G. Ash, "Verordnete Umbrüche – Konstruierte Kontinuitäten: Zur Entnazifizierung von Wissenschaftlern und Wissenschaften nach 1945," Zeitschrift für Geschichtswissenschaft 43 (1995): 903-23.

9. For the source of the concepts see E. Anrich, Die Idee der deutschen Universität. Die fünf Grundschriften aus der Zeit ihrer Neugründung (Darmstadt, 1956). Cf. also C. Oehler, Hochschulentwicklung in der Bundesrepublik Deutschland seit 1945 (Frankfurt, 1989), 125ff.

well as some medical fields were so highly developed that the victors rounded up German scientists and exported them to their own countries.[10] But scholars in the humanities finally wanted to read forbidden emigre writers and needed to catch up with international artistic and philosophical discussions. At the same time, the social sciences such as political science or sociology, decimated by the Third Reich, actually had to be refounded in order to stabilize the fledgling democracy. The postwar decade was therefore marked by a paradoxical blend of conservative modernization. Because of the restoration of autonomy, democratization efforts could only succeed in part. In the first postwar years many students felt a veritable hunger for meaning, for trying new, non-authoritarian forms of learning in a community of scholars, to which some sensitive professors chose to respond. Together with American and British authorities, this progressive minority worked out impressive plans for democratizing German higher education in the Schwalbacher Guidelines and in the *Blaue Gutachten*. But the compromise formula of "putting the healthy core of tradition at the service of the needs of our time" and the relative reserve of the occupation authorities allowed the accustomed structure of the *Ordinarienuniversität* (university dominated by full professors) to revive.[11] Self-government and professorial privileges led to a return of older forms of deference and dependence that vitiated most efforts at institutional democracy.

The contradiction between Humboldtian rhetoric and modernizing reality that had been growing since 1900 was resumed with the postwar restoration of the German universities. Critical initiatives such as the lectures by Karl Jaspers or the foundation of the Free University in Berlin might soften some authoritarian features but could not altogether prevent their reestablishment. The Indian summer of the Humboldtian vision did inspire idealistic efforts at a *studium generale* and at personal self-development; but

10. H.-W. Prahl, *Sozialgeschichte des Hochschulwesens* (Munich, 1978): 383; and N. M. Naimark, *The Russians in Germany: A History of the Soviet Zone of Occupation, 1945-1949* (Cambridge, MA, 1995), 205ff.
11. H. Rudolph and R. Husemann, *Hochschulpolitik zwischen Expansion und Restriktion. Ein Vergleich der Entwicklung in der Bundesrepublik Deutschland und der Deutschen Demokratischen Republik* (Frankfurt, 1984), 23ff.

it failed to keep professional training (fachliche Berufsausbildung) from becoming the actual goal of the majority. The democratization impulse of the progressive minority might motivate the reestablishment of student self-government, but it could not compel the university to confront its own complicity with the Third Reich.[12] Instead of initiating reform, the recovery of the neohumanist discourse largely served as justification for the reaffirmation of a German academic Sonderweg.

Expansion

The revival of Humboldtian rhetoric became even more problematic with the extraordinary expansion of higher education during the 1960s. Demographic reasons such as the arrival of the strong Third Reich birth cohorts propelled a growth of the primary and secondary sectors, which increased the pool of potential applicants for tertiary institutions.[13] Social factors such as increasing aspirations for upward mobility as well as more resources to pay for further training motivated a higher proportion of secondary school graduates to go on to the university. Moreover, Georg Picht's warnings that a shortage of professionals would lead to an "educational catastrophe" and Ralf Dahrendorf's plea for "education as a civil right" created the political will to meet these challenges.[14] While conservatives advocated responding to technological manpower needs, liberals supported increasing educational opportunities (Chancengleichheit) through a national scholarship program (Bafög).

A new kind of cooperative federalism also facilitated the growth of higher education. In the 1950s the universities began to work together in developing common policies through a Conference of

12. K. Jaspers and K. Rossmann, Die Idee der Universität, 2nd ed. (Berlin, 1980). Cf. also K. H. Jarausch, Deutsche Studenten 1800-1970 (Frankfurt, 1984), 213ff.

13. P. Lundgreen, "Bildungsnachfrage und differentielles Bildungsverhalten in Deutschland," in H. Kellenbenz, ed., Wachstumsschwankungen. Wirtschaftliche und soziale Auswirkungen (Stuttgart, 1981), 61ff. Cf. H. Titze, Der Akademikerzyklus. Historische Untersuchungen über die Wiederkehr von Überfüllung und Mangel in akademischen Karrieren (Göttingen, 1990).

14. G. Picht, Die deutsche Bildungskatastrophe (Olten, 1964) and R. Dahrendorf, Bildung ist Bürgerrecht (Hamburg, 1965).

Rectors (*Westdeutsche Rektorenkonferenz*). The creation of independent, tax-supported foundations such as the German Research Council (DFG) or the German Academic Exchange Service (DAAD) supported academic endeavors. Similarly, the individual states, called *Länder*, which were responsible for funding and oversight, decided to coordinate their efforts in a consultative Science Council (*Wissenschaftsrat*), created in 1957. The federal government expanded its scientific role when the 1969 revision of the Basic Law authorized joint tasks such as the construction of buildings, the promotion of research of national importance, and the issuing of framework regulations. The new federal ministry of science and research aided expansion by funneling resources into the higher education sector.[15]

Increased demand produced a burst of experimentation that exceeded Humboldt's institutional bounds. For instance, the *Technische Hochschulen* started to expand their scope by adding other subjects in order to turn into full fledged universities. At the same time, the teacher unions succeeded in getting most pedagogical academies integrated into regular universities as faculties of education. In order to bridge the gap between applied training and scholarship, SPD-led governments in North Rhine-Westphalia and Hesse developed a new institutional type, called *Gesamthochschule*, that purported to be a comprehensive tertiary institution. Traditional universities responded by upgrading older subjects like dentistry or creating new programs in journalism, biochemistry, etc. To provide a new degree for graduates not interested in public service, universities also revived the ancient *Magister Artium*.[16]

The ensuing rapid growth fundamentally transformed the system from *elite to mass higher education*. Through the expansion of existing institutions and the doubling of their number with new foundations, the supply of tertiary training grew dramatically. During the three decades between the early 1950s and the early 1980s, student enrollments exploded about ten times, rising from around one hundred thousand to over one million. The increase in size

15. U. Teichler, *Higher Education in the Federal Republic of Germany: Developments and Recent Issues* (New York, 1986), 13ff, 93ff.
16. Oehler, *Hochschulentwicklung*, 17ff; Rudolph and Husemann, *Hochschulpolitik*, 56ff.

also meant a change in composition to roughly 40 percent women and a diversification of backgrounds, increasing the number of students from the working class to about 14 percent. In consequence, the proportion of the age cohort in higher education jumped from about 5 percent to over 25 percent, transforming tertiary training from an exclusive preserve to a more broadly accessible path. With this social opening the Federal Republic finally caught up with developments that had been underway in other Western countries since the 1930s.[17]

In hindsight, the result of this expansion of tertiary studies appears somewhat paradoxical. No doubt, the enormous growth initially provided many people who would otherwise have been excluded with new opportunities to gain jobs in the expanding system itself. But mass enrollments also produced overcrowding that led to limited admission *(numerus clausus)* in some subjects, with places assigned by a central federal authority (ZVS), and reduced the quality of available instruction. More importantly, the job market could only absorb the flood of newly certified graduates in the beginning and the oil recessions of the 1970s created mass unemployment, raising the specter of an academic proletariat. The oversupply of teachers points to an ironic devaluation of degrees that lost their automatic claim to a government position when public funding for further expansion of schools dried up.[18] This relative overproduction broke the crucial nexus of the entitlement system *(Berechtigungswesen)* that had guaranteed the educated jobs during the past century.

The expansion from elite to mass higher education effectively eroded the institutional underpinnings of the neohumanist vision. A liberal reinterpretation of Humboldt could be used to justify making educational opportunities available more equally. But recruitment from more diverse social backgrounds undercut the cultural resonance of the ideal of cultivation, while the overcrowding of

17. W. Albert and C. Oehler, *Materialien zur Entwicklung der Hochschulen 1950-1967* (Hanover, 1969); F. K. Ringer, *Education and Society in Modern Europe* (Bloomington, 1979), 70ff, 272ff.
18. K. Hüfner, J. Naumann, H. Köhler, and G. Pfeffer, *Hochkonjunktur und Flaute: Bildungspolitik in der Bundesrepublik Deutschland 1967-1980* (Stuttgart, 1986), 200ff.

seminars and libraries meant that most students lost contact with actual research. An ever increasing majority of the consumers of higher education therefore no longer followed the precepts of *Bildung* but demanded competent professional training instead. Yet overburdened professors and harassed assistants continued to cling to the Humboldtian research ethos, afraid that they would lose their privileges if they became mere advanced teachers. No wonder that expansion further increased the discrepancy between a his-toricized academic rhetoric and a modernized scientific practice.[19]

Reform

The youth revolt of the late 1960s brought the crisis of the tradi-tional conception of cultivation into the open. A combination of societal and educational factors propelled the mass protests that have, with the passing of a generation, assumed a mythical char-acter. In political terms, students mainly objected to the Vietnam War, the Nazi remnants in the Bonn establishment, the emergency legislation, and the conservative Springer press empire. In social respects the satisfaction of material needs allowed the postwar cohorts to challenge the conventional lifestyle and control of their parents. Within the universities the influx of newcomers from the lower classes and the deterioration of study conditions due to over-crowding led to acute alienation. In contrast to the conformism of the 1950s, the rebellious students of the late 1960s took democ-racy literally and no longer put up with what they considered the hierarchical authoritarianism of the university.[20]

The student movement denounced the shortcomings of higher education as exemplar of capitalist exploitation in general. In the walled-in city of Berlin, sit-ins, strikes, and demonstrations began

19. Locating the rupture during the postwar expansion does not seek to relativize the earlier erosion of the Humboldtian legacy, but rather emphasizes the final stage of its collapse. For a revealing reappraisal of the tradition see H. Schel-sky, *Einsamkeit und Freiheit: Idee und Gestalt der deutschen Universität und ihrer Reformen* (Reinbeck, 1963).
20. K. Allerbeck, *Soziologie radikaler Studentenbewegungen* (Munich, 1973); and P. Mosler, *Was wir wollten, was wir wurden. Die Studentenrevolte – zehn Jahre danach* (Reinbeck, 1977).

to expose the discrepancy between Humboldtian idealism and the frustrating reality of the university in such slogans as "*Unter den Talaren, der Muff von Tausend Jahren*" ("Under the robes, the stuffy air of a thousand years"). With the death of Benno Ohnesorg during an anti-Shah demonstration in 1967, the protests became more general in scope, spread like wildfire to other campuses, and challenged the political system as such. It is often forgotten that student activism actually combined three distinctive strands: an anti-authoriarian lifestyle rebellion with anarchist overtones (the communards); a neo-Marxist critique of capitalism in a variety of orthodox KP, Maoist, or Trotskyite guises; and finally a radical democratic attempt to rescue existing structures through fundamental changes.[21]

Each faction developed a particular critique of the self-conception and practice of the German university. The anti-authoritarians called for the liberation of learning from all of its formal constraints, making it a spontaneous interaction of equals. The neo-Marxists denounced the bourgeois university as an agent of monopoly capitalism and preached a conception of emancipatory partisanship. Only the concerned democrats were interested in improving extant institutions through reforms such as the creation of smaller units, a voice in university decision making, fewer exams, and the like. While the *Wissenschaftsrat* tried to defend academic pluralism, rebellious students sought to overthrow such objectivist standards by calling for greater social relevance of scholarship. The demands for more participation and equality among all ranks culminated in the resolutions of the assistants, formulated in Bad Kreuznach during the spring of 1968.[22]

Confronted with such vocal pressure, progressive professors and politicians promoted the necessary changes by founding reform universities. Though conceived as relief for overcrowding, new institutions in Bochum, Bielefeld, Bremen, and Konstanz sought to

---

21. H.-A. Jacobsen and H. Dollinger, *Die deutschen Studenten. Der Kampf um die Hochschulreform*, 2nd ed. (Munich, 1969). See Beth Peifer's forthcoming dissertation on the mythologization of the German student movement (Chapel Hill, NC, 1997).

22. Bundesassistentenkonferenz, *Kreuznacher Hochschulkonzept. Reformziele der Bundesassistentenkonferenz* (Bonn, 1968); Jarausch, *Deutsche Studenten*, 226ff.

recreate an intellectual community between teachers and learners by accentuating research. Their liberal constitutions gave students a voice in decision making; their departmental structure created smaller and more coherent units; their thematic concentration and other arrangements (such as the Center for Interdisciplinary Research (ZiF) in Bielefeld) facilitated interdisciplinary cooperation; their campus layout concentrated teaching and research in one pleasant location; and their structured curricula as well as closer faculty advising improved study quality.[23] The appointment of younger and more critical professors created an open atmosphere that made some of these new institutions synonymous with innovative and socially engaged scholarship.

The reform ferment ultimately resulted in modest innovations that abolished some of the worst abuses. Supported by liberal professors and the powerful education union (GEW), many changes were enshrined in the *Hochschulrahmengesetz* (HRG) of 1976 that created a federal framework for local regulation. In recognizing the practical purpose of study, this law proposed that a student "be made capable of scholarly or artistic work and of responsible behavior in a free, democratic and social state, ruled by law." In most *Länder*, institutes were depersonalized with responsibility shared more widely among their members; the department was introduced as the basic unit, replacing the broader faculties; university presidents were elected for longer terms and a professional administration was created; self-government was broadened to include not only full professors, but also lower faculty, students, and staff; and the second dissertation *(Habilitation)* was made optional, while assistants were elevated to assistant professors.[24]

These changes markedly improved the functioning of the universities, but did not succeed in supplanting the Humboldtian legacy with a more democratic vision. This failure stemmed from a fundamental disagreement on which new conception should supersede the old ideal. Conservative professors defended tradition

23. See for example P. Lundgreen, ed., *Reformuniversität Bielefeld 1969-1994. Zwischen Defensive und Innovation* (Bielefeld, 1994).
24. Kommunistischer Studentenverband, ed., *Die formierte Universität. Hochschulreform in der BRD und Westberlin* (Cologne, 1977), 133ff; and Peisert and Framheim, *Systems of Higher Education*, 117ff.

by invoking slogans such as the "loneliness and freedom" of research, though at the same time advocating technocratic solutions. Progressive academics attempted to jettison the content of the Humboldtian rhetoric, while searching for a modern equivalent to its once-liberating ethos – a difficult quest. Radical critics defined the neohumanist rhetoric itself as the culprit, but their anarchist or neo-Marxist proposals did not provide a compelling alternative.[25] Ironically, the reform era ultimately rescued the Humboldtian discourse from extinction by alleviating some of its gravest problems through the adoption of largely imported American solutions.

Consolidation

In the mid-1970s, a shift toward gradual consolidation permitted the embattled tradition to reassert itself. On the one hand, enrollments continued to grow by hundreds of thousands and some innovative efforts, especially on the curricular level, persisted. But on the other hand, the oil shocks tightened financial resources while growing unemployment for university graduates due to a slowdown in government hiring ended the higher education boom. Because vocational school graduates tended to find jobs immediately, public priorities shifted to the upgrading of lesser postsecondary institutions such as engineering or social work schools, accessible without a regular high school diploma, into full-fledged *Fachhochschulen*. Although ever larger student numbers thronged into the lecture halls, the euphoria of growth slowly gave way to retrenchment and inaction during the 1980s.[26]

Remnants of Humboldtian rhetoric helped legitimize the *retreat from the reform agenda* that resulted from the excesses of the student movement. In trying to rally moderate professors, the *Bund Freiheit der Wissenschaft* propagated a return from politicization to the legacy of competence and authority. In response to a constitutional challenge, the Federal Supreme Court (BGH) in 1973 overturned the controversial *Drittelparität* arrangement, which had

25. J. Habermas, *Protestbewegung und Hochschulreform* (Frankfurt, 1969), 9ff; O. Negt, *Achtundsechzig. Politische Intellektuelle und die Macht* (Göttingen, 1995).
26. Rudolph and Husemann, *Hochschulpolitik*, 96ff.

given equal standing to professors, nonprofessorial teaching and research staff, and students and other university workers, and mandated that full professors have a majority in all commissions dealing with research and teaching. Extremist resolutions also brought the political mandate of student government so much into disrepute that South German states simply dissolved the AStAs. In struggling for recognition from their peers, the *Gesamthochschulen* also reverted to the regular university pattern. Finally, the 1985 revision of the HRG fundamentally differentiated between the theoretical orientation of the universities and the more practical character of the *Fachhochschulen*.[27]

Fiscal constraints also led to a freeze in public funding for higher education. Compared to keeping the economic engine running during the transition to postindustrial society, expenditures for teaching and research seemed less important. Since demographers predicted that student numbers would recede when the two-fifths smaller birth cohorts of the 1970s arrived, it seemed logical to "tunnel under" the enrollment peak without further institutional buildup. Therefore faculty positions were held constant from 1975 on, at about 80,000 for all ranks, while construction was limited to replacement and modernization. Unfortunately student choices rendered the figure of 850,000 places illusory, since a higher proportion chose to go on to advanced training, thereby driving up enrollments toward double the planning target.[28] The shortsighted parsimony of the CDU/FDP coalition aggravated the underfunding by actually decreasing higher education spending as part of the GNP.

The consequences of financial stringency further reduced the chances for implementing any aspirations of cultivation. The virtual hiring freeze for full professors created a large backlog of qualified younger scholars waiting for appointment and slowed progress toward gender equality. Lack of funding led to the rapid deteriora-

27. H. Maier and M. Zöller, eds., *Bund Freiheit der Wissenschaft. Der Gründungskongreß in Bad Godesberg* (Cologne, 1970); and Oehler, *Hochschulentwicklung*, 21ff.
28. Peisert and Framheim, *Higher Education in the Federal Republic*, 28ff, 80ff. Cf. Rainer Künzel, "Political Control and Funding: The Future of State Support," in this volume.

tion of facilities, especially in the humanities and social sciences, increasing their technological obsolescence (personal computers, fax machines) and making research, whenever possible, move out of the universities. The result was overcrowding in seminars with over one hundred participants, competition for scarce books in uncooperative libraries, and a general sense of neglect. The reduction in numbers and transformation of student stipends into loans also led to much part-time work (called, interestingly enough, *Jobbing*), which extended the already excessive length of study to an average of over fourteen semesters.[29]

Solutions for such problems had to work within the existing rhetoric and the resources available. While hopes for mobilizing donors by founding private universities such as the college in Witten-Herdecke were misplaced, the public correspondence program at the *Fernuniversität* (Open University) in Hagen was quite successful. Large foundations such as the DFG tried to help with initiatives such as the *Sonderforschungsbereiche*, which supported interdisciplinary cooperation on common research themes at existing universities. Also the Fiebiger fellowship program for promising *Privatdozenten* sought to ensure a supply of future professors for the retirement wave at the end of the century. Similarly the *Graduiertenkollegs* intended to offer tighter graduate training, somewhat on the American model. Finally, the Erasmus program provided support for study in other European countries.[30] Though such innovations provided welcome improvements, they were unable to cure the underlying problems of the German system.

Instead of fostering further innovation, a reformulation of the Humboldtian discourse largely came to serve as a cover for institutional inaction during the 1980s. The research imperative was often invoked to justify the reimposition of professorial power within the decision making of institutes and departments. Neohumanist phrases were also helpful in defending German peculiarities

29. P. Glotz and W. Malanowski, *Student heute. Angepaßt, Ausgestiegen?* (Hamburg, 1982); and W.-D. Webler, "Individualität und individuelle Gestaltungsmöglichkeiten von Studierenden in der Massenuniversität," in *Universitäten im Umbruch: Zum Verhältnis von Hochschulen, Studenten und Gesellschaft*, eds. F. W. Busch et al.(Oldenburg, 1992), 175ff.
30. Oehler, *Hochschulentwicklung*, 233ff.

such as the *Habilitation* against international criticism. Though liberals might employ the implicit egalitarianism of *allgemeine Menschenbildung* to ward off attempts at reinstitutionalizing academic elitism, severe underfunding rendered any pretensions to cultivation through scholarship illusory. Because the Humboldtian discourse blocked a realistic perception of mass white-collar training, it contributed to bringing the German university system to a state of latent crisis on the eve of unification.[31]

Conclusion

This rapid overview suggests that German higher education developed in a paradoxical fashion during the postwar period. On the one hand, pragmatic modernization made its structures and content so attractive that they pulled twice as many foreign students into the FRG compared with West Germans who studied abroad. Student enrollments grew roughly fifteen times, advancing the share of tertiary training from one in twenty to one in three of an age cohort. The number of institutions more than doubled from 25 to 68 universities, while their character diversified to include reform foundations, technical universities, and comprehensive and special institutions.[32] Research quality improved and approximated its former prominence in some special fields, as recognized by the continuing awarding of Nobel prizes. These startling changes brought the German system closer to Western patterns and practices than ever before.

On the other hand, adaptation was hampered by a false consciousness, created by the discursive framework of cultivation. In the immediate aftermath of the war, a return to Humboldt's grand vision legitimized the restoration of the *Ordinarienuniversität* and excused the university from confronting its own responsibility for the Third Reich. During the expansion, a radical reinterpretation of neohumanist egalitarianism helped to justify the growth of higher education to unprecedented levels. But in the student revolt, the

31. M. Daxner, "Hochschullehrer in der Massenuniversität," in *Hochschule im Umbruch*, 234ff.
32. Peisert and Framheim, *Higher Education in the Federal Republic*, 15ff.

rigidity of the Humboldtian legacy became the target of protest and served as a negative foil for the formulation of reform demands. Finally, during the consolidation of the 1980s a resort to traditional formulas served as a cover for the restoration of professorial power and prerogatives. In spite of its implicit liberalism, the practice of neohumanist rhetoric often justified an academic "special consciousness" *(Sonderbewußtsein)* that supported a separate German path.[33]

This discrepancy between reality and rhetoric in higher education should, perhaps, be called the *"Humboldt syndrome."* Such a label might refer to the ritualization of a vision into a set of empty slogans such as "loneliness and freedom" that no longer inspire in practice. This notion would also highlight the priority of norms of cultivation and research over the needs of professional training, which actually dominate the practice of mass higher education. At the same time, this concept could allude to the power of a historical legacy to prevent the formulation of a modern democratic self-conception, more adequate in solving current problems. And finally such an expression might hint at some of the reasons for the success of the rhetorical strategy of professors in regaining their institutional authority. The price of the continued tyranny of the Humboldt syndrome over the German university has been an unacknowledged deficit of legitimacy.[34]

In recent decades, the discursive framework of cultivation has mainly served to block necessary reforms. Since the 1960s the *Wissenschaftsrat* has recommended countless remedies for the intractable weaknesses of the German system. For instance, the introduction of an intermediate degree like the BA could resolve the contradiction between mass training and elite research by sequencing both. A frank recognition of prestige hierarchies among institutions and departments could safeguard minimum standards while advancing instruction in a few selected centers.

33. For the concept see H. Grebing, *Der 'Deutsche Sonderweg' in Europa 1806-1945* (Stuttgart, 1986).
34. The key question is therefore not what did Wilhelm von Humboldt really think, but why did his ideas develop such a powerful hold over a system whose practice grew ever more distant from their prescriptions. Cf. C. Menze, *Die Bildungsreform Wilhelm von Humboldts* (Hanover, 1975), 469ff.

Moving some humanities and social science research out of the universities would relieve overstressed faculties and upgrade its quality. Improving study conditions, tightening curricula, or reintroducing tuition might shorten the seemingly endless time to degree.[35] But such constructive proposals have been blocked time and again by accusing them of violating the hallowed Humboldtian legacy. The result of this reform blockage (Reformstau) is a loss of competitiveness and a sense of pervasive malaise.

The only way out of this vicious cycle is the recognition that the Humboldt syndrome is itself part of the problem. No doubt the inspiring rhetoric of early ninetenth century idealism revitalized the university as institution and propelled German scholarship to the forefront.[36] But in a late twentieth century postindustrial society, its idealistic maxims no longer adequately describe reality and, instead of liberating as intended, help cement outworn patterns and irrelevant practices. The original emancipatory impulse of self-perfection through cultivation and scholarship needs to find a new formulation that is both intellectually convincing and politically appealing. If they do not want to founder in the future, German universities have to enunciate a fresh democratic and social vision that harnesses the potential for human improvement through systematic reason in the face of mounting irrationality. Do the endemmic complaints about malfunctioning not suggest that the time has come to break through the confines of the Humboldt syndrome?[37]

---

35. See the almost annual recommendations of the Wissenschaftsrat, starting in 1960 with Empfehlungen zum Ausbau der wissenschaftlichen Einrichtungen, Teil I, Wissenschaftliche Hochschulen (Tübingen, 1960).

36. F. K. Ringer, The Decline of the German Mandarins: The German Academic Community, 1890-1933 (Cambridge, MA, 1969) versus R. vom Bruch, Wissenschaft, Politik und öffentliche Meinung. Gelehrtenpolitik im Wilhelminischen Deutschland (Husum, 1980).

37. "Überfüllt und kaputt," Der Spiegel, 1995, No. 42: 58-67. See also P. Lundgreen, "Mythos Humboldt Today: Teaching, Research, and Administration," in this volume.

Session Two

DISCUSSION

GERALD RIEMER: You said something about the relationship between sympathetic faculty and students in the 1960s. I am wondering if you have any thoughts on what the situation is like today. For the one semester I spent teaching at a German university, I was struck by what seemed to me a kind of complacency, basically among the younger faculty who in fact are there now, to a large extent because they were the student rebels in the 1960s. To put it almost cynically, it seemed to me that the effect of their rebellion was basically to grant them many of the same privileges of the old *Ordinarienuniversität* (university of full professors). To students of another generation, who have problems with resources and malaise, they really did not seem to be offering much, except some sort of vaguely idealistic, Humboldtian kind of rhetoric. I was also struck by how the students seemed to accept this; all anybody could agree on was that everyone involved was a victim of budget cuts. The sort of elementary reform proposals that would have occurred to me, for example to emphasize more responsible teaching, just did not seem to occur to them. What do you think about the interaction between presumably sympathetic younger faculty and the students with the new malaise today?

KATHERINE OLESKO: My question concerns the intellectual landscape accompanying all of these structural changes. We are now at the end of the twentieth century, confronted with the breakdown of the traditional disciplines and the rapid rise of interdisciplinary research, particularly in the United States. Yet from 1945 to 1989, the German universities were not as open to that kind of interdisciplinary research. To what do you attribute that, and how do you see things changing after 1989?

MITCHELL ASH: I am sympathetic to your suggestion that the Humboldt syndrome, that is, the rhetorical self-blockage you describe under that name, was part of what inhibited reform in the pre-1989 West German university. But I would like to suggest that, following the logic of your own argument, there may also be an institutional dimension to this. Thinking of the university as a collection of client groups rather than as a community may help us to understand it as kind of a microcosm of West German society. As we know, West German society changes slowly, in part because consensus is required amongst large numbers of often antagonistic groupings before anything can move forward. It seems that in the university a similar problem also exists. How much of a role do you give the conflict of groupings within the university – each grouping with a veto or at least the possibility of blocking change or reform?

BRUCE SMITH: I was a student at the Free University and I also attended the Humboldt University occasionally in 1958 and 1959. Then I had some involvement in the late 1960s at the time we formed the International Councils on the Future of the Universities during the Marxist uprisings of the day. Then, in 1980, I visited nine universities, and did a study for the National Academy of Sciences. I think there is some overintellectualization of the problem here. At the time I was a student, I had some wonderful professors. I always loved all of my professors, because I loved learning. The problem was the students were no good; my fellow students were not serious. They were guzzling beer. It's not that they were just by nature no good. Part of it was that there were no exams, except for the two months before the final exam, when students studied like crazy to try to make up for their total inertia and neglect the four previous years when they should have been working. So I thought that if they had exams at the end of the year or at the end of the semester, it would have been a lot better. And I also remember calculating one time with Erwin Scheuch the monetary benefits given to students, which were and are absolutely appalling. The money rewards in terms of free tickets and free transportation and free everything else are incredible.

Let me jump ahead to the 1980s. The problem then in visiting these universities, and the money was still going pretty well at that time, was that there was generally good quality, I think, in the major universities, but there wasn't exceptional, superior performance. Part of the reason for this was the fact that if you were a scientist – and mostly I visited scientists – after four years of maintaining a research technician, that person got tenure. It was just absolutely unbelievable. They could not get any flexibility or new starts because of this incredible rigidity, with everybody in the whole system getting tenure. I think you have to consider the fact that this is an upward redistribution of income from the poor to the wealthy. Having universities where you are paying students from the upper classes and do not have tuition helps bog down the whole thing. I think that these practical problems need to be considered as well.

KONRAD JARAUSCH: The 68'er question, that is, what has happened to them now that they are themselves established is, of course, full of ironies, and one is tempted to be very cynical about this result. Some of it has to do with age and with the issue of who has the privileges, whether you have them or the other people have them and you want them. But I do not think that is enough. My experience has been that a lot of the younger *Assistenten* in Germany are people who care about instruction, and they work very hard. But the system is set up in such a way right now that it defeats this feeling of commitment; if you have a seminar or a discussion section with fifty people in it, you are working in an impossible situation. The result of the recent budget cuts in Berlin is the sorriest thing I have seen in a long time. If any of you have been there recently, you will understand why I say this. It is just a disaster, and it is in some ways outrageous to have that at a leading academic institution. If you have to work with situations like that and you have idealism and want to do something for people, you get systematically turned off. The fact that people put their own academic development with their second dissertation or *Habilitationsschrift* before their teaching commitments seems to me to be understandable in that context. There are smaller institutions, such as Trier and Constance, in which the facilities are very nice and in which things are going well. Most of my comments have to do with places like Munich, Berlin, Münster, and Cologne, the really big universities.

The issue of interdisciplinarity is tricky; of course, the traditional faculty system was supposed in theory to foster that, because it

brought a wide range of disciplines together. On some level of collegiality, it probably worked; that is, professors saw each other on a
fairly regular basis, in the salons and so on. But I doubt whether
there was any spill-over into real scholarly work. We can document the roles of leading professorial houses, where there was this
kind of interchange around the turn of the century, but I am skeptical about its impact over time. My own experiences have been
with the ZiF (Center for Interdisciplinary Research) in Bielefeld
and with the ZI6 (Central Institute for Social Scientific Research)
in Berlin, which show that during the 1970s there were already
efforts to reach a new level of modern interdisciplinarity. It's just
that German structures are fairly rigid both administratively and
fiscally, and to get any of this going means overcoming enormous
resistance. So the practice of interdisciplinarity was not very extensive, and that is of course the reason why the institutes I just named
and the *Sonderforschungsbereiche* (special research areas) were
invented, so that there could be a bridge beyond the disciplines.

The question about the institutional aspect of the discourse
problem is quite correct. Discourses are also material. They are
not just things floating around in rooms, like our discussion today,
but involve interests and the groups that have such interests. That
is, of course, what makes the system so immobile, because these
discourses can be used and are being used by various kinds of parties for their own ends. One of the great ironies of the democratic
reform of the late 1960s and early 1970s is that the *Gruppenuniversität*, which appears democratic in its structure because not only
full professors, but also junior faculty, students, and even the
nonacademic staff are represented on various kinds of commissions, has led to a kind of gridlock in academic self-government.
Many institutions are thus dominated by the people who manage
to be (and stay longest) at meetings. It is ironic that sometimes
democratic impulses can have the opposite result.

Taking the practical questions at the end, my first impulse is to
say that student attitudes have of course to do with the fact that
the classical Gymnasium, with Greek and Latin, was a fairly regi-
mented institution in which people were drilled. Therefore, when
they finally got out of that with the *Abitur* and experienced *Lern-
freiheit* (freedom to choose one's own course of study), which is a

practical version of the larger concept of academic freedom, this was something which students conquered for or relegated to themselves. It became a set of social customs, which was in some ways necessary. Therefore the professoriate agreed with it and said, implicitly, you guys go around and drink and carry on and play pranks, because you've been drilled for so long. Then you get serious again when you begin the more advanced part of your studies. That worked with this sort of background. In the meantime, of course, secondary schooling has changed, and has become much more modern. The Gymnasium with *Leistungskurse* (advanced specialized courses) has become a kind of college-preparatory unit in which there is already a lot of selection and not nearly as much drilling any more. This behavior is still around among students as a social custom, but it has become dysfunctional.

Anybody in the German system who wants to tighten up anything at all in terms of curriculum is always accused of violating academic freedom. This is amusing particularly for Americans, because it implies a definition of academic freedom which does not exist in our country. Even in a democracy, we do not think that telling an undergraduate to take X, Y, and Z courses for distribution requirements is an infringment of academic freedom. Making students do their homework, making them do their reading, show up for the mid-term and final exams, and write papers is not seen as such a violation either. Actually, German practices are more diverse than one thinks, because in the sciences and in various other areas like medicine, this version of academic freedom has never existed in that way. There are tests, there are specified curricula, and so on. So this is a disease, I think, which affects the humanities and the social sciences. It is one of the traditions which is, I think, understandable and has a kind of charm in its nineteenth-century subcultural foundation, but it is counterproductive today.

Chapter Three

HUMBOLDT COOPTED

East German Universities, 1945-1989

⟳

John Connelly

B efore there was an East German state, there was an East German identity. Soon after its formation in 1946, the Socialist
Unity Party of Germany (SED) began concocting an identity for its
subjects from the "progressive" legacies of German history. At first
this meant Müntzer, Goethe, and Marx; in the early 1980s, a more
self-confident SED added Luther, Frederick the Great, and even
Bismarck. In university policy, the SED claimed to pursue the
ideals of Wilhelm von Humboldt.[1] The Unity Socialists ritualisti-

---

1. On 26 October 1948, the Academic Senate of Berlin University Unter den
   Linden made a unanimous request of the German Education Administration
   (DVV) that it be granted the name "Humboldt University" in honor of the
   brothers Alexander and Wilhelm von Humboldt. On 8 February 1949, at the
   inauguration of the new rector, Communist Walter Friedrich, Berlin University
   became Humboldt University. H. Klein, ed. *Humboldt-Universität zu Berlin.
   Dokumente 1810-1985* (Berlin, 1985), 82. Ritualistic Humboldtian invocations
   of the "unity of research and teaching" or the need for the "education of the
   complete individual" appeared scattered throughout the higher educational
   literature of the German Democratic Republic. See for example some of the
   pronouncements of leading GDR higher educational specialist Otto Rühle:
   "Fortschritt in der Wissenschaft und Weltniveau," *Das Hochschulwesen* 14, no.
   4 (1965): 236; "Humboldts Universitätsidee – Tradition und Aufgabe," in

cally invoked "Humboldt" at every marker in East German university history. Yet their active philosophy, namely that universities should serve the state as directly as possible, stood in sharp contradiction to "Humboldtian" thinking.[2] For that reason, Western observers have never honored the SED's claim to have realized the ideals of Wilhelm von Humboldt.[3]

Yet the SED invested great energy in breathing life into Humboldt and the other gods of the German Democratic pantheon, and one is justified in asking why. After all, no other East European state so carefully preserved a cult of an educational reformer, though such reformers did indeed exist. One need think only of Lomonosov, Comenius, or Konarski. What set East German higher education apart, I would like to suggest, was the more general East German complex of living mentally in the West, yet physically in the East. Humboldt – like Goethe and Luther – was made for Western consumption, and for an East German population, which itself consumed the West every evening through television. Invocation of "progressive" legacies was a vital part of the German Democratic Republic's competition with the West. The point is not that this Western image was without substance, the point is

Wilhelm von Humboldt 1767-1967: Erbe – Gegenwart – Zukunft, eds. W. Hartke and H. Maskolat (Halle (S), 1967), 162-94. See also the article of the Honecker-era Minister of Higher Education Hans-Joachim Böhme, "Erbeaneignung und Traditionspflege in der Wissenschaft," *Das Hochschulwesen* 34, no. 8 (1986): 187-92, cited in Gerlind Schmidt, "Aspekte der Hochschulpolitik in der DDR," in *Das Profil der DDR in der sozialistischen Staatengemeinschaft*, eds. Ilse Spittmann and Gisela Helwig (Cologne, 1987), 78.

2. At the SED Sixth Party Congress in 1963, Walter Ulbricht proclaimed principles that would guide university reform in that decade. Universities had the function of "training highly educated cadres who have mastered the scientific way of thinking and work creatively and economically for the attainment of the highest social use (*Nutzen*)." Cited in G.-J. Glaessner and I. Rudolph, *Macht durch Wissen: Zum Zusammenhang von Bildungspolitik, Bildungssystem und Kaderqualifizierung in der DDR. Eine politisch-soziologische Untersuchung* (Opladen, 1978), 119.

3. Western students of GDR higher education never took seriously the SED's commitment to the "freedom to study and teach" or to the "unity of research and teaching." See for example R. Rytlewski, "Studienorganisation in der DDR," in *Vergleich von Bildung und Erziehung in der Bundesrepublik Deutschland und in der Deutschen Demokratischen Republik*, eds. O. Anweiler et al. (Cologne, 1990), 449; and M. Usko, *Hochschulen in der DDR* (Berlin, 1974), 25-26.

that the substance was Eastern. This essay will attempt to peel away the Humboldtian mask, and show East German higher education's Eastern substance.

East German higher education was distinctly, even preeminently, East European.[4] It used the elements of Soviet-style education to the greatest effect because it possessed unusual advantages. On the one hand, East Germany was the first place in Eastern Europe to begin constructing of a Soviet-style higher educational system. As early as 1946 the SED was taking important measures to recast both student body and faculties. On the other hand, there were in East Germany's history no significant breaks in development. This meant that unlike other East European communist parties, the SED never experienced a replacement of the old Stalinist era leadership. The people who made ideological policy in the early 1950s continued in power through the 1980s. There was never a point in East Germany's development when it became permissible to reexamine the foundation period.[5] The foundation remained, and never could one question, let alone dismantle, what had been placed upon it. The result was continuous growth, and continuous perfection of the originally Stalinist regime.

The First Higher Educational Reform

At the center of Stalinist socialism was the question of cadres. In a 1935 speech Stalin had proclaimed that "cadres decide everything."[6] In the Soviet Zone of Occupation in Germany (SBZ),

4. For discussion of the meanings of the term "Eastern Europe," see the essays in *Eastern Europe ... Central Europe ... Europe*, ed. S. R. Graubard (Boulder, 1991).
5. Unlike Polish, Czech, or Hungarian colleagues, East German historians were not permitted to discuss the Stalinist period critically. For examples, see the last two important collected works of GDR historians: H. Heitzer, ed. *DDR-Geschichte in der Übergangsperiode (1945 bis 1961)* (Berlin, 1987); *Deutsche Geschichte Band 9: Die antifaschistisch-demokratische Umwälzung, der Kampf gegen die Spaltung Deutschlands und die Entstehung der DDR von 1945 bis 1949*, Autorenkollektiv unter Leitung von R. Badstübner (Berlin, 1989).
6. These words were meant to "emphasize the urgency of the need for better-qualified and trained staffs." A. Nove, *An Economic History of the U.S.S.R.* (Penguin Books, 1969), 233.

Soviet and German higher educational officials began working on the two major "cadre" issues at universities by early 1946: student admissions policies and faculty recruitment. The SED defined these policies in retrospect as constituting a "First Higher Educational Reform." Nowhere else in Eastern Europe, with the possible exception of Yugoslavia, had communists gotten off to such an early start in settling personnel matters in higher education. The policies which permitted early attention to cadre development derived from Germany's status as defeated nation, and were two of the Potsdam Accord's "four d's": "democratization" and "denazification."

For the Soviets democratization meant increasing the representation of the most numerous group in society, the working class. Every social class could partake in power, but the working class and "its" party, the SED, would have majority representation. At universities, this meant "breaking the bourgeois education monopoly," by introducing sons and daughters of workers and peasants into the student body, and by introducing into the curricula the "scientific worldview" of the working-class, Marxism-Leninism. "Democratization" helped resolve the all-important "question of power" at universities. Student council elections that failed to turn out majorities for the SED in 1947 were declared undemocratic and students supporting the oppositional Christian Democratic Union (CDU) or the Liberal-Democratic Party (LDP) were suspected of anti-Soviet and therefore fascistic tendencies. Beginning in 1946, Soviet and German communists expelled and arrested noncommunist student leaders in order to frustrate such "undemocratic" manifestations.[7] By 1948 "democratization" had permitted the SED to attain the positions of formal power from which to initiate far-reaching changes. Official GDR historiography described the events of the early postwar years as an "antifascist democratic upheaval," but they had the effect of the first stages of socialist revolution.[8]

---

7. Methods used included election fraud and terror. See J. Connelly, "East German Higher Education Policies and Student Resistance, 1945-1948," *Central European History* 28:3 (1995).
8. Ernst Richert described early SED university policy as "Ausschaltung – nicht Eroberung" in *"Sozialistische Universität" Die Hochschulpolitik der SED* (Berlin, 1967), 69.

Creating majorities of "worker-peasant" students required concerted efforts, because universities had been the preserves of the middle and upper classes. In 1932, 3.0 percent of Germany's students were of worker, and 2.2 percent of peasant background.[9] Beginning in late 1945, Social Democratic, communist, and trade union functionaries, particularly in the industrial southern regions of East Germany, began seeking out workers willing and able to enroll at university. They found few suitable candidates, however, because children from the lower social strata had been underrepresented in the Gymnasia as well. Thus it became necessary to devise means for preparing young workers for college studies. The means found were at first called *Vorstudienanstalten,* and then from 1949 *Arbeiter-und-Bauern-Fakultäten.* Initially they provided one, later two, and by 1949 three years' preparation. These courses had an almost immediate effect on the composition of the student bodies of the Soviet Zone. By 1947 at every university save Berlin numbers of students of worker-peasant origin were approaching one-third the total. The figures rose steadily, reaching a peak near 58 percent in 1958, and then leveling out to about half the student body in the 1960s; they declined thereafter, as the new elite protected its privileges.[10]

"Denazification" in East Germany aimed at the supposed roots of fascism. Soviet occupiers sought to destroy the economic power of fascism through large-scale expropriations of "war and Nazi criminals," as well as a land reform. They also struck devastating blows against the state apparatus: administrations of justice and education were all but depleted of the heavily Nazified staffs. The uncompromising denazification did not spare universities. The Soviet Military Administration in Germany (SMAG) did not permit East German universities to reopen *(neueröffnen)* until every former NSDAP member had been removed from the faculties. In

9. "Zehn-Jahresstatistik des Hochschulbesuchs 1943." Zentralarchiv des FDGB, Bundesvorstand, 11/-/785, cited in H.-H. Kasper, "Der Kampf der SED um die Heranbildung einer Intelligenz aus der Arbeiterklasse und der werktätigen Bauernschaft über die Vorstudienanstalten an den Universitäten und Hochschulen der sowjetischen Besatzungszone Deutschlands (1945/46 bis 1949)" (Ph.D. diss., Bergbauakademie Freiberg (S), 1979), 269.

10. H. Stallmann, *Hochschulzugang in der SBZ/DDR 1945-1959* (St. Augustin, 1980), 305, 307.

Berlin 427 professors and docents were dismissed (78 percent), in Leipzig 165 (67 percent), and in Rostock 67 (55 percent).[11] The number of full professors active in the Eastern Zone and Berlin sank from 615 to 279.[12] This weakening of teaching staffs was so severe that even "progressive" German professors, such as Günther Rienäcker in Rostock, did not see how university instruction could continue. But it did, and professors in the Soviet Zone learned early that political considerations would have precedence over academic considerations in the reconstruction of universities.

It is true that many of the East German professors dismissed during denazification would return to teaching positions. By the mid-1950s almost 30 percent of the teaching staff at higher schools in the Soviet Zone were former NSDAP members.[13] But these were former NSDAP members that the SED and Soviets had permitted to return, and they did not necessarily return to their former places of work; therefore the attenuation of university milieus was not reversed. Robert Havemann would later refer to former NSDAP members as the "Stalinist SED's most submissive servants."[14] They had been readmitted to teaching on the condition of good behavior, as understood by the SED.

"Denazification" also meant that East Germany's rulers could use political criteria in student selection from the start. According to guidelines released in December 1945, former members of the Nazi Party as well as military officers were excluded from university admission. Promoted were those who had suffered discrimination for "political or racial" reasons. From mid-1946 onward, those who could demonstrate so-called "antifascist, democratic basic convictions" (*antifaschistisch-demokratische Gesinnung*) also enjoyed

11. M. G. Ash, "Denazifying Scientists – and Science," *Technology Transfer Out of Germany after 1945*, eds. M. Judt and B. Ciesla (Amsterdam, 1996), 66.
12. Bundesarchiv, Abteilungen Potsdam (BAAP), R2/1060/21.
13. By 1954 the percentage of former NSDAP members in the East German professoriate had climbed to 28.43 percent. The numbers were highest in medicine and the natural sciences. R. Jessen, "Professoren im Sozialismus. Aspekte des Strukturwandels der Hochschullehrerschaft in der Ulbricht-Ära," in H. Kaelble, J. Kocka, and H. Zwahr, eds., *Sozialgeschichte der DDR* (Stuttgart, 1994), 226.
14. R. Havemann, *Fragen-Antworten-Fragen: Aus der Biographie eines deutschen Marxisten* (Munich, 1970), 85.

preferential treatment. Because the SED dominated admissions committees, these "convictions" meant little more than unwavering support of the SED.[15] From the dawn of East German statehood, a close relationship therefore existed between demonstrated conformity to the expectations of the SED, and access to higher education. As is well known, among the strongest inducements for conformist behavior among young East Germans were fears that certain statements or actions – like refusing the atheistic confirmation (*Jugendweihe*) – might jeopardize their ostensible right to equal education.[16] Education was a desperately desired good throughout the history of East Germany. In the 1940s, higher education was still very scarce. A reflection of this broadly shared desire to enter college was the high number of students entering the SED: as early as the winter semester 1946/47, close to one-third of the students of Leipzig, Halle, and Jena were SED members.[17] Students believed that SED membership would greatly increase their chances of college admission. These were by far the highest totals in East Central Europe at this point. Though not yet officially a "people's democracy," by 1948 East Germany was well ahead of the other Eastern European states in the construction of a loyal elite.

The transformation of student bodies was greatly aided by the SED's almost complete domination of educational administration. From 1945 the KPD, and later the SED, held every position of influence in *Land* education ministries. Education was always a high priority for the East German communists. In this they differed from their Polish and Czech counterparts, who in 1945 and 1946 temporarily abandoned the education ministries. In the immediate postwar years, the SED was imperfectly centralized, and so from 1947 onward the SED leadership (through the German Central Education Administration in Berlin, or DVV) took steps to coordinate the policies of the education ministries in the Zone. The transition to complete centralization of higher educational admin-

15. Connelly, "East German Higher Education Policies."
16. See G. Helwig, ed., *Schule in der DDR* (Cologne, 1988), esp. 90-110; F. Klier, *Lüg Vaterland. Erziehung in der DDR* (Munich, 1990).
17. In the winter semester 1946/47, 41.4 percent of Leipzig students, 34.8 percent of Halle students, and 30.7 percent of Jena students belonged to the SED. BAAP, R2/1060/46; Kasper, "Der Kampf der SED," 272.

istration with the Second Higher Educational Reform of 1951 would thus be a smooth one. Because of the heavy blows of denazification, and the pervasive terror of Soviet secret police, East German universities were little able to offer resistance.

The Second Higher Educational Reform

Not until 1951 did universities truly feel a change take place in the way they carried out instruction. Until that point, university teachers could mostly determine for themselves what they taught. The law on the reorganizing of higher education of 22 February 1951 carefully restructured East German higher education according to Soviet models. A so-called "state secretariate for higher education" was formed, which assumed direction of all six East German universities. It began to introduce a number of Soviet-style changes into the East German higher educational landscape. Ironically, the SMAG had almost completely withdrawn from day-to-day management of higher educational affairs by the time the Soviet system was duplicated in East Germany.

The most radical changes were to students' time. A ten-month academic year replaced the traditional German semester system with its seven-month year. Plans of study, carefully regulating the sequence and type of course to be taken in each major during each of the four years of study, were imposed upon all students. In a major break with German university tradition, students would no longer be able to attend lectures outside a tightly organized schedule of classes. Attendance at lectures now became mandatory, and was "controlled" by the newly created Free German Youth (FDJ) "seminar groups" of about fifteen to twenty students, with whom East German students spent all four undergraduate years. Particularly onerous were the lectures in social sciences, later known as "Marxist-Leninist basic studies." At first, these consumed up to 20 percent of students' class time, but as a result of continuing protests from faculties and students, this proportion gradually dropped to about 10 percent. More and more, East German students resembled their Soviet counterparts; their task was to obediently gain the qualifications that would make them useful

for the state. By German standards, they began more to approxi-
mate *Schüler* than *Studenten*.[18]

Through mandatory membership in the Free German Youth,
the SED began extending its control to students' free time. The
FDJ had very radical expectations of student involvement. In early
1953, a functionary wrote in the official FDJ monthly that

> Many students think of dance, like every other kind of amusement, as a
> special sphere of life, which exists independent of everything else, inde-
> pendent of their studies and sociopolitical activity. They are of the opin-
> ion that after fulfilling their tasks at university, in the FDJ etc., they have
> fulfilled their obligations and have the right to "relax" as they please.[19]

By the 1980s, as a rule at least one member of the seminar group
was also an "informal" informant of the secret police (*Stasi*).

Students' schedules, and indeed all of higher education, were
subordinated to the needs of economic planning. This meant a
drastic shift of resources from the traditionally strong humanities
to technical and natural sciences. The plan for 1953 allotted the
Technical Higher School in Dresden almost one-third of the entire
state budget for higher education. It received more than twice as
much as the Humboldt University in Berlin, and as much as the
universities of Leipzig, Jena, and Rostock combined. From 1951 to
1955 the number of students in technical sciences rose 463 percent, while those in philosophy, languages, and arts went up by
only 112 percent.[20] Of the 33 new higher schools opened between
1951 and 1970, 16 were technical higher schools, 2 schools of agriculture and forestry and 3 were medical academies.

The structures of higher education were altered to facilitate
central control of both teaching and research. Like their Soviet
models, newly founded institutions of higher education typically
had very narrow specializations (for example, higher schools of
transportation, finances, heavy machine building, and chemistry).
They entered the jurisdiction of respective ministries, and were

18. Richert, *"Sozialistische Universität,"* 81.
19. *Forum*, No. 4 (31 January 1953), 7 cited in M. Müller and E. E. Müller," ...
    *stürmt die Festung Wissenschaft!" Die Sowjetisierung der mitteldeutschen Univer-
    sitäten seit 1945* (Berlin, 1953), 348-49.
20. BAAP, E1/17038/113; E1/9107/7.

therefore more easily amenable to central planning. In flagrant transgression of the Humboldtian ideal, research facilities were increasingly transferred from universities to the Academy of Sciences and other research institutions.[21] Higher schools became ever more institutes for training the narrowly defined specialists required by Soviet-style economic plans. Thus one no longer studied Russian (*russisch*), for example, but rather "Russian teacher" (*Russischlehrer*). Traditional organs of university self-governance, such as academic senates and faculty councils, remained, but they became dominated by the SED. The true power at universities was the SED university directorate, which received instructions from the Department of Science of the SED Central Committee.

The Third Higher Educational Reform

The Third Higher Educational Reform of the late 1960s was part of the SED's larger reform agenda. The Sixth SED Party Congress of 1963 drew up plans for a unified system of education, which would feature earlier and more precise educational specialization. The entire East German educational system was subjected to a series of rationalizations. In 1965 a ten-year general polytechnical school (POS) was introduced, taking the place of a complicated mixture of primary and secondary schools. After the POS about 10 percent of the students now proceeded for two years to an extended high school (EOS) for the *Abitur*. They were granted spots at universities according to the needs of the plan; agitation for less desired professions – in particular the military – began in the sixth class. It also became possible to earn an *Abitur* outside the EOS while completing an apprenticeship. The system kept career paths open, and those who had gone directly into unskilled trades could still qualify for higher education through a range of adult education and correspondence

21. Until 1955, Ph.D. dissertations were defended almost exclusively at universities. This gradually changed. Between 1956 and 1959 9 percent of all history Ph.D.'s were taken at the SED Central Committee's Institute for Social Sciences or at the Parteihochschule "Karl Marx." Between 1960 and 1963, that number grew to 23 percent. I.-S. Kowalczuk, "'Wo gehobelt wird, da fallen Späne,' Zur Entwicklung der DDR-Geschichtswissenschaft bis in die späten fünfziger Jahre," *Zeitschrift für Geschichtswissenschaft* 42, no. 4 (1994): 303.

courses. Indeed, many citizens of the GDR took advantage of these broad offerings for further professional qualification. In 1986 one in five employees in East Germany was involved in some form of further professional training. Both the East German population and the state were in agreement on the value of formal education.

In 1966, as a sign of the greater expectations vested in higher education, the regime converted the state secretariate into a ministry of higher education. The first minister was physicist Ernst Giessmann, who had replaced ideologue Wilhelm Girnus – also a sign of the times.[22] A thorough restructuring of universities followed two years later. The most significant change was the introduction of an exceptionally manageable basic organizational unit at universities, the so-called *Sektion*. The *Sektion* replaced large and cumbersome faculties with their often unwieldy institutes. In Leipzig 16 *Sektionen* with 6 centrally directed institutes took the place of 10 faculties with 114 institutes, 24 clinics, and 3 centrally directed institutes. *Sektionen* were arranged according to professional designations and therefore made planning of university operations even easier. There were chemistry, physics, mathematics, history, and Marxism-Leninism *Sektionen*.

Sektionen also made it easier for universities to establish contractual relations with industry; best known were the intimate relations of various *Sektionen* at Friedrich Schiller University in Jena with the Carl Zeiss Optical Works. Walter Ulbricht had declared in 1965: "*Sektionen* are centers which serve research and teaching equally. They contribute to the emergence of larger work collectives which can go beyond the boundaries of existing faculties. They make possible a higher level of socialist communal work of scientists from similar or related fields." A communique of the following year more carefully defined the role of university research: "Scientific disciplines at universities are to concentrate upon complex basic research. The major exertions of the higher educational reform should be directed at research tasks that create true scientific preparation *(Vorlauf)* for industrial production."[23]

22. M. Rexin, "Die Entwicklung der Wissenschaftspolitik in der DDR," in *Wissenschaft und Gesellschaft in der DDR*, ed. R. Thomas (Munich, 1971), 105.
23. *Ibid.*, 107-10. In the late 1960's faculties in West Germany were also broken down into smaller units called *Fachbereiche*. Like its East German counterpart,

The reform also had an impact upon university power relations. The rector, in pre-Nazi days elected by the university faculty council *(Konzil)* and a sort of primus inter pares, was now little more than a state bureaucrat, whose task was to realize state policy at the university, rather than to represent the interests of the university to the state. The real power in the university had long been the Party first secretary. Because of the effective cadre policies, large pools of loyal and competent functionaries were becoming available for the staffing of growing SED university committees.

The GDR education reforms of the 1960s were the most ambitious in the Soviet Bloc. Poland's leadership attempted a similar educational reform in 1973, which included a shift toward the ten-class general school, but failed because of insufficient investment.[24] Following Jeffrey Kopstein's depiction of the economic reforms of that decade, one might label the East German educational restructuring the most serious attempt at "in-system" reform in the Soviet Bloc.[25] As a whole, the East German education system was perhaps the best adapted to the demands of the command economy, producing a relatively balanced mixture of qualifications.[26] The *Sektion* proved so suited to the requirements of central planning that other East Euro-

---

the West German reform aimed at enhancing state planning of university operations. It had, however, an additional aim that was lacking in the East German reform, namely to enhance possibilities of self-governance at universities, especially for the so-called *Mittelbau*. C. Oehler, "Hochschulverfassung, Planung, Verwaltung und Finanzierung in der Bundesrepublik Deutschland," in Anweiler et al, *Vergleich von Bildung und Erziehung*, 428-29.

24. O. Anweiler, "Bildungssysteme in Osteuropa – Reform oder Krise," in *Bildungssyteme in Osteuropa – Reform oder Krise?*, eds. O. Anweiler and F. Kuebart (Berlin, 1984), 16-17.

25. J. Kopstein, "Ulbricht Embattled: The Quest for Socialist Modernity in the Light of New Sources," *Europe-Asia Studies* 46, no. 4 (1994).

26. In contrast to many counterparts in Poland and Yugoslavia, East German university graduates found employment commensurate with their training. G. Schmidt, "Reformtendenzen im Hochschulwesen einiger sozialistischer Länder," in *Bildungssysteme*, ed. Anweiler, 253. Partly due to continuing German traditions of apprenticeship, GDR education managed to satisfy the professional aspirations of the population relatively well. It avoided the great pressures exerted upon higher education in the Soviet Union, where many more high school students desired university education than either universities or indeed the economy could accommodate. Anweiler, "Bildungssyteme in Osteuropa – Reform oder Krise?" 16.

pean states attempted to imitate it.[27] Nowhere else in Eastern Europe was the educational system so well coordinated with the system of labor allocation. Professional planning began early in the GDR; because it concentrated the tasks of student selection and preparation, the EOS permitted uniquely smooth transition between secondary and higher education.[28] The East German state devoted impressively high levels of resources to higher education. This fact is reflected in the consistently lowest student-teacher ratios in the Bloc. Another indication of the high relative quality of GDR higher education is the high percentage of daytime students in the student population, which in the 1970s was second only to Czechoslovakia.[29] Throughout the Soviet Bloc, heightened emphasis on economic efficiency in the 1960s had diminished earlier concerns to use higher education as a tool of affirmative action; yet here too East Germany revealed impressive results: together with Poland, its higher educational system produced the least disparity in Eastern Europe between the nonmanual and worker proportions of the population as a whole, and the non-manual and worker proportions of the student body.[30]

During the Honecker years higher education growth tapered off. This was consistent with a general effort in East European higher education toward intensive growth in the face of economic stagnation.[31] As a whole, East German society tended to a high degree of professional qualification, and by 1989, 22 percent of East German employees held diplomas either of higher schools or of technical

27. G. J. Giles, "The Structure of Higher Education in the German Democratic Republic," Yale Higher Education Program Working Paper, YHEP-12 (New Haven, 1976), 12.

28. Schmidt, "Aspekte der Hochschulpolitik," 77. Idem., "Reformtendenzen im Hochschulwesen einiger sozialistischer Länder," 252.

29. In 1975/76 there were 4.0 daytime students per academic teacher in the GDR. In Bulgaria the figure was 8.2, Czechoslovakia 7.2, Hungary 5.3, Poland 5.8, Rumania 8.2, and Soviet Union 8.3. Stefan Kwiatkowski, "Recent Trends and Issues in Higher Education in Eastern Europe," Paedagogica Europaea 13, no. 1 (1978): 161.

30. J. C. McClelland, "Proletarianizing the Student Body: The Soviet Experience During the New Economic Policy," Past and Present 80 (August 1978): 142. With the exception of Yugoslavia, the data are from 1963-65.

31. Anweiler, "Bildungssyteme in Osteuropa – Reform oder Krise?" 11, 14; Eduard Mühle, Hochschulreform in Ungarn. Das Hochschulgesetz vom 13. Juli 1993 (Bonn, 1994), 22-24.

schools. There were, however, stark imbalances. The percentage of East German students in the humanities and fine arts – at 4.0 percent in the mid-1970s – was among the lowest in all Europe.[32] The dialectics of detente also made the Honecker era a time of increasing political regimentation. The importance of ideological education was stressed more than ever, and the educational system was militarized.[33] The *Stasi* also took particular interest in universities, especially their electronics, biological technology, physics, and AIDS research. Only the army and the police were more thoroughly penetrated by the *Stasi* than were universities.[34]

A Loyal Academic Elite

The impressive integration of GDR higher education into the regime's economic plan was matched by higher education's subordination to the regime's political agenda. These two uses of higher education reinforced each other, so much so that it is hard to conceive of either separately. Certainly SED policy makers thought of higher education in broad terms. From the early postwar days, they assigned higher education a central role in the formation of the

32. In the Federal Republic, the total was 33.3 percent. Unesco Document ED-78/WS/24, *Statistical Study on Higher Education in Europe 1970-1975* (Bucharest, 1978), 42. Yet relative to other countries in the East Bloc, few GDR students were enrolled in technical sciences. In 1985, 29 percent of East German students studied technical sciences, compared to 22 percent in Hungary, 24 percent in Poland, 41 percent in the Soviet Union, 43 percent in Czechoslovakia, and 61 percent in Rumania. Schmidt, "Aspekte der Hochschulpolitik," 75.
33. On the logic of increasing repression at home while pursuing detente with the West, see K. W. Fricke, *Opposition und Widerstand in der DDR* (Cologne, 1984), 156-61. For the militarization of GDR society, see W. Buescher, P. Wensierski, and K. Wolschner, eds., *Friedensbewegung in der DDR: Texte 1978-1982* (Hattingen, 1982). During the 1980s, cohorts of college-age men began to drop in size, and the military could exert extraordinary pressures upon high school students to "volunteer" for three years military service in exchange for university admission. By law, young men were required to serve only 18 months. At university, female students were compelled to participate in uniformed summer paramilitary training.
34. R. Eckert, "Die Humboldt-Universität im Netz des MfS," in *DDR-Wissenschaft im Zwiespalt zwischen Forschung und Staatssicherheit*, eds. D. Voigt and L. Mertens (Berlin, 1995).

new society, and they did so with greater consistency than any other communist party in Eastern Europe. Because East German historical development evinced the fewest breaks in East Central Europe, the GDR's higher educational edifice of the 1980s rested upon the solidest foundations in the region. No fundamental structural elements had ever been removed, and building had started earliest. The mortar holding this structure together was cadre policy.

The most dependable indicator of the political loyalty of the East European academic elite was the behavior of students and teachers in times of general crisis. In 1956, 1968, and 1989 significant movements of political opposition had emerged in academia throughout the Bloc, except in East Germany.[35] Much attention has been paid to the role of the *Stasi* in suppressing dissent at GDR universities, but certainly the more important factor in achieving such impressive political support was the high degree of students' and professors' identification with the system. They had been chosen to meet not only economic, but also ideological needs. East German cadre policy was successful, thanks to the worker-peasant faculties.

Every communist party of the Soviet Bloc – including the Soviet one – had set up worker-peasant faculties, but none outdid the SED in devoting resources to their perfection. From the start, worker-peasant students could take full advantage of university resources. They had the strength, and frequently the confidence, of numbers: in the early 1950s, close to one-quarter of university entrants came from worker-peasant faculties. In neighboring Poland and Czechoslovakia, the figures hovered near 10 percent; in neither place could worker-peasant faculties make full use of university facilities. East German worker-peasant faculties continued operating into the 1960s; in Poland and Czechoslovakia they were closed down quietly in the mid-1950s.

After 1956 the Czech leadership abandoned the goal of socially recasting the Czech student body. This meant that the students of

35. In Hungary, Poland, and Czechoslovakia, university communities assumed leading roles in social movments for reform throughout the communnist period. See J. Connelly, "The Origins of the East German Peculiarity: Communist Higher Education Policies in Eastern Europe, 1945-55," in *Science und Socialism: East Germany in Comparative Perspective*, eds. K. Macrakis and D. Hoffmann (Cambridge, MA, forthcoming).

1967 or 1989 were drawn from the same sociocultural milieus as those of 1948. In 1948 students had been the only group in Czech society to protest the communists' seizure of power; in 1989 they were the leading force pressing for return to democracy. In East Germany too, students of the early postwar years had been unwilling to submit to increasingly dictatorial SED rule, as they demonstrated by handing the SED losses in student council elections of 1947. But the sophisticated general university admissions policies gradually weeded out potential antiregime demonstrators. Here too, the SED showed greater resolve than its fraternal parties. The Czech Party failed to mobilize its trade union apparatus to comb factories for workers suited for studies. Though Poland's communists scored greater successes in enlisting young workers for studies, unlike the SED they did not make visible and constant conformity – organizational membership, attendance at work brigades, election agitation, signature-collecting, or writing reports on one's fellow students – a condition for university graduation.

The SED took often culturally and politically uncommitted workers, whose education had taken place largely in delegitimized Nazi environments, and promised them participation in a grand struggle to build socialism, as well as concrete material rewards. All this for the price of loyalty and hard work, which for many workers were deeply held values. Yet beyond such basic values, worker students were often very impressionable. Their situation has been captured well by the writer Gerhard Zwerenz, who described his first encounter with Ernst Bloch in the following words:

> After the first lectures we stood out in the corridor and shook ourselves off like wet dogs. What were we supposed to think of these odd and novel things? These things were novel for us Saxon proletarians and sons of proletarians. We had no clue that what we had encountered was a two to three thousand year old tradition of philosophy. The Western tradition did not count us among its sons. Of course we had been born in the latitudes of the West, but it had not granted us its goods or its thoughts. We stood naked in this world, and of its culture we had assimilated no more than one needed in order to prosecute war.[36]

36. H. Krüger, ed., *Das Ende einer Utopie: Hingabe und Selbstbefreiung früherer Kommunisten* (Olten und Freiburg im Breisgau, 1963), 179-180.

Unlike Zwerenz, the overwhelming majority of worker students never had the opportunity of hearing, let alone being influenced by, an Ernst Bloch. Most were students of the technical sciences, and could ingest ideology in bite-size pieces through compulsory Marxism-Leninism instruction.

The successful transformation of student bodies permitted the successful transformation of professoriates. Graduates of worker-peasant faculties would form the core of the socialist academic elite; after 1965 over 50 percent of new professors were of worker-peasant background, and after 1970 over 80 percent of new professors belonged to the SED. This progress was astonishing, given that less than 2 percent of the professors appointed in Germany before the Second World War came from the working class.[37] Numbers of Communist Party members were if anything lower.

The presence of the new elite was visible earliest in ideologically sensitive areas. In 1947 political criteria were made preeminent in selection for graduate training in the humanities and social sciences. That same year the SED appended Marxist-dominated social science faculties to traditional university structures, and subsequently closed down several law faculties. Much of legal education was then transferred to extra-university institutions, such as the Walter Ulbricht Administration Academy. After 1947, growing ideological pressures caused a number of the Zone's best-known philosophers and social scientists to depart for the West; examples include Hans-Georg Gadamer, Theodor Litt, Hans Leisegang, and Eduard Spranger. *This* development did not trouble the SED. But the departure of "bourgeois" specialists in other disciplines did. As Anton Ackermann told SED higher education functionaries in May 1949, "When a reactionary philosopher or historian leaves, this can only make us smile. But the situation is different with physicians, mathematicians, or technicians, whom we need and cannot replace."[38]

37. R. Jessen, "Zur Sozialgeschichte der ostdeutschen Gelehrtenschaft (1945-1970)," in *Historische Forschung und sozialistische Diktatur. Beiträge zur Geschichtswissenschaft der DDR*, eds. M. Sabrow and P. Th. Walter (Leipzig, 1995), 122, 137.

38. Stenographische Niederschrift des Referats des Genossen Anton Ackermann auf der Arbeitstagung über die Frage der Auswahl und Zulassung zum Hochschulstudium, 6 May 1949, Stiftung Archiv der Parteien und Massenor-

Indeed, the SED made great financial exertions to retain these highly qualified specialists, paying them many times the average worker's salary. To the regime's displeasure, however, the "technical intelligentsia" continued leaving the GDR throughout the 1950s. Often the great financial incentives could not mute the effects of other SED policies, for example discrimination against religiously inclined children, or the simple harassment of low level officials that was already part and parcel of GDR life in the 1950's. Beginning in 1955, the SED leadership commissioned reports from the Central Committee Science Department on the reasons why "members of the technical intelligentsia" were leaving East Germany. In 1960 it was told of a head doctor *(Chefarzt)* in Schwerin who had applied for permission to visit his gravely ill father in West Germany. A People's Police official had given the doctor the following advice: "You had better wait until he dies, because you won't get permission to travel a second time." Instead, this doctor "fled the Republic."[39]

Repeated exhortations to lower-level functionaries to stop such petty harassment achieved little. In August 1961 the regime chose to build a wall between East and West Berlin in order to halt the population losses. Now the consolidation of a distinctly East German academic elite could begin. The 1950s had been a period of transition. Throughout that decade, university teachers were still largely drawn from bourgeois backgrounds. But already in the late 1950s, the SED had begun to erode the ability of "bourgeois" professors to choose their successors, even in the hard sciences. Increasingly, worker-peasant cadres were imposed upon universities, and by 1971 close to 40 percent of all professors were of worker-peasant background.[40] The Third Higher Educational Reform created the structures that permitted these well-trained worker-peasant cadres to assume positions of influence.

---

ganisationen der DDR im Bundesarchiv Berlin (SAPMOZPA [Zentrales Parteiarchiv]), IV 2/904/464 (unnumbered), 9.

39. Notizen über Republikflucht, 29 October 1960. Anlage 3: Beispiele sektiererischen Verhaltens gegenüber der Intelligenz. SAPMO ZPA, IV 2/904/669 (unnumbered).

40. R. Jessen, "Die 'Entbürgerlichung' der Hochschullehrer in der DDR – Elitewechsel mit Hindernissen," *hochschule ost*, no. 3 (1995): 68-70.

Shortly after the Wall went up, the Central Committee ceased receiving reports on "flight from the Republic" *(Republikflucht)*. No longer would it have to worry about sectarian excesses of the People's Police against scientists, because scientists were now held hostage. Nevertheless, the 1960s are recorded by historians of East and West as a time of reform. Relieved of the massive loss of population, and hoping to remain competitive during a worldwide "second scientific-technical revolution," the SED could experiment for several years with economic reform. Yet free of the need to be sensitive to grass-roots dissatisfactions, the SED leadership could also squelch reform initiative. Precisely this occurred in 1970, when the leadership feared that reforms might jeopardize its hold on power. True reform would become possible again only with the reopening of the border in 1989.

The pre-1961 open border was not only a problem for the SED, however. Though it helped destabilize the East German regime by loss of skilled labor, it also acted as a sort of safety valve. This fact becomes apparent when one sees East Germany in its East European context. Throughout Eastern Europe, communist leaderships were forced to make accommodations to traditionally influential elites. In Czechoslovakia, the middle classes refused to be budged from higher education and the routes leading to it. In Poland, the intelligentsia continued to dominate intellectual life. In Poland, Hungary, and Czechoslovakia, members of the old middle classes and gentry were heavily overrepresented in the dissident movements. The East German leadership did not have these problems. The old educated elites to a large extent emigrated to West Germany.[41] Sociologically speaking, East Germany thus became the place in Europe most suited to the construction of socialism. Those members of the middle class who remained had chosen to do so. After the building of the Berlin Wall in 1961 it was they, and not the regime, who would have to make accommodations.[42]

41. In 1961, 3.4 percent of the male population of West Germany was college educated. Of the male refugees from East Germany, the percentage was 7.2 percent. H. Heidemeyer, *Flucht und Zuwanderung aus der SBZ/DDR 1945/1949 – 1961* (Düsseldorf, 1994), 50.
42. The high degree of allegiance to the SED helps explain the peculiar nature of East German intellectual dissent in the 1980's. Alone among East European

Finally, the East European background also highlights the importance of denazification in permitting the SED to create a loyal elite.
The denazification of universities in East Germany marked the
most radical break in continuity suffered by a higher educational
establishment in Eastern Europe. In no other place had the preexisting elite been so heavily compromised as in East Germany;
nowhere else did an elite have fewer resources with which to defend
its positions. Denazification meant that the SED, with SMAG help,
could immediately destroy intact educational establishments, and
begin building its own academic elite. German university professors,
of course, had never had an absolute right to determine succession
to vacant university positions; but never before had state intervention been so pervasive. This was true not only for the professoriate's
self-reproduction, but also in student admissions.

Czech communists waited until 1948 for the chance to break
universities, but would need to repeat the effort in 1969. For
Poland's communists such an opportunity never arose. The Polish
professoriate was never purged, and managed to preserve its
integrity even in the social sciences and humanities, a fact that
helps explain the continued high regard that Polish sociology or
history have enjoyed in the West. The partially transformed Polish
professoriate was in turn poorly suited to assist in the ideological
transformation of Polish students (in East German parlance, the
Erziehungsauftrag), though by the late 1950s most of these students were drawn from worker and peasant strata.

Conclusion

East German higher education possessed several features that
made it unique within Eastern Europe; these features also made it
uniquely East European. East Germany was the only state in Eastern Europe faced with a daily need to compete with the West;
"Humboldt" became a mask worn for Western eyes. The more

---

dissidents, East German dissenters professed commitment to "socialism." See T.
Judt, "The Dilemmas of Dissidence: The Politics of Opposition in East-Central
Europe," in *Crisis and Reform in Eastern Europe*, eds. F. Feher and A. Arato
(New Brunswick and London, 1991).

fiercely East German higher education competed with its West German counterpart, the less Humboldtian, and the more Eastern it became. Indeed, since they were most effectively subordinated to the agendas of a socialist state, East German universities were arguably the least Humboldtian in Eastern Europe. In the 1980s, Polish and Hungarian experts even criticized the GDR for excessive instrumentalization of higher education.[43] The East German leadership could make use of several unique advantages in constructing its Soviet-style educational system: the early policies of democratization and denazification, the absence of destalinization, and the open border.

Denazification permitted the SED and its Soviet patrons to make a stronger break in the continuity of the preexisting academic regime than any other East European communist party. From 1946 the SED could become heavily involved in issues of faculty recruitment, and could begin to shape a new elite. For the first two postwar decades it still relied heavily upon "bourgeois" professors, many of whom had been compromised by NSDAP affiliation. Yet "democratization" of student bodies via worker-peasant faculties had created a reservoir from which the SED would draw its own academic elite. The new elite, often from underprivileged or compromised backgrounds, had received everything from the SED: education, material rewards, status, and ideology. The SED had not only made this new elite, it had made these people. They were the most loyal academic elite in Eastern Europe, and after the Third Higher Educational Reform they came to hold influential positions at universities. In recognizing the value of education for creating a supportive elite the SED had no rival in Eastern Europe.

The history of East Germany was the most linear of any East European society. The SED leadership faced several crises – in 1953, 1956/57, 1961 – but emerged from each strengthened, so that the men who made educational and cultural policy in the 1950s were still making educational and cultural policy in the 1980s.[44] Three higher educational reforms were stages in a unitary

43. Schmidt, "Aspekte der Hochschulpolitik," 77.
44. The Hungarian and Polish regimes were profoundly shaken by the events of 1954-56, and the Czechoslovak regime by the events of 1967-69. For discussion of the relative meaning for higher education of breaks in political continuity, see

process of increasing rationalizations of power. They constituted a perfecting of the original regime. Thus the "neostalinism" of the 1980s could pursue a Stalinist agenda with greater efficiency; this "late-socialist" (Charles Maier) SED controlled East German society more effectively with less resort to terror. East German university instruction and research in the humanities and social sciences during the 1980s was more carefully controlled than in the 1950s. The substance of continuity in higher education was cadre policy. During the Third Higher Educational Reform worker-peasant cadres came to achieve important footholds throughout academia, effecting what Ralph Jessen has termed a "de-bourgeoisification" of the professoriate.[45]

Finally, the SED leadership reaped both the disadvantages and advantages of an open border to the West. For over a decade, valuable specialists, but also potential political opposition, were drained westward. No other East European regime could so easily dispense with preexisting elites. East German universities were thoroughly depleted of alternatives to Marxist-Leninist approaches to scholarship. In 1947 the SED economist Fritz Behrens, later known as a revisionist, had proclaimed:

> I am not entirely in agreement with Comrade Rompe when he says we must create free competition between our science and bourgeois science. To the contrary, I believe that we must limit competition at least for some time, because the bourgeois ideology is so deeply engrained in people's minds ... I would find it appropriate to limit competition systematically and to create for ourselves a monopoly for a time. Later, when positions have been occupied by our people we can, for all I care, reintroduce free competition, if it should still be necessary. (laughter)[46]

In 1989 free competition again became necessary, and East German universities faced grave difficulties in reintroducing it.

S. Baske, "Die Konzeptionen der Hochschulpolitik und Hochschulgestaltung in der DDR und in der Volksrepublik Polen," in *Bildungssysteme*, ed. Anweiler.

45. Jessen, "Zur Sozialgeschichte," 137-40.

46. "Stenographische Niederschrift über die Konferenz von Angehörigen der Hochschulen (Hochschulausschuss) am Sonnabend, dem 22. November 1947 und Sonntag, dem 23. November 1947 im Hause des Kulturbundes, Berlin," 162, SAPMO ZPA, IV2/9.04/6 (unnumbered).

Session Three

DISCUSSION

HANS-JOACHIM MEYER: This was really a brilliant and thoroughly analyzed report about the East German academic scene. I would like to emphasize this because, of course, my comments will refer to problems which I would view in a different way.

First of all, in my view, you underestimate the importance of the so-called third university reform of 1968. It is my impression that for the situation in the individual universities, particularly in the technical sciences, the natural sciences, or linguistics, that was really the turning point. I admit that all of the things you mentioned prepared this change. But until 1968, it would have been comparatively easy to take up the German university tradition again, with the exception of such academic fields as law, economics, philosophy, basic educational science, and history to a very large extent. There are some exceptions, which I could also name. Among the student body, the political situation was not very supportive of the regime up to the years immediately after 1968 in these fields. I could cite a number of personal examples of this. A friend of mine who studied medicine told me that, when the students had to go to some military exercise, it was commanded by a student from the law faculty; and one of the teachers told them, be careful, those people mean what they say. So this was the really general situation.

The second thing I would like to say is that you also underestimate the opposition in the East German universities, particularly among the students. Let me remind you that the chairman of the elected students' council of Leipzig University went to prison in Bautzen, as did Natonek and others; the student representative from Rostock was executed, if I remember correctly; and there are other examples. This was up to 1949, but even after this time the political position of the SED in the universities was not too strong. Also, people coming from the Workers' and Peasants' Faculties, if they chose to take up science or engineering subjects, quite smoothly took up the ideas and views of traditional academic life; we find quite a lot of SED documents in which this is severely criticized.

The last comment I would like to make is that in the Ulbricht era, particularly in its last years, the attempt of the SED to influence the political and social composition of the student body by means of admission criteria was severely hampered by their intention to achieve a rapid increase in student numbers. University policies had two aims: First of all, of course, to see to it that the political and social composition of the student body was according to the SED wishes, but at the same time to fulfill their state planning targets. Quite often in the second or third round of admission young people got into the universities who, according to SED criteria, should not have been admitted. There was a drastic change in the early Honecker years, because this policy of increasing student numbers came to an abrupt end. The number of young people admitted to the so-called extended secondary school (EOS) and then to the universities and colleges was reduced and kept at a comparatively low figure. Of course, this made it easier for the SED to influence the student body and their views. But nevertheless, also at that time, particularly in the technical and scientific subjects, it was still possible for young people to get in simply because university bodies offering admission had to fulfill their state plans. Even so, it was much more difficult after 1968 and in the following decades.

GREGORY HENSCHEL: It seems to me that there is a mystery that has not been addressed by your presentation that I am very curious about. You describe the situation in Eastern Germany as being quite unique, where a very small proportion of the faculty was retained after 1946, most of them being purged, followed by a progressive draining away to the West of dissidents in order to maintain the ideological purity of the East German faculty. Yet it seems that East Germany was able to maintain a rather high technological standard. I don't know a lot about Eastern European technology, but given that the standard of living was in most regards, I believe, higher in Eastern Germany than it was even in the Soviet Union, which was of course the epicenter of the sphere of homogeneity of which Eastern Germany was a part, it is somewhat mysterious how the Eastern Germans were able to maintain that technological standard that I presume was there.

MITCHELL ASH: In a certain sense, my comments continue the lines of thinking that Minister Meyer and Gregory Henschel have been pursuing. Just to make it extremely brief, I have two points. One is more supportive of your analysis in a certain sense and another somewhat more critical.

You said that after the initial purge, there was a certain reintegration of former members of the NSDAP, particularly in the natural sciences. That is quite true, and indeed I think that the data show that it was actually a more powerful reintegration than the number you reported. You gave the correct number for the percentage of former NSDAP members in the early 1950s at 28, but that was for the university as a whole. If you exclude the expressly ideologized and targeted disciplines, that is, the humanities and the social sciences, and just focus on the natural sciences and medicine, the figure of former NSDAP members rises rapidly. In engineering, it is in the mid-thirties. For full professors of medicine, it is 45 percent. We are talking about a policy of controlled integration of former members of the Nazi party as a kind of gap filler until one could train a new intelligentsia in the natural sciences as well as in the other fields.

This brings me to my more critical question. I am a little puzzled how you could say that the open border could be an advantage to the SED, whereas you then say in another part of your paper that the closed border assured the stability of the regime. I would like a bit more enlightenment as to how you can maintain these two things at the same time. My own impression, on the basis of other research that I have done, is that the open border was an extreme problem for the East German leadership, especially in the natural sciences. It gave the "bourgeois" professors a high level of bargaining power, which they used by deliberately getting offers from the West and using them to improve their standing in the Soviet Zone.

PETER QUINT: I would just like to make one brief remark and then ask a question related to it. I think that it is fair to say that even in the faculties of law, there were still some people, a small number of people, but very eminent people, who were pushing against this uniformity from the Babelsberg Conference of 1958 really until the end. I also think that there must be similarities that are perhaps even more notable in other areas. In this connection, I would like to ask a question. If I remember correctly, you have not really discussed the role of the Academy of Sciences. Certainly in law and perhaps in other areas, it became a kind of refuge for people who were reformers, or at least against the prevailing trend but not so completely outside the realm of discourse that they were going to be silenced completely. The institutes of the Academy may have also acted as a kind of safety valve in a way for the SED. But they also retained people who were somewhat in opposition, who thus played, I think, an interesting double role.

JOHN CONNELLY: In general, I should say in response to all of these questions that my own subject of research has been the 1940s and 1950s, and thus my concentration upon that period may make me a bit myopic regarding the third higher education reform. Nevertheless, I would argue very strongly that without these earlier measures, the third higher education reform would not have been possible. And in all of its basic aspects, it seems to me that it was a further pursuit of the principles established in the Stalinist period, namely the attempt to utilize universities and higher education for the goals of the state. It was in some senses a rationalization that the East Germans got to making that other East European parties had already attempted in the 1950s by, for example, transferring much more research from the universities to academies of sciences. The East Germans lagged a little bit in that regard. In that sense, they did require the third higher educational reform.

With reference to opposition, I agree wholeheartedly that there was a very strong and impressive student opposition in the 1940s, but it was squelched. It was heavily terrorized, hundreds of students were arrested. Many disappeared, of whom some were executed; some of their fates are not known. I agree with you entirely, Minister Meyer, and I think it is a very important point to make, because otherwise one could have the impression that what we are dealing with here is really just some form of continuation of National Socialism or of the repressive order associated with it. That is not the case. I think that there was a very impressive manifestation of liberal will in the Soviet Zone in the early postwar years. Many brave people said some very daring things. Most of these people were very young. They did not enjoy the degree of support from their professors that one would have liked. And I think that that is something that is problematic that needs to be studied. But I would still insist that by 1952 or 1953, students were relatively quiescent; the only large scale event of opposition after this was in Greifswald in 1955 or 1956. When the medical academy was converted to a military medical academy, there was a student strike. But it was a very focused kind of strike, and was not directed at broader issues of reform.

Moving forward, it is well known that in 1968 many East German intellectuals and students had strong sympathies with the Prague Spring. There is no doubt about that. But the thing that is striking, if you compare this with the situation in any other country of the region, such as Hungary, Czechoslavakia, or Poland, is that the SED could pinpoint the so-called leaders of these groups, take them away, and the rest of the people fell into order. You know the stories of seminar groups being called together to vote to expel a member. With grave pangs of conscience, they did so. So my argument would be that there are grave disparities in East German intellectuals between what they were thinking and how they were behaving. That is a very broad topic which we cannot discuss more completely here.

Nevertheless, I would agree with you that if one could imagine East Germany falling apart in 1968, the transition would have been a relatively easy one before the third higher educational reform, not only for structural reasons, but also because some economists, historians, people like Ernst Engelberg, who, if you can imagine, had been trained in the prewar period, even the pre-Nazi period, were still there. There were certain still existing traditions, links to an earlier academic system that would have permitted, I think, a more successful transition than we've witnessed at present. So there are certain generational reasons that certainly support your point. Nevertheless, I would say that the larger truth for me, given that in 1968 the GDR did not fall apart, is that there was this large reservoir of very loyal people, the worker-peasant cadres, who had to be created in the 1950s or else they would not have existed, that made it possible in the Honecker era to consolidate further the kinds of things that had been established in the 1950s.

The mystery of the high technological standard in East Germany is only apparently a mystery. I do not know that there is a necessary correlation between political democracy and the level of technological sciences. I know for a fact that GDR mathematics, for example, was world class. So was GDR gymnastics; the GDR had some success stories, no doubt. I am not an expert on the relation between political democracy and the ability of a system to generate good, hard science, but I would suggest that this is only a pseudomystery. The real problem in East Germany was the way in which ideology hampered open and free research in the social sciences and humanities. And I would insist upon a very strong distinction between the humanities, social sciences, and the rest of the sciences, technological, medical, and otherwise.

The next question is how the border could be stabilizing and destabilizing simultaneously. Well, this claim was meant to be provocative, because it has always been mentioned in the literature that the open border acted to drain East Germany. People talk about East Germany hemorrhaging. Well, the first thing I would do is look at population density; this is not a very strong argument, but I would at least offer it for your consideration. East Germany in 1961 still had a higher population density than that region had in 1939. In other words, the influx of refugees had caused the population to go from about 17 million to close to 20 million by 1950. Then in the 1950s, it was reduced to the level of 1939. I am not saying that that was good or bad, but it simply is interesting to know. More important and to the point is the fact that the border was stabilizing to the degree that it permitted old elites, the so-called "bourgeoisie" – this needs to be studied in greater detail – to go westward. This was something that the Czech party could not do. It had other ways of dealing with its bourgeois elites, but it was a major task that all of these parties had that the East German party was relieved of. By the late 1950s, this had become destabilizing, because the people going over were increasingly young. They were specialized, freshly educated in Dresden and other places, and East Germany could not absorb these kinds of losses for much longer. One could then make an argument about the timing of the Wall in 1961 being related to that factor. But that is obviously a larger subject.

Lastly, regarding the Academy of Sciences, again I have not studied this in detail, although I would tend to agree with you that indeed comparatively speaking there was more freedom for research in many fields, the historical sciences and others, at the Academy of Sciences. But, again, in comparison with Eastern Europe, I am struck by the hesitance of supposed reformers like Uwe-Jens Heuer, Michael Brie, Reiner Land, and others to go beyond certain kinds of mental barriers in their thinking of reform. East Germany was the only place in that region – and this is something that even students of Eastern Europe often do not understand – where in the 1980s, supposed dissidents were still closely allied to the Marxist-Leninist party and really did not get beyond that in their thinking.

Chapter Four

UNIFICATION IN GERMAN HIGHER EDUCATION
"Renewal" or the Importation of Crisis?

☞

Mitchell G. Ash

Debate on the transformation of social and cultural institutions in the former GDR and its impact on Germany as a whole since unification is dominated by three lines of thought. One view, advanced by some eastern Germans and foreign observers, contends that West German institutions and procedures have been imposed in a form of "colonization."[1] An opposing view, advocated by many West and East German politicians, officials, and academics responsible for actual policy, affirms that, given the intellectual, moral, and economic bankruptcy of the previous system, it was necessary to make the transition to democracy and to what are called legal state institutions as quickly and effectively as possible.[2] Recently, as the

1. See, e.g., D. Rosenberg, "The Colonization of East Germany," *Monthly Review* 43 (September 1991): 14-33; K. Macrakis, "*Wissenschaft* and Political Unification in the New Germany," in *From Two to One: U. S. Scholars Witness the First Year of German Unification*, ed. K.-J. Maas (Bonn, 1992): 72-85; *Unfrieden in Deutschland: Weissbuch 2, Wissenschaft und Kultur im Beitrittsgebiet* (Berlin, 1993).
2. See, e.g., W. Frühwald, "Erneuerung oder Kolonialisierung? Forschungs-förderung in den neuen Bundesländern," *Nova Acta Leopoldina*, Neue Folge, No. 290, vol. 71 (1994): 131-40.

results of earlier decisions become clearer, a third line of thought has emerged, which combines affirmation and resignation, and could be summarized briefly as follows: What has been done is both right and good; even if there were some mistakes, there was no alterna- tive in the circumstances to the policies chosen.

In this essay, I will argue that in higher education, some aspects of each of these views are correct, but none is unproblematic. Many developments in this field appear at first to speak for the "coloniza- tion" interpretation. In the late 1980s, commentators generally agreed that the West German universities and scientific research establishment were in a state of crisis; and yet, precisely this system became the unquestioned model for the full-scale restructuring of higher education and scientific institutions in the new states. In a recent article, geneticist Jens Reich calls this "the cloning of a dinosaur."[3] Ironically, the more common term for the process is "renewal." As I will try to show, the picture in higher education is more mixed than either the "colonization" or the "renewal" per- spectives would suggest.

Specifically, the essay presents and attempts to support two theses. The first is that the term "renewal" itself has been and remains deeply contested, and has undergone significant changes of meaning since 1989. Thus, the question of whether what has happened can be called "renewal" depends on the positions of the speakers using the term, and on the situations in which it has been used.

The second thesis is that developments since unification are best understood both in relation to the situation in the two Ger- man states in the late 1980s and as a process of change over time since 1989. The process began as an effort to produce large-scale changes with a few sweeping measures (conveniently summarized by the term *Abwicklung*), based in part on stereotypes about the political corruptibility of certain academic disciplines and the value neutrality of others. The effort to confront the legal and political consequences of these early decisions as well as the polit- ical and administrative challenges of structural reform and person- nel "renewal" with tightly limited financial resources then yielded

---

3. J. Reich, "Die Einheit: gelungen und gescheitert," *Die Zeit*, Vol. 50, No. 38 (15 September 1995): 58.

a patchwork of policies and a mixture of results in the East German states and Berlin, purchased at a high social cost.

The Situation in 1989

In view of what has happened since unification, it is important to remember just how wide agreement was by the late 1980s that the West German universities and scientific research establishments were in deep trouble.[4] As anyone who had studied or taught at a West German university could see by that time, the expansion of higher education in the Federal Republic was financed largely by overloading the existing infrastructure, despite the large number of new universities. One statistic will make this point clear. In 1970, expenditure per student in West German higher education in constant marks was 21,600 marks; in 1987, that figure was 14,800 marks.[5] Among other things, it was that discrepancy between vast expansion in enrollments, slower growth in institutional capacity, and real decline in financial resources devoted to higher education that led many West Germans to begin saying that the university was no longer *im Kern gesund*, or basically healthy, as complacent conservatives had said at the end of the Second World War, but rather *im Kern verrottet*, rotting at the core. By the late 1980s signs of fatigue were unmistakable even among the most committed reformers. In 1988, for example, Social Democratic higher education specialist Peter Glotz complained that, in contrast to the widely shared hopes of the 1960s of achieving social change by expanding access to and reforming higher education, by the late 1980s there was no longer any political capital to be acquired here.[6]

After unification, talk of this kind ceased for awhile, at least in the public sphere. Hans-Joachim Meyer, the last education minister of the GDR and the first minister for science and art in Saxony,

---

4. For further discussion see K. Jarausch, "The Humboldt Syndrome: West German Universities 1945-1989 – An Academic *Sonderweg?*" in this volume.
5. P. Windolf, *Die Expansion der Universitäten 1870-1985: Ein internationaler Vergleich* (Stuttgart, 1990), 237.
6. P. Glotz, "Die Universitäten und die Neurose der Linken," in *Hochschule 2000. Zukunft der Bildung zwischen konservativer Hochschulpolitik und Gegenbewegung*, eds. M. Gorholt and G. Seidel (Marburg, 1988), 19-30.

spoke in 1991, in an ironic reference to Nietzsche, of a "transvaluation of values."[7] A higher education system that had been in crisis only a short time before suddenly became the best of all possible higher education systems. This radical change of perspective was closely associated with a corresponding set of negative qualities attributed to the East German system, qualities that allegedly made it ripe for "renewal."

The prevailing image of higher education and science in the GDR is that of a system thoroughly dominated by ideological indoctrination, in contrast to the alleged emphasis on objective science and scholarship in the West. The legislation that introduced the so-called "third higher education reform" in the late 1960s did state that one of the primary goals of higher education in the GDR was to develop "socialist personalities."[8] It is important to emphasize that in employing this terminology the Socialist Unity Party made no disciplinary distinctions. Students in the natural, medical, and engineering sciences as well as those in the humanities and social sciences were required to take courses in Marxism-Leninism. However, it is also important to remember that "objective reality" was one of the central categories of Marxist thought as well as Marxist-Leninist ideology, and that science and technology were recognized and supported in the GDR as "productive forces" essential to the operation of a modern planned economy. Thus, membership in the natural, medical, and engineering sciences hardly guaranteed political neutrality. Indeed, prominence in SED party organizations was often necessary for leading scientists in order to ensure the continued flow of resources. There was no *necessary* relationship between scientific or scholarly competence and its absence and political engagement or its absence in the GDR.

Another widespread opinion that played, and still plays, an important role in higher education policy is that teaching and research were separated in the GDR, with research concentrated in the Academy of Sciences and teaching and professional training

7. H.-J. Meyer, "Higher Education Reform in the New German States," paper presented to the German Studies Association, Los Angeles, California, 24 September 1991.
8. For further discussion, see J. Connelly, "Humboldt Coopted: East German Universities, 1945-1989," in this volume.

left to the universities. In its broadest form this claim is simply untrue. The emphasis on science and technology as "productive forces" just mentioned did mean that university education in the GDR was more closely tied to practical skills than it was in the Federal Republic. The priority of highly specialized training was especially evident in the so-called *Fachschulen*, narrowly specialized training institutions that were established alongside the universities. Nonetheless, in the 1980s research productivity measured in publications per researcher was actually higher in GDR universities than in the Academy of Sciences, though the bulk of resources for research and development outside the industrial sector went to the more than seventy Academy institutes.[9]

Finally, in discussions of the East German system after unification, references abound to the alleged "overstaffing" of university and other research institutes and to the school-like character of university instruction. The criteria that underlie such claims are rarely specified, let alone justified. Given the chronically overstuffed and understaffed classrooms in the old Federal Republic, West German talk of "overstaffing" in East German universities, resulting in student-faculty ratios as low as five to one, was more envious than accurate. Reality in this case appears to have been Janus-faced. Small classes made it easier to enforce both academic and political conformity and discipline. However, combined with a clearly defined programs of study and livable, if low stipends, smaller classes also made it possible for students in the GDR to complete their studies on time.[10]

Higher education in the GDR was surely in crisis by 1989, but not for the same reasons as the Federal Republic's system was perceived to be in crisis. Deterioration of university infrastructure and increasing lack of resources for teaching and research were due not to overloading and underfunding existing facilities, as in West Germany, but to the worsening finances of the GDR itself. A further

9. C. Weiss, "Der Erneuerungsprozeß an der Universität Leipzig," *Nova Acta Leopoldina* (cit. n. 2): 96. For more detailed discussion see R. Bentley, *Research and Technology in the Former German Democratic Republic* (Boulder, CO, 1992).
10. G. Buck-Bechler, "Das Hochschulwesen der DDR am Ende der 80er Jahre," in *Aufbruch und Reform von oben: Ostdeutsche Universitäten im Transformationsprozeß*, ed. R. Mayntz (Frankfurt a.M., 1994): 11-31, esp. 21, 23.

sign of deep crisis, also not limited to higher education, was the contradiction between the rigidities of state planning and tight security regulations and the free flow of scientific information.

Unification and Its Contradictions

The development of higher education and science policy in East Germany since 1989 can be divided into three somewhat overlapping phases. After an initial period of attempts at reform from within before unification, dominated by various conflicting conceptions of "renewal," came what could be called a "heroic" phase, beginning after the adoption of the Unification Treaty in the fall of 1990 and lasting until the spring and summer of 1991. This was characterized by attempts to restructure the entire higher education and research landscape of the former GDR with a few spectacular measures, including the dissolution of the GDR Academy of Sciences – the only specific reference to a scientific body in the Unification Treaty – and the abolition and refounding (the so-called *Abwicklung*) of selected academic disciplines in the universities.

In the spring and summer of 1991, a third, "prosaic" or "legalistic" phase began, with two related aspects. So-called "higher education renewal laws" were passed in the East German *Länder* by July 1991, and remained valid until the adoption of permanent higher education legislation in the years 1993 and 1994. These laws represented both an attempt to resolve the myriad difficulties created by the "heroic" policies enacted in the fall of 1990 and an effort to put higher education policy on a more detailed and coherent legal basis than that provided by the Unification Treaty alone. The second aspect of the "prosaic" phase, that of personnel and structural renewal and reconstruction, also began in the spring and summer of 1991, but is only now nearing completion. This is marked by the elimination and consolidation of some institutions and the founding of new ones, but most of all by the dismissal of many faculty and staff for political and moral reasons, and the competition of the remainder with West Germans for a greatly reduced number of positions.

Particularly with regard to the two aspects of phase three, it is somewhat misleading to call this a phase model, which would imply a linear succession. In theory, personnel and institutional restructuring represented the execution of legal mandates legitimated by overwhelming parliamentary majorities. In reality, personnel and institutional restructuring and the creation of new, more permanent higher education laws designed to legitimate the results proceeded *at the same time*; all the while financial constraints forced deep cuts in state budgets in this as in other areas. Deeply politicized debates over those cuts tended to undermine the consensus for renewal, however understood. Precisely this attempt simultaneously to restructure, legalize, and drastically reduce the size of the higher education system in the new states under severe time and financial constraints, without stopping instruction, was what made the whole process so problematic and difficult – and also accounts for its mixed results.

Contesting "Renewal," October 1989–October 1990

Even a brief discussion of preunification attempts at reforming East German higher education from within is sufficient to show that both these efforts themselves and the term "renewal" used to describe them were hotly contested. The term "renewal" appeared in discussions of GDR higher education policy even before the fall of the Berlin Wall, in September and October of 1989; however, it was used by many different speakers and conveyed multiple meanings. Gerhard Maes writes, for example, that administrators at the University of Rostock quickly presented "renewal" as an urgent need and ideal goal; but their actual intent was to keep control of the process in their own hands. It is unclear whether "renewal" in this usage was ever more than a slogan.[11]

The term had quite different meaning for the initiators of reform efforts that sprang up within the university, led by members of the so-called *Mittelbau* – permanent instructional staff who were not professors – and students. For these actors "renewal" meant restoring the freedom of teaching and research and democratizing university governance, for example by subjecting institute heads to votes of confidence by their own staff, or by restructuring univer-

11. G. Maes, "Die Universität Rostock auf dem Weg in die Bundesrepublik Deutschland," in *Aufbruch und Reform von oben*, esp. 137ff.

sity governing bodies. Various models were proposed for accomplishing these aims even before unification, with and without West German advice; whether the Federal Republic's Framework Law for Higher Education *(Hochschulrahmengezetz)* should or should not be used as the guideline for these efforts was a passionately debated issue.[12]

The third meaning of the term "renewal" was advanced by ministry officials in the newly created East German states and by policy makers in Bonn even before unification. Seen from the standpoint of those working for reform from within the universities, "renewal" in this case meant reorganization from above and without; and this came to be the dominant meaning of the term. However, many of the people who advocated reform from above, particularly officials in the ministries of the new German states, were themselves former GDR academics, who were deeply skeptical of the ability of the East German university establishment to reform itself from within.

The "Heroic" Phase

The struggle for control over the meaning and content of the term "renewal" was by no means decided by October 1990. But the sweeping measures taken in the first months after unification had the effect of deciding the outcome in favor of reorganization from above and without, thus basically supplanting initial attempts at reform from within. These measures were driven by different forces and were also justified rather differently than the dissolution of the Academy of Sciences mandated in Article 38 of the Unification Treaty. Under more general provisions in Article 13 of that docu-

12. Maes, "Die Universität Rostock"; G. Machnik, "Der Erneuerungsprozeß an der Friedrich-Schiller-Universität Jena," *Nova Acta Leopoldina* (cit. n. 2): 76f.; J. Mehlig, "Die 'Wende' von 1989/90 aus der Sicht der Nicht-Etablierten," in *Martin-Luther-Universität: Von der Gründung bis zur Neugestaltung nach zwei Diktaturen*, eds. G. Berg and H.-H. Hartwich (Opladen, 1994), 167-202; P. Pasternack, "Studentisches Bewegtsein in der DDR/in Ostdeutschland 1989/90," in *IV. Hochschulreform: Wissenschaft und Hochschulen in Ostdeutschland 1989/90 – Eine Retrospektive*, ed. P. Pasternak (Leipzig, 1993), 57-70; H.-J. Meyer, "Zwischen Kaderschmiede und Hochschulrecht," in *IV. Hochschulreform*, 121ff.

ment governing the closing or continuation of administrative and other public institutions in general that appeared to sanction this procedure, entire university departments were declared tainted by their previous affiliations with Marxism-Leninism and designated to be "wrapped up" by December 31, 1990, in order to be refounded under new auspices. Even six years later, it is already becoming difficult adequately to evoke or even to remember the atmosphere of anxiety that surrounded these events at the time, the passionate student protests that resulted, particularly in Leipzig and East Berlin, or the fears of false solidarity with the old GDR elite that those student protests elicited in some quarters.

The decisions involved were made with extraordinary speed. Hans-Joachim Meyer recalls that when he got to the ministry in Dresden, he and his staff had one month to decide whether and how to eliminate particular institutes or fields of study.[13] The decision-making processes involved remain largely unresearched – if one can speak of processes at all in such chaotic circumstances. A deliberately tendentious approach to political education, impatience with or an inability to see the results of the slow, difficult internal reform efforts just mentioned, a desire for a clean sweep to clear the ground for major changes, and practical considerations may all have played a role in these actions. There had been little protest against such sweeping decisions in the case of Marxism-Leninism itself, which had ceased to be a required course already before unification, or in the case of disciplines like criminology, where connections with the Stasi were too obvious and pervasive to ignore. The problems came and still exist in other fields where this clean sweep approach was attempted – in philosophy, law, history, pedagogy, and the social sciences.

The legal difficulties with the undertaking became clear quite quickly. Most prominent was the Humboldt University's lawsuit that resulted in a higher administrative court decision in Berlin declaring the *Abwicklung* in that institution to be an unconstitutional reading of the Unification Treaty. In the opinion of the court, the Treaty had outlined only two alternatives, *Abwicklung* with no successor institution or *Übernahme* – taking over the exist-

---

13. H.-J. Meyer, "Zwischen Kaderschmiede und Hochschulrecht," 132.

ing institutional structure, with personnel decisions to be made afterward on the basis of case-by-case evaluations.[14] In Saxony, this difficulty appears to have been dealt with by the decision of the ministry to evaluate personnel individually even in those fields listed for *Abwicklung*. In practice, however, the *Abwicklung* faced fundamental legal challenge only in Berlin, perhaps because independent West German legal advice was more available there. Even in Berlin, the decision had little practical impact. By the time it came down, in June 1991, structure and appointments commissions were already at work, and Rector Heinrich Fink explicitly requested that they continue.[15] In the other new states, court challenges were largely limited to individual cases and confined to issues of labor law, which are complicated enough and still bedevil the *Länder* bureaucracies today.

Aside from these legal difficulties, there were obvious inconsistencies in the lists of departments designated for *Abwicklung*, which differed in different states for no obvious reason. For example, whereas all of history appeared on the list in some states, only some historical specialties were "wrapped up" in Saxony.[16] No discipline other than Marxism-Leninism was *abgewickelt* in Mecklenburg-Lower Pomerania. Interestingly enough, apart from certain exceptions, the "cultural sciences" (*Kulturwissenschaften*) – that is, German and foreign languages and literatures, art and art history, music or ethnology – appear on only a very few lists, even though Marxist-Leninist dictates were as firmly established in these fields as they were in the ones listed. As will be shown below, the decision to list only certain disciplines would have a significant impact on later personnel restructuring.

Of central importance for the perceived democratic legitimation of policy is that in the heroic phase, conclusions about individual scholars were often drawn from broad general statements about their disciplines, regardless of what those individuals themselves

---

14. For discussions of the court decision and its impact, see M. Küpper, *Die Humboldt-Universität* (Berlin, 1993); I. Markovits, *Imperfect Justice: An East German Diary* (New York, 1995); P. Quint, *The Imperfect Union: Constitutional Structures of German Unification* (Princeton, 1997), ch. 13.
15. Küpper, *Die Humboldt-Universität*, 57f.
16. Sächsisches Ministerium für Wissenschaft und Kunst, *Sächsisches Hochschulerneuerungsgesetz vom 25. Juli 1991*, Anlage zu 145 Abs. 3 & 4.

had actually done. Here *science policy* – that is, policy addressed to the organization or funding of research institutions, the research topics to be supported with state funds, or the subject matter to be taught in universities – became confused with a *personnel* issue, the political assessment of civil service employees.

Third, these decisions created considerable practical problems. Because students continued to have a constitutional right to education, and no one proposed actually closing the universities, courses needed to be offered and examinations held in the fields affected. The response was the engagement of dozens of visiting professors, mainly from West Germany but in some cases from other countries, funded primarily by the Deutsche Forschungsgemeinschaft (DFG) and the German Academic Exchange Service (DAAD). Most, though not all, of these faculty continued to teach full time at their home institutions, and commuted for a few days each week to the East. Because they often traveled by air, one popular term for them was *Lufthansaprofessoren*. However, many later joined structure and appointments commissions, and some even moved permanently to the East. Thus, what began as an improvised coping strategy became the first step of a long-term science transfer.[17]

Fourth and most important, policy in the heroic phase failed to take sufficient account of the way the social system of science actually worked in the GDR. Policy makers proceeded on the assumption that there was a distinction between allegedly ideologized social and human sciences and the supposedly objective natural, medical, and engineering sciences. However, as mentioned above, the authors of the third higher education reform in the GDR had made no such disciplinary distinctions. In this stage, then, many scholars in supposedly "clean" disciplines who were highly regarded internationally, but who also had important connections in the science section of the SED and the GDR science and education ministries, and in some cases, as later transpired, also to the Stasi, escaped close personal scrutiny.[18] This would change during the later phase of more complete personnel restructuring.

17. B. Muszynski, ed., *Wissenschaftstransfer in Deutschland: Erfahrungen und Perspektiven* (Opladen, 1993).
18. For an early warning of this outcome, see W. Lepenies, *Folgen einer unerhörten Begebenheit. Die Deutschen nach der Vereinigung* (Berlin, 1992), esp. 25ff.

The "Prosaic" Stage I: Legalization

This stage can be described as an attempt to deal with the problems created by policies of the "heroic" stage, while at the same time giving these measures a more detailed and coherent legal grounding than that offered by the Unification Treaty alone. So-called "higher education renewal laws" were in place in all of the new states by July 1, 1991. Permanent higher education legislation has appeared with widely varying speed since then. Precisely this variation is one indicator of a fundamental tension at work here, between the constitutional principle of state autonomy in cultural affairs (*Kulturhoheit der Länder*) and continuing financial dependence on the federal government.[19] That dependence is expressed in the policy sphere, for example, by a massive inflow of research grants from the DFG, support for visiting and temporary professorships by both the DFG and the DAAD, mentioned above, and last but not least in the federal subsidy program for higher education construction. This tension is surely the strongest of many forces driving the imposition of West German structures and norms in the new states in general. The result in higher education was a set of laws and policies that had in common the effort to conform with the federal framework law for higher education (*Hochschulrahmengesetz* or HRG); but the considerable variation among the states indicated the impact of countervailing forces for local autonomy.

One common feature of these laws, and a carry-over from the heroic phase, was the sweeping legal move on which all of them were based. The "renewal laws" of 1991 created a two-class professoriate composed of "HRG professors" – that is, professors named by specially authorized structure and appointments commissions and positively evaluated from both political/moral and competence standpoints – and "professors under previous law" – that is, GDR appointees not yet reconfirmed. Karl Heinrich Hall, the ministerial official responsible for this area in Saxony-Anhalt, refers to this feature when he speaks of "a nearly revolutionary act," in which "the idea of self-purification and self-renewal after

---

19. For a general account of this issue, see A. B. Gunlicks, "German Federalism after Unification: The Legal/Constitutional Response," *Publius: The Journal of Federalism* 24 (1994): 81-98, esp. p. 82.

the *Wende*" found legal expression.[20] Also mandated was the reorganization of university governing bodies to assure professorial majorities, as required by the HRG. This had the ironic effect of undoing the internal reform efforts undertaken since 1989, already mentioned, that were aimed at democratizing university governance by giving students and nonprofessorial staff greater representation in order to counterbalance SED dominance in the existing professoriate. In this respect, these provisions mark a further step in the process of state-level centralization at the expense of university autonomy already begun during the heroic phase.

A second common feature of this legislation was the continuing distinction between political/moral standards and scientific competence in the assessment of GDR professors and academic staff. In all "renewal" laws these criteria were kept separate, though the way in which the assessments were actually carried out differed. Consistent with provisions of the Unification Treaty, a third standard – that of need *(Bedarf)* for the position in question was mentioned, as well. Whether "need" referred to any sort of objective criterion or was only a code word for financial limitations was left, surely intentionally, unclear.

A third common feature of policy making, only partly incorporated in legislation, was the creation of organs designed to improve policy coordination and cooperation among the new states. All of the new laws mandated participation by science or education ministers and university rectors in regular all-German conferences with their West German colleagues, which they had been doing in any case. In addition, conferences of science and education ministers in the new states and parallel conferences of university rectors from these states began in Berlin in March of 1991. Far more important, however, was the vast array of structural and appointment commissions named by state ministries either to make policy recommendations for entire institutions or to name new personnel in individual departments. This array of barely formalized institutions, often only subsequently sanctioned by the "renewal" laws, marks the limit of common policy in the new states. In contrast to the situation at the rectoral or ministerial level,

---

20. K. H. Hall, "Die Hochschulgesetzgebung der neuen Länder als Rahmenbedingung der Neustrukturierung," in *Aufbruch und Reform von oben*, 179f.

there was little formal coordination among these commissions from state to state, a problem which led to the perception at least of different standards being applied in the different states. Impressive as the common aspects are, both the differing speeds of change and the policy differences among the new states are equally striking.[21] The earliest of the "renewal" laws to be enacted, Mecklenburg-Lower Pomerania's law of February, 1991, was also the first to prescribe individual assessments (*Einzelfallüberprüfung*) for all university staff according to political/moral and competence standards, regardless of discipline. In this case, separate commissions for each set of standards were established, with the competence assessment (*Überleitungsverfahren*) following the political-moral one (*Ehrenverfahren*). In theory, final decisions to retain or release teaching personnel at the rank of Professor or Dozent were to be made in a third stage (*Übernahmeverfahren*), in which the "need" criterion, and therefore the state government, would also be involved. Other staff and middle-level instructors at the rank of *Mitarbeiter* went through only the first two assessment stages.[22]

Both Saxony-Anhalt's "renewal" law of July 31, 1991 (passed on June 21) and Saxony's law of July 25, 1991 also adopted separate political-moral and competence standards for personnel, but specified simultaneous rather than successive evaluations. While separate personnel commissions were created for moral-political evaluations, more numerous structural and appointments commissions determined the number and occupancy of new positions in all fields. This made it more than likely that personnel evaluated positively from a political/moral standpoint and perhaps also for their competence would still find their positions declared unneeded.[23]

21. Only a few examples can be discussed here; the case of Thuringia has been excluded for reasons of space. For more extensive overviews see Hall, "Die Hochschulgesetzgebung," and R. Myritz, "Zwischen Umbruch und Konsolidierung: Zur Entwicklung der Hochschullandschaft in den neuen Bundesländern," *Deutschlandarchiv* 26 (1993): 657-73.
22. Gesetz zur Erneuerung der Hochschulen des Landes Mecklenburg-Vorpommern – Hochschulerneuerungsgesetz – vom 19. Februar 1991, Art. 1, 2-3, Mitteilungsblatt des Kultusministers von Mecklenburg-Vorpommern, No. 1/1991, 31-32.
23. Gesetz zur Erneuerung der Hochschulen des Landes Sachsen-Anhalt (Hochschulerneuerungsgesetz), Abs. 7, 64-68; *Sächsisches Hochschulerneuerungsgesetz* (cit. n. 16), Abs. 8, 75-81.

One policy applied in Saxony and Saxony-Anhalt deserves particular mention. A significant proportion of teaching staff (about 25 percent in Saxony and 20 percent in Saxony-Anhalt) was to be appointed in extraordinary procedures – that is, to positions advertised only in the state in question.[24] This was done, it was said, to assure a reasonable amount of continuity and a better mix of East German and West German personnel. We can assume that another motive was to reduce public protest against measures that were disruptive enough in any case, and to assuage fears of a complete takeover of higher education by West Germans.

The Berlin law of June 24, 1991 (promulgated on July 18) was passed as a supplement to West Berlin's existing higher education law. Here, as in Saxony and in contrast to Mecklenburg-Lower Pomerania, all positions at professorial rank were redefined by structure and appointments commissions and then publicly advertised. Also unique to Berlin was the mandate given to the state-level structural commission to develop proposals for restructuring the entire higher education landscape of the city-state, including the West as well as the East. Unfortunately, the document that the commission finally produced in late summer 1993 was a dead letter almost as soon as it appeared due to radical funding cuts enacted that fall.[25]

Brandenburg is in many respects a special case. Because the region lacked universities before 1989, the new state was able to skip over the transition stage and pass a regular higher education law as early as June 24, 1991. Since the law established three new institutions, it could be called a university establishment law rather than a "renewal" law. A full university was founded in Potsdam unifying the pedagogical academy there, the Academy of Law and Administration in Babelsberg and the former training academy of the Stasi in Golm; in the latter case only lower-level, not academic staff were taken on. The second institution was a new Technical

24. See, e.g., Hall, "Die Hochschulgesetzgebung," 182.
25. Ergänzungsgesetz zum Berliner Hochschulgesetz vom 18. Juli 1991; Hochschulpersonalübernahmegesetz vom 11. Juni 1992; *Berliner Hochschulstrukturplan 1993* (Berlin, 1993); M. Erhardt, "Der Erneuerungsprozeß aus der Sicht der Senatsverwaltung für Wissenschaft und Forschung des Landes Berlin," *Nova Acta Leopoldina* (cit. n. 2): 37-40.

University in Cottbus taking over the former *Bauakademie* in that city. The third was a new European University, the Viadrina, in Frankfurt/Oder. Guidelines for evaluations of personnel to be taken over from earlier specialized technical schools in Potsdam and Cottbus were similar in form to those elsewhere.

The "Prosaic" Phase II: Structural and Personnel "Normalization"

The term most frequently associated with this stage, aside from "renewal," is "reconstruction" *(Umbau or Neubau)*, which is used mainly for structural or institutional change. Among the structural reforms enacted in the new higher education legislation were the dissolution of many specialized training institutions *(Fachschulen)*, including but not limited to those linked with the SED *(Partei-hochschulen)*, and the folding of other specialized schools into the full and technical universities. This was a painful process, accompanied at times by rancorous debate. The tension between financial necessity, local politics, and individual justice was no easier to resolve in these cases than within the universities themselves.

For personnel, the most common term is "mixing" *(Durchmischung)*; this refers to the hope of achieving "renewal" by combining East and West German teaching and administrative staff. Such language suggests a straightforward execution of policies carefully planned in advance and clearly defined in the laws just described. Terms like "exchange of elites" *(Elitenaustausch)*, first used by Jürgen Habermas, or the less forceful term "change of elites" *(Elitenwechsel)*, mark the counter-discourse.[26] Neither of these grandiloquent formulations fully describes what has happened. Rather, as Hans-günter Meyer writes, a renewal process that began with large hopes has been reduced "to a detail-puzzle, in which disciplinary structures decided upon in great haste are now being filled with content in remarkably pragmatic fashion, one appointment at a time."[27]

26. See, e.g., J. Habermas, "Die normative Defizite der Vereinigung," in idem., *Vergangenheit als Zukunft*, ed. M. Haller (Zürich, 1990); K. König, "Bureaucratic Integration by Elite Transfer: The Case of the Former GDR," *Governance* 6 (1993): 386-96.
27. H. Meyer, "Hochschulerneuerung Ost," *WZB-Mitteilungen*, No. 60 (June 1993): 39.

The measurable results available thus far show a variation among the new states and among disciplines that is even wider than the variation among the legal texts just discussed. Nonetheless, a number of trends can be distinguished. Most obvious are three developments that began already in 1989 and thus set the scene: a drastic drop in total personnel, a redistribution of personnel among the new states, and a shift in the relative weighting of the disciplines in the mix.

Even before higher education renewal laws began to take hold, from 1989 to 1991, there was a total personnel reduction of 21.6 percent in the higher education institutions of the new states. Among professors the reduction was 26.4 percent.[28] After 1991 the reduction continued apace, due mainly to the financial squeeze already mentioned, and has reached 40 percent in some fields. Regional redistribution is shown by the fact that the largest personnel reductions by far were in Saxony (6,291, or 49 percent), and in Berlin (2,714, or 54 percent) – the two regions that had had the highest concentration of higher education and research personnel in the GDR. In contrast, in this early period there were minimal cuts in Thuringia (128, or 4 percent), and a strong net gain in Brandenburg (169, or 10 percent) due to the founding of new universities there.[29]

Indicative of a certain continuity in attitudes and policies from the heroic phase are the data showing redistribution among disciplines. Put very briefly, the natural, medical, and engineering sciences were reduced barely at all, whereas the social sciences were cut the most (from 5,483 to 2,212, or 60 percent). In contrast, the number of positions in the "cultural sciences" (languages, art history, theology, etc.) dropped only slightly more than that of teaching positions overall (from 6,922 to 4,671, or 33 percent). The size of the asymmetry between the natural and social sciences plainly reflects the closing of institutes for Marxism-Leninism and SED

28. A. Burckhardt and D. Scherer, "Hochschulpersonal Ost im Wandel: Zwischenbilanz," *Das Hochschulwesen* 42 (1994): 277f.; cf. D. Scherer, "Personalbestand an den ostdetuschen Hochschulen 1989, 1990, 1991," in *Hochschule im Umbruch – Zwischenbilanz Ost*, ed. H. Schramm (Berlin, 1993), 154-59; U. Jahnke and H. Otto, "Stellen- und Personalabbau an den ostedeutschen Hochschulen 1989-1993 – Zwischenbilanz 1992," *ibid.*, 414-17.
29. A. Burckhardt and D. Scherer, "Hochschulpersonal Ost im Wandel," 277, Table 1.

academies. Even after adjusting for this, however, it is fair to say that unification has resulted in a relative reduction in the weight of the social sciences (from 14 percent to 7 percent of all positions) and a relative increase in the weight of the natural sciences and medicine in the new German states (from 16 to 20 percent and from 21 to 25 percent, respectively).[30]

Compared with such large shifts in both the size and the structure of higher education institutions, the quantitative impact of political dismissals has been far less than the emphasis given to them in the media would suggest. Public discussion of this issue has focused almost obsessively on the unmasking and dismissal of informers for the Stasi and other politically compromised academics; but the measurable outcomes observed are both ambiguous and ironic. On the number of political firings in the narrower sense – that is, for work in SED organizations in prominent positions or for collaboration with the Stasi – figures now available from the universities of Rostock and Jena may serve as rough indicators. These mark the full range from very high to relatively little turnover in teaching staff; but in both cases the results show that, contrary to widespread beliefs, firings for political reasons as such account for only a small part of the total.

In Jena, of 263 teaching staff as of January 1, 1990, a total of 195 (72 percent) have since left the university. Early retirement accounts for the largest number of these, 35 (13 percent); some "political" professors may well have put themselves in this category. Departures due to *Abwicklung* of whole disciplines and to the dissolution of the institute for Marxism-Leninism, that is, for political reasons in the wider sense, numbered 62 (23 percent). There were only 26 dismissals for political reasons in the narrower sense (10 percent of the total). It should be emphasized that this figure is plainly *not* an indicator of the actual number of Stasi collaborators or committed SED party activists in Jena. How many such people left the university precisely to avoid dismissal cannot be determined with any precision.[31]

In Rostock, the university's "honor commission" (*Ehrenkommission*) examined a total of 6,248 university staff (not only teaching

30. *Ibid.*, 278, Table 2.
31. G. Machnik, "Der Erneuerungsprozeß an der Friedrich-Schiller-Universität Jena" (cit. n. 12), 77.

staff), ranking its findings on an eight-point scale ranging from "no false behavior" to immediate dismissal. The category "no false behavior" was by far the largest (5,547, or 88.8 percent). The categories "slight false behavior" and "disapproval" or "reprimand" account together for 361 (7.7 percent). Only 191 people (3.1 percent) fell into those categories that led either to permanent restriction from university governance or to dismissal.[32] Unfortunately, these data are not differentiated by rank and are thus not compatible with those just reported for Jena. Nonetheless, the general trend is clear; polemical accounts implying that all those dismissed from East German universities were either SED activists or were working for the Stasi are wildly off the mark. Such – unfortunately quite widely accepted – claims have the effect of distracting public attention away from the far larger numbers of dismissals of scholars and teachers not deemed politically or morally compromised, who could not be retained for financial or structural reasons.

Turning to the disciplinary dimension, the available data plainly show that none of the key words mentioned above ("exchange of elites" or *Elitenaustausch* versus "mixing" or *Durchmischung*) applies across the board. Rather, both processes have taken place, but to different extents in different disciplines. Contrary to the simplistic stereotypes that governed policy in the "heroic" stage and clearly influenced personnel restructuring decisions in the normalization or legalization stage as well, it is not possible to make a straightforward distinction between politically "tainted" and value-neutral disciplines. The numbers suggest that a threefold scheme is more precise, one that distinguishes the "wrapped up" (*abgewickelte*) disciplines mentioned above (law, the social sciences, pedagogy, philosophy and history) the "cultural sciences" (ethnology, languages and literatures, art and art history, theology, etc.) and the natural sciences, medicine, and engineering. The following data for Halle (from October 1994) and Berlin (from February 1995) indicate what is meant.

In Halle, there were a total of 63 appointments at professorial rank in the fields of law, economics, education, history, philosophy and social science by October 1994. Of these, only 7 (12.5 percent) came from the new states, and of these only one was

---

32. *Bericht der Ehrenkommission der Universität Rostock über ihre Arbeit* (30 June 1995). Cf. Maes, "Die Universität Rostock."

appointed as full professor (with non-HRG status). The number in the "cultural sciences" (theology, languages and literatures, art and ancient studies, and applied language instruction) was 16 of 29 (55.1 percent). In contrast, 75.5 percent of professors in the natural sciences and engineering came from the new states.[33] Thus we have more a sliding scale than a yes-no result.

This threefold schema also comes through, though somewhat less clearly, in the most recent available figures for the Humboldt University in Berlin (HUB). By February 1995 there were a total of 115 appointments at professorial rank in law, economics, education, history, philosophy, and social sciences at the HUB; of these only 21 (18.3 percent) were from the new states. The number of Eastern Germans in the "cultural sciences" (theology, languages and literatures, Asian and African studies, and other cultural sciences) was 53 of 122 (43.4 percent). In medicine, mathematics, and natural sciences, the number was 77 of 147 (52.4 percent) – a far lower percentage of East Germans than in Halle.[34]

These data are only partial indicators, but the evidence clearly suggests that *Durchmischung* is most consistent in the social sciences and humanities that were not among the disciplines "wrapped up" in the "heroic" phase. Since, as noted above, these disciplines (with the exception of theology) were no less infused with official SED doctrine than were the listed fields, it follows that in this respect the results are as much an artifact of policy decisions in the "heroic" phase as of essential truths about the moral or political corruptibility of science as such under socialism.

Social Impacts

The social impacts of these policies appear comparable in some respects to those of policies in other areas in the new German states. The overall attrition rate of about 40 percent in the univer-

33. Martin-Luther-Universität Halle-Wittenberg, *Rektoratsbericht für den Berichtszeitraum Dezember 1992 – September 1994* (October 1994), Statistischer Teil. A potential source of error in these data is that all professors listed as employees, i.e., with non-HRG status rather than as civil servants, have been counted as East Germans.
34. Unpublished statistical data from the Senat of the Humboldt-Universität Berlin.

sities appears enormous to Western eyes, but it is considerably lower than in industrial research, which was decimated by the sell-off of East Germany's state-run enterprises.[35]

Who the losers were has been clear for some time – middle level teaching and research staff and women.[36] In the universities, the imposition of West German personnel structures that feature more senior and fewer middle-level positions has led to far-reaching reductions in the *Mittelbau* (nonprofessorial teaching staff), the people who had carried much of the teaching load in the GDR. This trend has been softened only somewhat by the retention of some older, positively evaluated middle-level staff with either permanent or time-limited contracts. The result is more than a little ironic, for it was precisely from these middle ranks that the early initiatives for reform from within had come in 1989 and 1990. There is no doubt that in this group far more academics whose work and behavior were positively evaluated have been affected than have been dismissed for political or moral reasons. Leipzig University rector Cornelius Weiss has openly, and rightly, called this an "injustice."[37]

The impact on women has been more ambiguous. Both early figures from the Humboldt University and later, more broadly based surveys indicate that the decline in women professors and permanent scientific staff roughly matches that of men in the same ranks. The percentage of women professors in the GDR was already low before 1989, though it was higher there than in the FRG; and it has gotten no lower since. The proportion of women in professorial rank in the new states was 9 percent in 1991, 50 percent higher than the level in West Germany. By 1994, it was 11 percent, a considerable gain in both absolute and relative terms, and still nearly twice the percentage in the West (6 percent in 1994). But the gender-specific pyramid that had been characteristic of the GDR as well as the FRG remained in place. The higher

35. H. Ziegler, "Ein Stück Zukunft vertan: Der Niedergang der Industrieforschung Ost," *Deutschlandarchiv* 26 (1993): 689-702.
36. See, e.g., D. E. Zimmer, "Wunder im Osten," *Die Zeit*, vol. 49, No. 21 (20 May 1994): 56-57; cf. S. Kiel, "Personelle 'Erneuerung' an ostdeutschen Hochschulen: Versuch einer ganzheitlichen Betrachtung," *hochschule ost* 4:1 (January-February 1994): 59-73.
37. C. Weiss, "Der Erneuerungsprozeß an der Universität Leipzig" (cit. n. 9), 97.

the rank, the lower the percentage of women in it, which is also true in the United States. As Anke Burckhardt points out, "Not only gender, but also the East-West problematic played a role here. But the West bonus did not suffice to break through the male phalanx."[38] Thus, being a woman from the West was a bonus in some disciplines, but the numbers of women involved were not large enough to affect the overall result.

Implications for Unification Policy Making

The overall result of unification in German higher education was neither complete "colonization" of the East by the West nor complete "renewal" from the ground up, but rather an extension of West German legal and institutional frameworks to the East, combined with cautiously introduced structural reforms drawn largely, though not entirely, from the agenda of a group that can be called conservative modernizers. Examples of this include the introduction of specialized professional training institutions (*Fachhochschulen*) in much larger numbers in the Eastern states than in the West; efforts to establish interdisciplinary research centers and to improve cooperation with extra-university research institutes, such as the Max Planck Institutes; and cautious initiatives to give more administrative autonomy, including in some cases control of admissions, to individual schools. The newly founded European University "Viadrina" in Frankfurt/Oder, already mentioned, is clearly a bolder initiative. Though small and by no means financially secure, it has reached out in innovative ways to Germany's eastern neighbor by enrolling hundreds of Polish students, and has promoted particularly promising interdisciplinary efforts in its new Faculty of Cultural Studies.[39]

A primary force behind the imposition of West German structures and norms in the new states, their financial dependence on

---

38. A. Burckhardt, "Besser als befürchtet – schlechter als erhofft: Zum Stand des Berufungsgeschehens an ostdeutschen Hochschulen aus Frauensicht," *hochschule ost* 5:3 (March/April 1995): 107-21.

39. H. Weiler, "The Changing World of Knowledge and the Future of Higher Education: Reflections on the Creation of a New Univesity," in *Universities in the Twenty-First Century*, ed. S. Muller (Providence, RI, 1995), 129-37.

the federal government, continues and shows no signs of abating. But the self-assertion of *Länder* autonomy and the force of local politics in the face of extreme financial constaints are equally evident. Examples include the effort to retain full universities, including faculties of medicine, in both Rostock and Greifswald in Mecklenburg/Lower Pomerania, despite contrary recommendations from the federal Science Council, or in the founding of three new universities in Brandenburg, already mentioned. These were clearly political acts in poor states.

Equally fundamental is the tension between *science* or *higher education policy (Wissenschafts-* or *Hochschulpolitik)* and *social and labor policy (Sozial-* and *Arbeits-* or *Beschäftigungspolitik).* The most embarrassing example of this is the so-called WIP im HEP program *(Wissenschaftler-Integrations-Programm im Hochschulerneuerungsprogramm).* Instituted in 1991 as a way of "salvaging" at least some research personnel from the disolved GDR Academy of Sciences, this program was based on the false assumption that, because there had been little or no research in the East German universities, personnel from the Academy should and could be integrated into the renewed universities. However, as we have seen, there already had been research in the GDR universities; and in any case, these institutions were not about to accept new staff at considerable direct or indirect costs to themselves. The result is that nearly 2,000 scientists who had been positively evaluated by the federal Science Council have been working since 1991 on short-term contracts with no obvious solution in sight.[40]

Though the cliche that GDR universities were overstaffed continues to circulate, no one dares to predict what effect the personnel reductions now underway will have on the quality of instruction. Fortunately, enrollments have not increased as quickly as originally feared. For now, at least, East German universities can boast both faculty-student ratios that compare favorably with most West German universities and a certain camaraderie born of common regional and GDR experiences. However, with the exception of Frankfurt/Oder, the Humboldt-Universität in Berlin, and a few

---

40. "WIP-Memorandum: Verwirklichung des Wissenschaftler-Integrationsprogramms (WIP) im Hochschulerneuerungsprogramm (HEP)," *Das Hochschulwesen,* 43 (1995): 95-100.

technical universities, the hope of attracting West German students has been largely a vain one thus far. Apparently the overcrowding in West German universities that had been a source of constant complaints before 1989 is not so bad as to overcome the reluctance of some West German students to undertake the challenge of studying in what some of them call "the Gobi Desert."[41] On the other hand, most German universities recruit students regionally; seen from that point of view, localism and Eastern German recruitment are only normalization in another guise.

Impacts on Political Culture

The most significant short-term impact of the transformation in higher education in the new states on the political culture of the new Germany is a negative one – the often-remarked loss of opportunities to reexamine and reform the scientific and scholarly landscape in the West as well as in the East. In fact, the opportunity for critical re-examination was not inadvertantly missed, but was stoutly resisted by many, though not all leading science and higher education policy makers in West Germany.[42] Whether the changes in the East will have any feedback effect on reform initiatives in the West German states remains to be seen. A recently published report by a reform commission in Hesse, for example, makes practically no reference to unification.[43] Both recent press reports on the malaise of the universities and a prominent counter-article stating that Ger-

41. T. Bargel and H. Peisert, "Studium im vereinten Deutschland," *Forschung und Lehre: Mitteilungen des Deutschen Hochschulverbandes* (September 1994): 389-92.

42. D. Simon, "Verschleudert und verschludert," *Die Zeit*, vol. 50, No. 15 (7 April 1995): 49; W. Schluchter, "Die Hochschulen in Ostdeutschland vor und nach der Vereinigung," *Aus Politik und Zeitgeschichte. Beilage zur Wochenzeitung 'Das Parlament'*, B 25/94 (24 June 1994): 12-22. For analyses of the reasons for this in science policy, see D. Simon, "Die Quintessenz – der Wissenschaftsrat in den neuen Bundesländern: Eine vorwärtsgewandte Rückschau," *ibid.*, B 51/92 (11 December 1992); R. Mayntz, *Deutsche Forschung im Einigungsprozeß: Die Akademie der Wissenschaften der DDR 1989 bis 1992* (Frankfurt a.M., 1994); J. Kocka, "Vertane Chancen? Thesen zur Vereinigung der Wissenschaftssysteme," in idem., *Vereinigungskrise: Zur Geschichte der Gegenwart* (Göttingen, 1995), 75-82.

43. Hessisches Ministerium für Wissenschaft und Kunst, ed., *Autonomie und Verantwortung – Hochschulreform unter schwierigen Bedingungen* (Frankfurt a. M., 1995).

man students are generally more optimistic than they had been in years refer almost exclusively to West German institutions.[44] Important in the future will be the effect of these transformations on what could be called the *political culture of academic life*. Will the emerging mixture of East and West German academics, largely unintended in this form, be able to work together either in research or in collegial bodies to create something resembling a functioning community of scholars, and thus provide a living example of democratic political culture? Will the smaller size of the Eastern German universities make possible greater solidarity between students, faculty, and administrators, perhaps in struggle against a common enemy, such as a budget-cutting state or federal government?

Results thus far have been mixed. The most extreme case of intrafaculty conflict was that of the historians at the Humboldt University, where newly appointed, internationally recognized West German scholars and younger, severely critical East German historians confronted court-reinstated East German professors head-on.[45] More common at present is a certain uneasy cooperation, fueled in part by many newly appointed West German academics' sincere desire for constructive change, and partly by the fact that – contrary to loose talk about "colonization" – East Germans remain in the majority in nearly all university governing bodies, which prevents even the most dynamic and aggressive West Germans from getting their way without resistance or compromise.[46] The major

44. W. Hoffmann, "Die Elite hat abgewirtschaftet. Hochschule: Knappe Finanzen, Studentenschwemme und egoistische Professoren ruinieren das Prunkstück des deutschen Bildungssystems," *Die Zeit*, Vol. 50, No. 13 (24 March 1995): 34; "'Überfüllt und Kaputt'," *Der Spiegel*, 42/1995, 58-66; N. Grunenberg, "Und der Zukunft zugewandt: Studenten in Deutschland – Sie haben Spaß am Studium und planen pragmatisch ihre Karriere," *Die Zeit*, Vol. 50, No. 53 (27 October 1995): 1.

45. K. Pätzold, "What New Start? The End of Historical Study in the GDR," *German History* 10 (1992): 392ff.; G. A. Ritter, "The Reconstruction of History at the Humboldt University: A Reply," *German History* 11 (1993): 339ff.; idem., "Der Neuaufbau der Geschichtswissenschaft an der Humboldt-Universität zu Berlin – ein Erfahrungsbericht," *Geschichte in Wissenschaft und Unterricht* 44 (1993): 226ff.

46. For a detailed analysis of these complex East-West and East-East negotiations in the early stages of unification, see F. Neidhart, "Konflikte und Balancen: Die Umwandlung der Humboldt-Universität zu Berlin 1990-1993," in *Aufbruch und Reform von oben*, 33-60.

lines of conflict run not only between East and West, but also among East Germans themselves, particularly between those who tried to maintain their integrity under the old regime and those former SED academics who somehow escaped dismissal. Whether and how the term "renewal" is used continues to depend on the position of the speaker. Thus, for some academics who were persecuted by the GDR regime, and also for some conservatives in the West, the dismissals that have already occurred have not gone far enough to earn the name "renewal."[47] For those who have been dismissed, terms like "destruction" *(Zerschlagung)* seem more appropriate. The lists of missed opportunities that are becoming common in discussions of this topic also tend to reflect the political positions of their creators. For example, when Manfred Erhardt, then Senator for Science in Berlin, pointed in June 1994 to the requirement to complete programs of study in a fixed number of semesters as a feature of the former GDR system that might have been retained, he was actually referring to something long advocated, albeit for different reasons, by conservatives in the West.[48]

Thus, with the imposition of West German models of higher education in the new states, West German problems and policy debates have also been introduced. "Normalization" in this case has meant the importation of crisis. Potential for significant innovation is evident, and is being realized in some cases; but widespread frustration remains. Perhaps it is unrealistic to expect a high level of careful planning in transition periods, when improvisation is the norm. What induces bitterness and cynicism is the contrast between the impression of rough and ready improvisation, or even arbitrary guesswork, and the technocratic rhetoric of rational control. When those adversely affected hear these messy and ambiguous changes being called "renewal," or even "modernization," that bitterness can only grow.

47. "Minister Frick und 'die Saubermänner,'" *Mitteldeutsche Zeitung*, 25 September 1993, V 14; P. Hahn, "Hohe Schule der Partei-Senioren. Die Universität Potsdam leidet unter ihrer Erblast an DDR-Professoren," *Frankfurter Allgemeine Zeitung* (1 October 1993); S. Schattenfroh, "Wenig tatsächliche Erneuerung," *Frankfurter Allgemeine Zeitung* (15 May 1993).
48. M. Erhardt, "Der Erneuerungsprozeß" (cit. n. 25), 40. In contrast to Berlin, Saxony's higher education law has introduced firmer time requirements for completion of studies.

Comment

UNIFICATION IN GERMAN HIGHER EDUCATION

Gunnar Berg

Science and education in the GDR were strongly inhibited by state regulation and by educator influence. All important decisions were made by the responsible members of the Socialist Unity Party. Professor Connelly has spoken about this. This was true especially for personnel issues, where universities, in contrast to the Academy of Sciences of the GDR, played a special role and thus attracted the special attention of the leading functionaries. The reason was that, unlike the Academy of Sciences, the universities had to teach students. It was a principle of all communist countries that, alongside justice and the military, all kinds of education were regarded as central state functions and were therefore strongly controlled. The result was that scientists at universities were often selected according to their attitude toward the state, and only secondarily according to their scientific qualifications. University autonomy did not exist. Renewal of personnel was therefore a necessity after unification. Professor Ash has spoken about this. In addition, it should be emphasized that the material basis of science in the GDR was inadequate. In contrast to official propaganda, administrative mismanagement led to insufficient financial support of science, and that means also of universities.

The main aim of the renewal now underway must therefore be new construction, the improvement of scientific equipment, especially in the computer field, and restoration of the buildings. It was necessary to achieve this in a short time, while at the same time introducing administrative and academic structures that were compatible with those of the universities in West Germany. The reason these things all had to be done at once is that during the whole time it was necessary to teach students, and these students had and have a right to finish their studies with results that are acknowledged in all of Germany. Also, it was necessary to assure that a student who transferred from one university to another could continue his or her education without interruption. It was therefore important that the structure of curricula should be similar in the East and in the West. There was no chance – and I think there is no disagreement here – that an entirely new type of university could be developed in East Germany. But renewal did offer possibilities of developing internal structures that are not usual at the older West German universities. The advantage of a comprehensive renewal is greater flexibility. At the same time, a large part of the faculty came in from the outside. So there were also good possibilities for building up new connections, especially connections between different branches of knowledge. The governing bodies of the East German universities support these tendencies.

At the University of Halle, for example, we have founded centers for interdisciplinary studies. These centers can apply for and receive financial and personnel support from the university. That means that the central administration of the university is willing to dedicate resources to supporting these centers. The supposition behind the founding of such centers is the readiness of scientists of different departments to work on a common research and teaching program. The centers will be evaluated after about five years, when a decision will be made whether to end or to continue each program. Now, we have seven such centers at the university. One of these is a center for research in school problems and for teacher education. Colleagues from different sciences, languages, natural sciences, history, and the allied fields of pedagogy or educational science are members of the center. One task of this center is the discussion and determination of new teaching content in the schools.

Other examples of cooperation of scholars from different disciplines are the topical seminars we have organized to treat problems of general interest. For example, a seminar on the risk society was carried out in 1994, with jurists, pedagogues, physicists, and theologians participating. A seminar on ethics in the sciences followed during the fall of 1995. A further example is the introduction of the tutorial system in fields where it was not used up to now.

So I can say in principle that, although the East German universities are rebuilding in ways similar to the universities in West Germany, many possibilities exist to establish interesting internal structures, which are flexible and readily adaptable to new conditions. As Professor Ash mentioned, low numbers of students favor this development, because this allows closer contact between students and scientific staff. Adequate financing is also important to maintaining universities in good order. In the new Länder, I must say, the situation in this respect is better than in the past during the GDR era. Nevertheless, we must improve this situation, because students can now compare the conditions in all of Germany with one another; when they think that support is inadequate in the East, they will go to the West. Also, we need new support for excellent research work. I already noted that financial deficits and mismanagement during the GDR era were the second reason, alongside the problems in the personnel area, that good research work could be done in only a few fields in East Germany.

Other problems of West German universities, such as the excessively high number of students and very long times to completion of degrees, do not exist up to now in the Eastern universities. But one must feel that in the future this also will become a problem for us, because the legal situation is the same in East and West. Saxony-Anhalt is trying to avoid this problem by establishing specialized higher schools (*Fachhochschulen*). Professor Ash spoke about this briefly.

In summary, I can say that the transformation of the universities in the Eastern part of Germany was, first of all, a reorganization of scientific structures. The model was the structure of the universities in West Germany. But we have also grasped many opportunites to build up new structures, especially institutional structures for interdisciplinary cooperaration in research and in teaching. However, the principal crises of German universities – the financial problems, the dramatically high number of students compared with the number of fully funded places for students, and the long times to degree – are common problems, at least for the future. No single approach can solve these problems, in the West or in the East.

Session Four

DISCUSSION

CLIFFORD ADELMAN: In the summer of 1993, I attended some conferences of European rectors. They like to tell stories. As you know, all college presidents like to tell stories. At the time, the German rectors from both sides were telling me about a phenomenon known as the "flying faculty." That is what they called them. In response to the sudden decrease of personnel in the East, professors would teach a course in Stuttgart in the morning and fly and teach another one in Leipzig in the afternoon. I would like to know to what extent the rectors were simply telling stories, and to what extent this was in fact a significant phenomenon.

Then I want to know the answer to another question, which carries forward from Professor Connelly's presentation. We have now had two purges of faculty by two different regimes, so to speak, in the same country over a period of forty years. In both cases, the science and technological faculties were somehow saved and set aside. Does that mean that it is an inevitable consequence of modern university systems, even democratic ones, to sacrifice anything in the name of science? Have we built up a false sense of what the position of science and technology means in university systems?

KONRAD JARAUSCH: This is for Mitchell Ash. You start with two or three different versions of how people think about this. The question I have is, what are the criteria for adjudicating between these versions? That is, according to what standards can we decide which of these versions is correct?

To resolve this issue I tried two or three things. The first one that I tried, you also used a lot, which is the structural issue. This obviously has to do with Paragraph 38 of the Unification Treaty, which mandates *Einpassung*, that is, taking Eastern structures and making them fit into the federal system, which of course to some degree is predetermined when you have new states joining a system which already exists. Then you can't meet halfway. There is some-where in the academic debate a kind of presumption that these two things should have come together at some sort of halfway point, but that of course was politically impossible. So I do not think we have any disagreement there.

The second kind of possible standard is the question of quality. How good really were Eastern institutions and in what areas, and how good were Western institutions? Eastern ones got evaluated to some degree, but Western ones have not really been evaluated in the same way. How do we measure that kind of quality? Is quality some-thing in the eye of the evaluating commission? Then it depends upon who is in the commission. Or is there something semi-objec-tive about such judgments? Has quality improved in the last several years? I think this is something that we might want to talk about.

The third issue that occurred to me was the question of politi-cization. Of course, the reform was started with the claim of get-ting rid of excessive politicization. However, you have established structures; how do you get rid of that politicization and those structures if not through political means? Of course, there are some ironies here, as you very well know, but I think we may need to talk about the processes at work. Can you respect faculty auton-omy in the case of faculties which never had this autonomy them-selves and which did not respect this principle before? What do you teach them about democratic procedures if you use administra-tive fear in order to get them to change? These are contradic-tions in the process of renewal that have made it a little bit more difficult, and I think these are also the reasons why people have such widely different views, not only because their experiences are different but also because it is not clear what standards there are and how these standards should be applied.

HANS-JOACHIM MEYER: First of all, I would like to congratulate Mitchell Ash on his fair representation of the problems involved. I would like to say a few words about it, taking first of all the ques-tion of renewal. For obvious reasons, this is decided on the basis of one's convictions and principles. If one regards - to put it a bit unfairly - excessive individualism as an ultimate goal of academic reform, then of course he would have a totally different position from people who regard a high degree of academic reforms, if not to say excellence, as a main criterion of renewal. So I think that it is unavoidable that there are totally different conceptions about what renewal is and also, of course, what the result of renewal policy of the East Germany university has been.

If I see it correctly, there are two fields in which probably most, if not all East Germans would agree. The first of course is the reduced position of the *akademische Mittelbau*. But this has not political, but financial causes, financial restraints which forced the East German governments to drastically reduce university staff. To give an example of Saxony; as it was already pointed out, Saxony, together with East Berlin, was one of the centers of concentration of high education in the GDR. Now, when we took over responsibility in November of 1990, we had as much academic staff as Baden-Würtemberg. The problem simply is that Baden-Würtemberg has double the size and population of Saxony, quite apart from the fact that the economic potential there is much higher than that of Saxony. So for quite obvious reasons we were forced to reduce our academic staff by half, still hoping that Saxony in a not-too-distant future would acquire the same economic potential as Baden-Würtemberg has at present.

The majority of those who have had to leave the universities and other higher education institutions did not have to leave for political reasons. Quite the contrary, all of them got a letter saying that, because of their integrity and their competence, they would be qualified for academic employment, and promising that as soon as there is a chance to give them work at an academic institution, they would get it. But, of course, there is no chance. To make this distinction is very important. Now, financial constraint – if I understood you correctly, Mitchell Ash, you implied that this was more or less due to the pressure of the federal budget. Is that what you said?

MITCHELL ASH: I said there was a potential dependence on federal money and the state in Bonn.

PROF. DR. MEYER: No, I don't think so, frankly speaking. You know, the federal budget is the source for financial means to set up university buildings, to renovate university buildings, to have new technical facilities, to have books for libraries, and so on. But all of these decisions are taken by the states. And there is a highly complicated process in Germany, as you know, that on the basis of all of the plans designed by the state governments an all-German plan is set up with the help of the Science Council. Then there is a constant debate between the federal government and the state governments to get the necessary money for each budget year. The drastic cuts in academic staff were due to the state budgets. Now, as the budgets of the East German states depend on an all-German arrangement of transferring money within Germany (*Länderausgleich*), the real pressure came from the West German states. I could put it this way. There was no finance minister for a West German state who was ready to give more money to the science minister of Saxony than to his own science minister. It was as simple as that. In fact, the so-called higher education renewal program was financed by the federal government and by the East German *Länder*, not by the West German *Länder*. It was quite helpful also for finding at least temporary places for people who otherwise would have been forced to go earlier than necessary.

Then I would like to say a few words about your phases. You mentioned the ninth of November. I know your sympathy for East Germany. Could I say East Germans are a bit sensitive about this date? On the one hand, the Wall went down, and so it was a big defeat for the communist regime. But it was not the day of a victory. The victory is the ninth of October, in fact. The ninth of October, not the third, the ninth of October. That was the day of the big demonstrations in Leipzig and in Dresden, and not the ninth of November, which was the only result of this, the consequence. So I would not mention this date in connection with the internal developments in East Germany. And if I remember correctly, the first student meetings in the Humboldt University of East Berlin, which then led to the disposal of the leadership of the communist organization and to the election of the student council, were earlier than the ninth of November.

I would like to say a word about the difference between the disciplines in need of renewal and also about the method of renewal. First of all, it would have been absolutely impossible for us to start with the renewal process in all academic fields at once, so we had to decide the dissolution of academic departments in law, economics, philosophy, and others. Given the need to organize study programs for the students who were there, this was such a tremendous task that it would have been impossible to start with all of the fields at once. We had a renewal process in all of the academic fields. But that the result is different is due to the total change of the political and social order. Not only personal integrity or political integrity is at stake, but also academic competence. Somebody who has taught socialist planning economics does not have the academic competence to teach business studies for a market economy, somebody who has taught socialist constitutional law is at least not necessarily well prepared for giving lessons and lectures in democratic constitutional law. So I think it is absolutely necessary that the effects of such a renewal process are more dramatic in fields such as law or economy or philosophy than in physics, or in linguistics, the field from which I come.

In this context, I would like to say a word about the increase or the decrease in the proportion of the natural sciences and engineering on the one hand and the humanities and social sciences on the other. Something cannot be correct with your figures. I am afraid, as you've already correctly guessed, that people simply counted as social scientists all of the people in the former departments of Marxism and Leninism which were dissolved in May of 1990. That was one of my decisions as the last GDR minister of education and science. Of course, for example, when one looks at the Technical University of Dresden, which today is still called by that name for historical reasons and because it provides a whole range of engineering degree courses, at the same time it is a full university with faculties in humanities, social sciences, law, economics, educational sciences, and medicine. As far as I can see, this reduction in the social sciences and humanities is particularly dramatic at Dresden, but this is an exceptional case for the East German states. My impression is that, for example, faculties of law, economics, and also the theological disciplines are today in fact larger than they were before 1989.

A last word about the influence of the federal university framework law, the *Hochschulrahmengesetz*. I would like to mention that I made it a point and I was successful in this in the course of negotiating the Unification Treaty, that the East German states had a phase of up to three years before they were legally compelled to have university acts along the lines of the university framework act. Up to that time, to the third of October 1993, the states only had to comply with the rulings of the Federal Constitutional Court. It was a ruling of the Federal Constitutional Court that in all matters relating to decisions on teaching and research, there should be a majority of professors.

Regarding the "flying faculties," well, what was a "flying faculty"? For example, we had the former Section of Law at the then Karl Marx University, that is Leipzig University. We dissolved this department and decided to set up a new faculty. Some of the professors got new provisional job contracts, but the majority did not get such jobs because that would have made practically no sense. That is, if all of the professors would have been in the position to go on with their teaching, then of course we would not have had the right to dissolve this department. So we needed help from West German universities. And I am really quite grateful that quite a lot of colleagues from West Germany were ready, in addition to their teaching commitments in their own universities, to take up additional commitments in East German universities. Usually this was done in the form of so-called block lectures or seminars; that is, they came for two days or a week and gave all of the lectures in these two days and then of course disappeared, as I have to admit, mostly by air. For this reason, Professor Schiedermeier, the president of the *Hochschulverband*, invented this terrible and highly misleading term, "flying faculty." And I had an argument with him about it. I told him, this is really nonsense and it creates illusions and wrong impressions. And he said, well, I never was so successful with an expression I coined and so I will stick to it.

By the way, Professor Jarausch, Article 38 of the Unification Treaty refers, if I remember correctly, not to universities but to extra-university research, that is to say, to the Academy of Sciences. Of course, I am still of the conviction that this was correct, that the highly centralized structure of the GDR Academy of Sciencey could not be continued, that it was necessary to be aware of or to take over models of extra-university research which had been developed in West Germany, the Max Planck Society, the Fraunhofer Society, and so on. And I still stick to this decision, because this is much more to the purpose than the highly centralized Academy of Sciences was, which comprised everything from basic research to the development of scientific equipment.

RAINER KÜNZEL: I would just like to add two short comments. The first pertains to the enormous importance of the shortage of time, the pressure of time, as Mr. Ash rightly pointed out. Because of that, many attempts to come to new solutions to a number of problems were not successful. For instance, the University of Osnabrück, where I come from, hosted a series of three conferences of university rectors of the state of Saxony and the state of Saxony-Anhalt, in order to discuss the possibilities of influencing the process of formulating new laws of higher education in the new *Länder*. It was very interesting to see that from the experience that we have had in the Western part of the country with our state laws and exchanging views with the rectors of East Germany, we came to a number of very interesting solutions. But none of these solutions was put in practice, because a year later most of the participants in this conference from the Eastern states were not in office any more, and the others that had replaced them told us that there was practically no communication or very little communication between university administrations and the respective ministries of higher education. So most of the laws were just passed without cooperation or without thorough discussion with the heads of the universities.

Another point I want to make is about the role of those "flying faculties." Some of these "flying faculties" did not have a chance to fly. For instance, our people from the University of Osnabrück set up a department of economics and business administration and a new department of law at the University of Greifswald. They had to drive to Greifswald, which is eight hours driving, and they did that for two and a half years, because the process of hiring new teaching staff took that long. It was very complicated because it was probably the poorest state in the country that had tried to set up two new faculties and, of course, it took them very, very long to fill the positions.

CLIFFORD ADELMAN: That question about the "flying faculty," which I'm delighted has had such wonderful ripples and smiles, was a question about how systems in periods of stress adopt a variety of interim measures to respond to imbalances, disequilibrium, and conditions that border on severe crisis. So the "flying faculty" is only a metaphor for a variety of measures that were taken at the time. If you are close to another country where they at least have competent people who speak decent German, you can bring them in to handle some of this material. The fact is that the system worked that way, and some integration, however painful, occurred. In Russia, you know, that still has not happened; they are still trying to give people in the technical institutes something to do, and they do not know how to talk to the people in the university. So one problem was solved in Germany.

GUNNAR BERG: The "flying faculties" have already been discussed; Minister Meyer has said what needs to be said about this. In Halle, especially in the law faculty but in other fields as well, such measures were simply necessary in order to maintain instruction. The consequences of doing anything else would have been closing the faculties and institutes and sending the students either home or to West German universities. The solution we chose was reasonable.

How can one measure quality? Naturally it is difficult to measure quality, and I do not want to claim that the quality of our universities has improved everywhere. This is something that will take many years, and that has to do with the reputation of a university as a whole. What I can say, however, and here I can agree with Professor Ash, is that there is now a new quality of academic life. Earlier it was not the case that different faculties worked closely together. This result is due in part to the fact that a large number of new people have come to the university in a short time. It is different when one new person comes into an existing, established institution and must adapt to the situation. In this case, numerous newcomers arrived in a situation in which everything was in motion, much was new, and everyone had the same problems. One can therefore say that in this ideal sense a new quality has emerged. I can only hope that this will eventually have an impact on the situation of the university as a whole.

Let me add something to Minister Meyer's remarks on the problems of middle-level staff (the *Mittelbau*). This is the largest personnel problem that we now have, and the fact that the structure must change simply adds to the difficulty. In the GDR it was the case that 70-80 percent of the *Mittelbau* had unlimited tenure. In that situation there was no possiblity of bringing in younger people. This blockage was not there at first. In the 1960s new positions were simply created for the younger staff, but over time this was no longer possible. By the 1980s the existing positions were practically blocked with people between thirty-five and fifty years old, which meant that they would remain filled for the next twenty years. Therefore the need arose to alter the structure itself, and at the same to make the process "socially bearable," as we say so nicely.

A final remark to Professor Künzel. One should certainly discuss how to change the higher education laws. Nonetheless, and in spite of everything, the changes in our case had to happen in a short time. I believe that it would not have been good to introduce something into the new *Länder* that did not exist in the others. Some aspects of these discussion did, I believe, enter into the new laws. It is true that some changes did not happen, but that is a problem of the German landscape in general. National solutions are needed, and any differences among the states must still produce results that are comparable from one state to another.

MITCHELL ASH: First, a quick point to Clifford Adelman. The term used by the head of the Rectors' Conference was "flying faculty," but the term that I heard most was the one I used in my remarks, *Lufthansaprofessoren.* As we heard from Rainer Künzel, obviously even that is not quite right, since some of them were Volkswagen or BMW professors.

I am more interested in the second question that you asked that no one has answered. That is the question about the difference, if any, between the two purges after 1945 and 1989 or 1990. I happen to be investigating that, and I am not going to tell you the results here, because this should be short. I just want to point out, as a point of understanding and clarification, that I spoke of the sparing of the natural sciences as characteristic only of the first stage after unification. Individual evaluations of all disciplines happened after the renewal laws were passed. After that, scientists were not spared any more, at least not by those criteria.

To Minister Meyer, I think I have really very little to say because I accept just about all of your points. How could I not? I am especially curious about one point, however. And that is your suggestion, which I find very interesting, that the actual source of the financial problems was the *Länderauslgeich* and not the federal budget. I had thought that the East German states were exempted from the *Länderausgleich* in the first years after unification, and were directly dependent on transfer payments from the federal government, which they still receive.

Shortage of money, shortage of time. It had to be like this. It had to be like that. The students had to get their degrees. These are all statements that sound objective, but in fact are representative of political choices that were made. This is why a discourse analysis is extremely helpful here, because it helps us to remember that these were political choices. Now, that does not mean that once the choices were made, they did not become constraints; they did. But they did not have to become such tight constraints, not necessarily. Whether they did or not is an issue that can be discussed, but one cannot discuss it if one uses these terms as though we were talking about laws of nature. I think it is very important to be clear about that.

The challenge of people who have carried out a policy to the critic always is, how would you have done it differently? All I can say in response to that is, that it is not my job to tell you that. I look as a historian at the alternatives that were in fact available, not the ones I would have invented out of whole cloth. That brings me to Konrad Jarausch's points.

Konrad Jarausch's effort to introduce possible criteria for adjudicating among the various ways in which the term renewal is given a content seems to me very admirable, and I do not want to dismiss it out of hand. But my fear is that what you have done is to introduce yet an additional set of terms which themselves are contested. Quality is one of them.

KONRAD JARAUSCH: But they come from the time. I didn't make them up.

MITCHELL ASH: Yes, of course, but their meanings were and are themselves contested. Dieter Simon has claimed that instead of grasping opportunities for innovation, all that has happened is that mediocre West German academics have gotten professorships in the East; his term, I believe, is "third rate." I suspect that what has resulted is a qualitative mix that is not very different in principle from that in the West, or in American state-supported universities, for that matter. Be that as it may, I am not sure it is possible in this particular situation to find the kind of firm, Archimedean point from which we can make clear assessments. I think the right metaphor is more like being on a greasy dance floor, holding on to each other for dear life. The only thing that can be done in such slippery circumstances, it seems to me, is to reflect on the categories, realizing that they are contested, and state one's own position as clearly as possible. That sounds very watered down and liberal, but I am not sure there is anything better than that that can be achieved. All that Francis Bacon ever expected of the new science in the seventeenth century is agreement, not certainty.

Part Two

THE PRESENT SITUATION
AND OUTLOOKS FOR THE FUTURE

Chapter Five

MYTHOS HUMBOLDT TODAY

Teaching, Research, and Administration

⊂∞⊃

Peter Lundgreen

Much can be said about the differences between the idea of the Humboldtian university on the one hand, and the reality of this university on the other. The German university of the early nineteenth century looks even more different from the one of the late nineteenth and early twentieth centuries than it does from today's university; this holds true both from the inside and with respect to the environment.[1] Nevertheless, such developments and changes appear to be minor compared with the dramatic transformation of the university in what Peter Moraw calls the "postclassical" period, since the 1960s. It is, therefore, no accident that reform debate and reform movements, although constant companions of university history, gained momentum precisely during the last three decades. Of particular interest is the well-known finding that many participants in this debate pay tribute to Hum-

---

1. R. vom Bruch, "A Slow Farewell to Humboldt? Stages in the History of the German Universities, 1810-1945," in this volume; cf. P. Moraw, "Aspekte und Dimensionen älterer deutscher Universitätsgeschichte," in *Academia Gissensis. Beiträge zur älteren Gießener Universitätsgeschichte*, eds. P. Moraw and V. Press (Marburg, 1982), 7ff.

boldt or the "idea of the (Humboldtian) university" when they argue in favor of, or against, a given proposal.

The present paper will study this *Mythos Humboldt* as a living part of the reform debate since the 1960s. For methodological reasons it is crucial to pay attention to the precise meaning of any reference to the "idea of the university." Is it part of Humboldt's thinking and writing, or is it an essential property of the image widely held as characteristic of the classical German university? Furthermore, does reference to Humboldt indicate a defensive stance in spite of mounting criticism and increasing deficits? Or do such references, alternatively, lead to an offensive search for solutions that are functionally equivalent to Humboldt's reforms? Questions of this sort will have to be borne in mind, when we concentrate on the three areas of teaching, research, and administration in the postclassical university.

Teaching

For observers from the outside, the contrast between the classical and the postclassical university is nowhere as sharp as with respect to the enrollment of students. Although "overcrowding" has been a public issue since the 1880s, only 2 percent of the pertinent male age cohorts (or 1 percent of these age cohorts comprising both sexes) attended an institution of higher learning (*Hochschule*) by 1900. During the twentieth century, and after the admittance of women, beginners among students still made up only 3 percent of their age cohort by 1930 and 5 percent by 1950, but constituted 8 percent in 1960 – enough to trigger a reform debate on how to cope with the expansion. Since 1960, however, enrollment figures for beginners have reached previously unimagined orders of magnitude: 15 percent in 1970, 19 percent in 1980, 32 percent in 1990; forecasts speak of 40 percent at the turn of the millenium. Concomitant symptoms of this mass university are well known: increasingly long periods of individual study; a high rate of dropouts; deterioration of student-faculty ratios; loosening of linkages between academic training and occupational opportunities; etc.

Deficits of this sort are widely acknowledged, as is the crucial importance of appropriate answers to the key question: How are the goals and functions of academic training to be defined, if the student population has risen to include every third person in an age cohort? Any answer to this question cannot but discuss the cherished principle of the "unity of teaching and research." Indeed, no other essential feature of the "idea of the Humboldtian university" has ever found as much attention and reference in contemporary reform debate as this core principle. Participants in the debate agree that at least two main teaching functions may be distinguished: the training of academic practitioners, i.e., of lawyers, physicians, teachers, etc.; and the training of "academic recruits," i.e., of researchers who, eventually, may become professors. Agreement also prevails that university teaching can never substitute for training on the job – that job skills can only be gained by practical training, whether formalized like preparatory periods for trainees leading to another examination (such as the *Referendariat* for lawyers and teachers) or not. Hence the distinction between occupational qualification *(Berufsbefähigung)* and job skills *(Berufsfertigkeit)* has entered common parlance. So far, so good; but the lines of this picture become blurred as soon as we realize that there is one academic career, the researcher, for whom the university provides both theoretical and practical training, or qualification and job skills: getting taught how to do research by gradually participating in research. Here we have the "unity of teaching and research" as seen from the perspective of particular students. Is this a valid model for university teaching in general?

To begin with, it should be noted that the famous formula of the "unity of teaching and research" is not a quotation from any of Humboldt's texts. The formula was coined by later historiography that connected two different thoughts with each other: Humboldt's definition of *Wissenschaft* as an ongoing and never-ending process of research, and Humboldt's conceptual distinction between high school instruction ("learning how to learn") and university instruction ("freedom and self-determined activity, inspired by a longing for *Wissenschaft*").[2] The traditional corporate *universi-*

2. W. von Humboldt, "Über die innere und äußere Organisation der höheren wissenschaftlichen Anstalten in Berlin [1810]," in idem, *Werke in fünf Bänden*, eds. A. Flitner and K. Giel (Darmstadt, 1969), vol. IV, 256f., 260; idem, "Der Königsberger und die Litauische Schulplan [1809]," in ibid., 169ff.; cf. M.

tas magistrorum et scholarium thus gained a new meaning: professors and students are both and together engaged in research. This "unity of teaching and research" was clearly governed by the two concepts of "*Wissenchaft* as research" and of "education by *Wissenschaft.*" A further reminder is necessary: Humboldt did not yet have in mind the modern concept of specialized research within the boundaries of a single discipline. His regulatory ideal was another formula, the "unity of *Wissenschaft,*" this time an original phrasing that he shared with philosophers of idealism such as Fichte and Schelling, but also with Schleiermacher and Steffens.[3] "Unity of *Wissenschaft*" paid some tribute to the older encyclopedic tradition, which was refreshed and newly clothed by the synthetic ambition of philosophical idealism. Teaching and research as governed by this ideal aimed at synthesis, at philosophical enlightenment about the world, and, thereby, at character formation.

It is well known that in reality the meaning of research at the "Humboldtian university" radically changed and was transformed into the present understanding over a long period of time. Key aspects of this development are the establishment of seminars and institutes, the rise of a competitive market in ideas based on the production of papers evaluated by peer review, the differentiation and specialization of disciplines, etc. At the same time the "Humboldtian university" remained, like many other universities, an institution for the training of pastors, judges, administrators,

---

Riedel, "Wilhelm von Humboldts Begründung der Einheit von Forschung und Lehre' als Leitidee der Universität," *Zeitschrift für Pädagogik*, 14. Beiheft (1977): 231-47.

3. Humboldt, "Organisation" (note 2), 258; idem, "Schulplan" (note 2), 170; J. G. Fichte, "Deduzierter Plan einer in Berlin zu errichtenden höheren Lehranstalt [1807]," in *Gelegentliche Gedanken über Universitäten*, ed. E. Müller (Leipzig, 1990), 84; F. W. J. Schelling, "Vorlesungen über die Methode des akademischen Studiums [1803]," in *Die Idee der deutschen Universität*, ed. E. Anrich (Darmstadt, 1956), 4, 16; F. D. E. Schleiermacher, "Gelegentliche Gedanken über Universitäten im deutschen Sinn [1808]," in *Gelegentliche Gedanken über Universitäten*, ed. E. Müller (Leipzig, 1990), 161, 169f.; H. Steffens, "Vorlesungen über die Idee der Universitäten [1809]," in *Die Idee der deutschen Universität*, ed. E. Anrich (Darmstadt, 1956), 320, 361ff.; cf. Riedel, "Humboldts Begründung" (note 2), 241ff.; L. Huber, "Bildung durch Wissenschaft – Wissenschaft durch Bildung. Hochschuldidaktische Anmerkungen zu einem großen Thema," *Pädagogik und Schule in Ost und West* 39 (1991): 193ff.

lawyers, physicians, and, since 1810, of high school teachers. From these circumstances stems the argument that at least the faculties of theology, law, and medicine were barely transformed by the Humboldtian "idea of the university" and may be regarded as belonging to the realm of "special schools." No doubt, if anywhere, the "idea of the (Humboldtian) university" found its stronghold in the newly prominent philosophical faculty (which then included natural sciences and humanities). Here we witness a pragmatic approach to the synthetic ideal of a "unity of *Wissenschaft*," embodied in the state examination for teacher training required to cover a wide, albeit narrowing, range of subjects. At the same time as they prepared for such examinations, these students attended a seminar or an institute and wrote increasingly specialized papers. It is this organizational identity that underlies the common parlance of a "unity of teaching and research."

How is this principle to be evaluated in historical perspective? In my judgement, the principle served excellently the function of recruiting scholars, and yet did not considerably harm the function of training practitioners, at least as long as we see such tiny minorities of an age cohort flocking to a university and entering one of the few academic professions around 1900. Close linkages between formal qualifications and entry to occupations prevailed, and professional skills were to be learned on the job anyway. During the twentieth century, conditions have dramatically changed, not only in terms of enrollment figures but also with respect to the labor market. There are many more academic (and semi-academic) professions, much looser linkages between qualifications and entry to occupations, much more competition of academic and nonacademic applicants for identical jobs, etc. It is this environment that repeatedly gives rise to the question of whether training academic practitioners and researchers in one and the same course of study should be continued at the (postclassical) university of our time. As has been said already, participants in the reform debate never forget to refer to the "unity of teaching and research" in the sense mentioned above, but their answers to the question just posed nonetheless differ.

A stronghold of the conservative position has been the (West) German Rectors' Conference (WRK, HRK). As late as 1988 the

WRK defended the "dualism of occupational qualification and research qualification" as a "common structural element of *all* university studies": "both objectives are as usual integrated in *one* program of study without any differences for all who graduate."[4] Ready to admit that these two objectives have been organized sequentially in most foreign countries, the rectors advanced three reasons for maintaining the German way. First, we find the inevitable reference to Humboldt in general and to his reform of the high school in particular. Historically correctly, they argued that the Gymnasium had substituted for the old faculty of liberal arts and hence had become the only and sufficient stage of general education preparing for professional studies. No attention is paid, within this context, to the exponential rise of the high school population; on the other hand, curricular reforms at the high schools toward a highly individualized selection of subjects are criticized as falling short of ensuring maturity for university studies. In other words, the introduction of some sort of "academic freedom" into the high school is seen to impinge upon "general education" as an objective. But reform (of a conservative orientation) is demanded for the Gymnasium, not for undergraduate study at the university.

Secondly, the rectors pointed to the professional colleges (*Fachhochschulen*) as an alternative to university studies; these offer fewer years of study and more orientation toward practice. *Fachhochschulen*, it will be remembered, only came into being by 1970 when former *Fachschulen*, i.e., higher schools of engineering, business economics, or social work, were upgraded. In taking this position the rectors deliberately overlooked the fact that for most university students there is no option to study their subject at a *Fachhochschule*, notwithstanding the desired expansion of this institutional segment. Furthermore, it seems to be characteristic that the problems inherent in university teaching are admitted, but the solution is sought again by referring to another institution outside the university.

Thirdly, the rectors defended their traditional position as a matter of acceptance or rejection by the people concerned. Shortened university studies, i.e., three instead of four years, they argued, will

4. Westdeutsche Rektorenkonferenz, *Die Zukunft der Hochschulen. Überlegungen für eine zukunftsorientierte Hochschulpolitik* (Bonn, 1988), 50.

be accepted neither by industry nor by professors and students. This argument has several flaws. To begin with, the main issue is the differentiation between occupational qualification and research qualification, not necessarily the number of years of study. But what about the acceptance? For industry, this question does not make much sense, because there will always be a supply of differently qualified manpower competing for similar jobs. Hiring and firing, after all, are more dependent on market conditions and individual performance on the job than on formal credits and diplomas. For students and professors, on the other hand, questions of distinction and prestige within a large educational system are at stake.

The transition from the integrated German way of teaching practitioners and researchers alike to the two-stage model of other countries is typically denounced as introducing a hierarchy between a school-like study for the masses and an elite program of study for the happy few. Historians and sociologists of education know that accusations of this sort are a powerful weapon wherever public opinion prefers "equality of opportunities" as a core value of liberal democracy. Similar reasoning applies, if we consider the institutional history of the educational system. In my reading we find two secular trends in this history: functional differentiation and academic upgrading. It can be shown that processes of (or pushes for) academic upgrading cause losses of functional differentiation, at least for some time. Why? Because the wish to belong to the higher (or highest) rank of institution implies adaptation. Consequently, people at the top tend to resist functional differentiation if it appears to introduce hierarchical internal differentials or to narrow external distances to other institutional segments in the system.

To sum up, the formula of the "unity of teaching and research" and its transformation into the principle of "identical training of academic practitioners and researchers" joined forces in West Germany with the belief in "equality of opportunity" and in the need for "academic upgrading." This coalition formed a strong defense of the postclassical German university against reform along the lines of functional differentiation of teaching. Advocates of such reforms, on the other hand, were not silent, and they intensified their activities from the 1960s onward. Interestingly enough, in doing so they again referred to Humboldt. Helmut Schelsky, for example, in his reading of Humboldt advised us that we should make a distinction between "antiquated institutional forms" and "still living ideas" when relating reform proposals of our time to the reforms of the early nineteenth century.[5] As a sociologist Schelsky was a strong believer in functional differentiation; he was convinced that the old demarcation line between high school and university must be redrawn across the university, i.e., between "training for academic occupations" and "research governed by academic freedom." In other words, Schelsky reminded us to ask for institutional reforms that are functionally equivalent to older ones and thereby keep alive their spirit.

The very same track of thinking was followed by the National Council for Science (*Wissenschaftsrat*). Founded in 1957 as a body for the coordinated planning of science policy, the *Wissenschaftsrat* brought together representatives of the science system and of the federal as well as state governments. After starting in 1960 to publish science and educational policy recommendations, the *Wissenschaftsrat* advocated as early as 1966 a restructuring of university studies according to the two-stage model, and reinforced this position in 1986.[6] The basic proposition states that the "unity of teaching and research" at the German university can only be upheld in the future if identical study programs for future practitioners and researchers are given up in favor of functional differentiation. Otherwise, teaching and research will harm each other. Several lines of argumentation may be distinguished here:

- During the nineteenth century, Humboldt's ideal of the "unity of teaching and research" was already more or less postgraduate in character. It found realization in some seminars and institutes, but mainly in the American graduate schools. This particular institutional development has been followed up in

5. H. Schelsky, *Einsamkeit und Freiheit. Idee und Gestalt der deutschen Universität und ihrer Reformen*, 2nd ed. (Düsseldorf, 1971), 256; idem, "Die Universitätsidee Wilhelm von Humboldts und die gegenwärtige Universitätsreform [1967]," in idem, *Abschied von der Hochschulpolitik oder die Universität im Fadenkreuz des Versagens* (Bielefeld, 1969), 157, 159.

6. Wissenschaftsrat, *Empfehlungen zur Neuordnung des Studiums an den wissenschaftlichen Hochschulen* (Bonn, 1966), 7ff.; idem, *Empfehlungen zur Struktur des Studiums* (Bonn, 1986), 33ff.

Germany only recently, through the introduction of graduate colleges (Graduiertenkollegs.)

- Differentiation and specialization of scientific disciplines have meant that the units an individual researcher can competently master have become smaller and smaller parts of a whole discipline or field of study. Participation in such specialized research requires a preceding program of study that is not dominated by the "unity of teaching and research."

- Differentiation and specialization of scientific disciplines have enlarged the distance, if not the difference, between disciplinary units of study and professional fields of practice. The older functional identity between disciplinary and professional orientation has become obsolete; no longer do students 'interests in existing knowledge at given research frontiers come close enough to other students' interests in knowledge required for professional life.

- These developments are not only a result of scientific progress, but also of dramatic changes in the labor market. A host of new academic occupations has come into being, with no established linkages between graduation from university and entry into practice, and thus no formalized stages for trainees. Hence both students and state administration call for more "practical orientation" of university studies. This is also justified on the ground, that a considerable proportion of the graduates will not have a chance, statistically, to enter any academic occupation, but will have to seek employment and fulfillment elsewhere.

For all these reasons, the Wissenschaftsrat proposed a functional differentiation between "basic study" (four years) and selective "graduate studies." If this proposal was to mean more than new language for existing practice, namely the sequence of study for a diploma (state exams, master's degree) and a follow-up period of research for the Ph.D., everything depended on a new definition of the four-year study program. In other words, the question is how far the Wissenschaftsrat distanced teaching and learning for occupational qualification from the inherent dynamics of the research imperative. Several dimensions may be observed that cannot be dealt with here extensively. Of particular interest is the decoupling of research and teaching by time allotted. Setting a given period of time for a program of study, it is correctly argued, must appear arbitrary, if viewed from the standpoint of research and scientific progress. There is simply no way to translate disciplinary interests into "necessary" time spans for study; rather, a decision of educational policy is called for that is guided by a conventional time frame (i.e., four years) and thus poses the need for appropriate teaching objects to become part of the curriculum. Obviously, the crux of the matter is to reach agreement about "appropriate teaching objects" on the level of particular fields of study, and the *Wissenschaftsrat* could only formulate guiding principles for a type of study that is still science based but nonetheless qualifying for professional life (apart from research).

In its concern to enable the student of average capabilities to finish such a study program on time, the *Wissenschaftsrat* took pains to encourage all sorts of help, e.g., lecture plans, tutors, small groups, additional examinations before the qualifying state examinations, etc. Interestingly enough, the decisive step to ensure compliance with the time frame was not taken: The introduction of "classes" of first-, second-, or third-year students was not considered. Maybe such a move would have meant too sharp a break with the Humboldtian tradition, although the *Wissenschaftsrat* came close to proposing it. In 1966, the authors were already convinced that the venerated "principle of individual responsibility" or "freedom of learning" could no longer guide students and hence would be of only limited value. One might expect that in 1986 such a conviction should have become even stronger; in the meantime the former *Fachschulen*, or higher schools of engineering, etc., had been upgraded to become *Fachhochschulen*. Among other changes, this meant giving up class instruction in favor of individual responsibility. But even in the light of this recent experience the *Wissenschaftsrat* did not dare to recommend uniform class instruction by sequencing years for any stage of university studies. There is good reason, then, to remain skeptical whether the campaign to shorten study time in Germany will succeed, even if the functional differentiation between "basic study" and "graduate study" should lead to a thorough reform of "basic study."

Chances at least for this part of the reform may have improved, since the German Rectors' Conference revoked its position of 1988 and converted to the *Wissenschaftsrat* proposals in 1992.[7] Why did the rectors do this? The diagnosis of symptoms, deficits, and causes was more or less identical in 1988 or 1992, but the conclusions differed. To put it pointedly: The rectors decided that the principle of "unity of teaching and research" can only be upheld as a constituent of the university if it is decoupled from the basic four-year study program for the masses and is limited only to the graduate study of minorities selected by performance. Structure and organization of the basic study program must allow the average gifted student, who is aiming – rightly – at an occupational qualification, to graduate after four years. Specialization for such students is generally a matter of practice afterward; one field of specialized practice is research in science, that is only to be learned in graduate study.

In spite of this recent agreement with the *Wissenschaftsrat*, the rectors devoted much less attention to the question of how a four-year program of study for the masses may become reality. Controversial debates and the search for a compromise formula can easily be imagined, if we read: "Differentiation of special studies and examining of specialties should be cut back. The resulting gains in time would enable interested students to participate in research in some cases."[8] Apparently, the rectors only reluctantly, and with a nostalgic mood of resignation, bid farewell to the concept of individual, self-determined, and responsible learning as a fundamental characteristic of all university study. In my interpretation, this is due to the fear of losing the *differentia specifica* between a university and the type of study prevailing at special schools. Similar reasoning applies, if the rectors consider that the basic study program may even allow graduation below the four-year benchmark. The rectors hastened to add that such "short programs," which had already been proposed by the *Wissenschaftsrat* in 1978, should not copy those offered at *Fachhochschulen.*[9]

7. Hochschulrektorenkonferenz, *Konzept zur Entwicklung der Hochschulen in Deutschland* (Bonn, 1992), 23f., 28ff.
8. bid., 29.
9. Ibid., 29; Wissenschaftsrat, *Empfehlungen zur Differenzierung des Studienangebots* (Bonn, 1978).

One may wonder why the Rectors' Conference converted to the position of 1992 at all. There is one obvious, but not very flattering answer. The pressing need for university reform had caused a change in pertinent state policies. Instruments limited in time such as "overload," "tunnelling" through a peak of enrollments, or "emergency programs" apparently did not suffice any longer. Conferences of ministers of finance and of cultural affairs agreed, in 1992, that a structural reform (along the lines of the existing *Wissenschaftsrat* proposals) was necessary, and that state action was called for. Under the pressure of such impending regulation by law or administrative decrees, and particularly in danger if the allocation of resources is increasingly based on output factors, universities had, and still have, no option but to participate in the reform business for the sake of influencing it. Since 1993, the official policy of all parties, i.e., the *Wissenschaftsrat*, the Rectors' Conference, and the Conference of Ministers of Cultural Affairs, is identical. All agree that functional differentiation of university studies should take place along the lines already proposed since the early 1960s. It remains to be seen whether or not this structural reform will succeed by becoming an accepted pattern in the future.

Research

The ongoing debate on the "unity of teaching and research" obviously can focus either on the adequate determination of study at the mass university or on the future of research at this institution. Dominant among this latter debate is a twofold conviction: (1) research is an indispensable function of the university, if only for the recruitment and training of future researchers; (2) research is gravely in danger at the present university and may fail to properly fulfill its function.

As to the first point, research in the modern sense of producing specialized new knowledge within a spectrum of scientific disciplines had clearly become part of the Humboldtian university back in the nineteenth century, although one might argue that Humboldt himself had something different in mind (see above). The contemporaneous phrasing of the research imperative during the nineteenth century was that the sciences should not only be transmitted, but also be "promoted," "enlarged," or "cultivated." It is this added research function that paved the way for technical colleges to gain university status from 1879 onward.[10] Research activities as an accepted and expected function of the university have triggered a dynamic, which has thoroughly transformed the German university. A prominent indicator is the big research institute that provoked the question of whether research could or even should be organized outside and independently of the university. The pertinent discussion of this issue in Germany dates back to the late nineteenth century; foreign patterns of more separation between teaching and research served as a constant point of reference. Nevertheless, there is not a single reform proposal since the 1960s that advocated that the modern mass university should no longer embrace research among its functions.

This finding brings us to the second point, the "dangers" confronting research at the university. Such dangers may be classified according to particular comparative shortages or disadvantages: (1) constraints of time available for research due to the demands of teaching, if compared with research outside the university; (2) limits of growth for big science, or for institutional emphasis on specific research areas, as they are caused by collegiate loyalties in favor of equal distribution of funds across existing chairs; (3) lack of funding. As a result of the cumulative effects of these dangers, research is seen to emigrate from the universities to nonuniversity institutions.

The last point deserves special attention because of the implications drawn from a statistical observation. For about one hundred years the national science system of Germany (and of other countries) has consisted of three major branches – the academic sector, the industrial sector, and the state sector.[11] Growth differentials

10. Cf. G. Schubring, "Spezialschulmodell versus Universitätsmodell – die Institutionalisierung von Forschung," in *'Einsamkeit und Freiheit' neu besichtigt. Universitätsreformen und Disziplinenbildung in Preußen als Modell für Wissenschaftspolitik im Europa des 19. Jahrhunderts*, ed. G. Schubring (Stuttgart,1991), 311f.; P. Lundgreen, "Technische Bildung in Preußen vom 18. Jahrhundert bis zur Zeit der Reichsgründung," in *Die Technische Fachhochschule Berlin im Spektrum Berliner Bildungsgeschichte*, ed. G. Sodan (Berlin, 1988), 33.
11. Cf. P. Lundgreen et al., *Staatliche Forschung in Deutschland 1870-1980* (Frankfurt/New York, 1986).

among these sectors tell something about functional differentiation and division of labor, but also about an increase in the science
base of industry and the modern state. A falling percentage of the
academic sector's share in the overall growth does not by itself indicate, however, any shortcomings of research at the university. A
conviction to the contrary, put forward by the Rectors' Conference
as late as in 1988, only testifies to the pseudo-Humboldtian ideology that the university should be the first address for research,
before other institutions may serve as substitutes.[12] It may very well
be that the dissolution of the Academy of Sciences of the former
German Democratic Republic paid some tribute to this ideology.

Quite apart from such comparative and statistically informed
reasoning there was and still is broad consensus about the dangers
confronting research at the German universities. Beginning in
1960, the *Wissenschaftsrat* took up this topic in a series of recommendations, and so did others. For the sake of brevity, I name only
some of the major and recurring reform proposals:

- Structural reform of university study, i.e., functional differentiation between basic and graduate study. This most far-reaching strategy of reform has already been dealt with extensively
  in the previous section.
- Growth of the academic sector by founding new universities
  in order to relieve older ones of their burden and create new
  research facilities.[13] This policy was followed during the 1960s
  and 1970s, but was swallowed by the upsurge of enrollments
  under conditions of fiscal restriction.
- Functional differentiation within the university sector by
  allowing some "research universities" as an exception.[14] This

12. Westdeutsche Rektorenkonferenz, *Zukunft der Hochschulen* (note 4), 41.
13. Wissenschaftsrat, *Empfehlungen zum Ausbau der wissenschaftlichen Einrichtun-
    gen. Part I: Wissenschaftliche Hochschulen* (Bonn, 1960), 53.
14. Wissenschaftsrat, *Anregungen zur Gestalt neuer Hochschulen* (Bonn, 1962);
    Schelsky, *Einsamkeit* (note 5), 235ff., 249f.; H. Schelsky, "Grundzüge einer
    neuen Universität. Eine Denkschrift [1965]," in *Grundzüge einer neuen Uni-
    versität. Zur Planung einer Hochschulgründung in Ostwestfalen*, eds. P. Mikat and
    H. Schelsky (Gütersloh, 1966); *Gebremste Reform. Ein Kapitel deutscher
    Hochschulgeschichte. Universität Konstanz 1966-1976*, eds. H. R. Jauss and H.
    Nesselhauf (Konstanz, 1977).

proposal of the early 1960s, which implied a general limitation for the enrollment of students, was realized, for some time, in the new universities of Konstanz (1966) and Bielefeld (1969), but was likewise swallowed by the pressing needs of coping with teaching demands.

- Succession of "teaching" and "research" on a year-by-year basis for professors.[15] Denounced as a privilege, this element of the original Bielefeld "structural characteristics" fell victim not only to the teaching imperative but also to the principle of "equal opportunities" among university professors.[16]

- Collective research planned and organized on the level of departments and guided by a research program.[17] This type of university research substituted neither for individual research nor for the oligarchy of chairholders and directors of institutes. However, it was more or less realized when the *Deutsche Forschungsgemeinschaft* (DFG) introduced *Sonderforschungsbereiche* (Special Research Areas) in the late 1960s as an additional part of the funding system.

- Institutional provision to encourage interdisciplinary research as a minor appendix to traditional research along disciplinary lines. The success story of the Center for Interdisciplinary Research (ZiF) at the University of Bielefeld, founded in 1968, is telling enough in this respect.[18]

- Functional differentiation within the university sector by promoting or neglecting research areas in a state- or nationwide division of labor. Keywords in this discussion are "profile formation" and "competition" among universities.[19] It may be

15. Schelsky, "Grundzüge" (note 14), 40f.; idem, "Universitätsidee" (note 5), 161.
16. *Reformuniversität Bielefeld 1969-1994. Zwischen Defensive und Innovation*, ed. P. Lundgreen (Bielefeld, 1994), 29f.
17. Schelsky, "Grundzüge" (note 14), 38ff.
18. H. Schelsky, "Das Zentrum für interdisziplinäre Forschung. Eine Denkschrift [1966]," in *Grundzüge einer neuen Universität. Zur Planung einer Hochschulgründung in Ostwestfalen*, eds. P. Mikat and H. Schelsky (Gütersloh, 1966), 71-87; *ZiF: 1968-1993. Daten aus 25 Jahren Forschung*, eds. M. Kastner and G. Sprenger (Bielefeld, 1993).
19. Wissenschaftsrat, *Empfehlungen zum Wettbewerb im deutschen Hochschulsystem* (Bonn, 1985); idem, *Empfehlungen zu den Perspektiven der Hochschulen in den 90er Jahren* (Bonn, 1988), 25.

doubted whether the potential economies inherent in this policy have already been tapped. Flexibility seems to prevail as long as contract money (limited in time) is involved. Much more difficult is a differentiation on the level of permanent staff, and this will remain the case as long as there is no clear differentiation between basic and graduate study.

- Functional differentiation between types of institutions of higher learning, i.e., between universities and *Fachhochschulen*.[20] This latest call may serve to prevent the *Fachhochschulen* from becoming too much like universities. The political decision to expand the *Fachhochschule* sector finds approval from all sides, but even such a desired development will not free the universities from rethinking the reform of research within their own walls.

Universities have of course participated in this reform discussion for a long time. At the core of their diagnosis lies, quite naturally, the issue of basic funding. Since these resources are given annually by state governments and governments make no distinction between teaching and research in allotting them, the relative share available for research is shrinking owing to the tremendous increase of students. Several specific observations and interpretations, as recently made by the Rectors' Conference, may be distinguished:[21]

- Growth of basic funding did not keep pace with growth of the student population since the late 1970s.
- In addition, basic funding is negatively affected by the desired profile formation within universities, but mainly by the pooling of resources for special research programs of the state government, because such policies are financed by a reallocation of existing funds.
- Developments of this sort are harmful for free research activities independent of existing programs. Nondirected, self-chosen research without a foreseeable practical relevance, however, has proven to be indispensable and beneficial in the long run.

20. Hochschulrektorenkonferenz, *Konzept* (note 7), 33f.; Wissenschaftsrat, *10 Thesen zur Hochschulpolitik* (Bonn, 1993), 31ff.
21. Westdeutsche Rektorenkonferenz, *Zukunft der Hochschulen* (note 4), 41ff.; Hochschulrektorenkonferenz, *Konzept* (note 7), 32f.

Such thinking pays some vague tribute to the traditional idea of the university, but mainly reveals typical institutional inertia. The expectation is that any new developments deemed necessary will be added on to existing practice; growth, not change, and provision of more funds rather than redistribution are the order of the day. The defense of the *status quo* and an egalitarian solidarity against an unfriendly world that denies the deserved support join forces in blocking intra-university redistribution. Between 1975 and 1990 German universities were only able to reallocate 5 percent of all positions; during the same time, state governments came up with 15 percent.[22] Universities would be well advised to gain the initiative by basing their research policy on autonomous decisions of redistribution instead of awaiting additional funds. Research at the university is certainly "in danger," but its future will depend to a great extent on the universities' ability to improve their own regulatory will and powers to make unpopular redistribution decisions.

Administration

On the surface, making an appeal for more autonomy for the individual university – as opposed to the interventionist policy of directing and decision making by state government – seems to be a very popular course. After all, autonomy has long been regarded as an essential part of the "idea of the university." Apart from the calamitous Nazi period, such autonomy is thought to have fallen victim only recently to a minute regulation by administrative decrees pouring down from above. In a way, this apparent loss of autonomy is sometimes considered as a major characteristic of the present postclassical university. The rhetoric of lamentation about the loss of autonomy tends to obscure, however, two facts: the autonomy of the Humboldtian university was never as great as alleged; more importantly, autonomy often implied weakness in decision making and invited state action.

True, Humboldt followed Schleiermacher's advice and pleaded for a continuity of corporate self-government as the basic constitu-

22. U. Schimank, "Probleme der westdeutschen Hochschulforschung seit den siebziger Jahren," *Leviathan. Zeitschrift für Sozialwissenschaft* 23 (1995): 74.

tional principle of old and new universities. Such internal autonomy was meant to include, ideally, the freedom of research, i.e., the independence from utilitarian objectives set by the state. On the other hand, Humboldt left no doubts that universities – unlike academies – "always keep a closer relation to practical life and the needs of the state" by fulfilling their teaching function.[23] Consequently, the external autonomy of the Humboldtian university was relatively limited: "The appointment of professors must exclusively remain with the state, and it is certainly not a good practice to allow the faculties more influence."[24] Similarly, the state kept control of all exams that were required for entry into professional life. Finally, funding was and remained part of the state budget, although Humboldt had played with the idea of financial autonomy. During the nineteenth century, state governments such as the Prussian one exercised, from time to time, a ruthless appointment policy against the will of faculties.[25] By the same token, performance and entrepreneurship of individual professors were honored and met by state-funded institute building.

Around the turn of the century it was clear to contemporaries that German universities were constitutionally governed by overlapping and partially conflicting principles: the corporate equality of chairholders on the level of faculties that housed more and more disciplines; and the hierarchies prevailing at the institutes that housed the big science of the day. With regard to autonomy and self-governed action, initiative and progress were mainly to be found on the level of institutes. Faculties and senates usually took a conservative or defensive standpoint. Two prominent examples are the long-standing opposition against some measure of "equal rights" for "applied science" (technical colleges) and for the non-professorial staff.[26] Reform was finally forced upon the universities by state governments in these cases as in others.

23. Humboldt, "Organisation" (note 2), 263.
24. Ibid., 264f.
25. R. S. Turner, "The Prussian Universities and the Concept of Research," *Internationales Archiv für Sozialgeschichte der deutschen Literatur* 5 (1980): 73ff.; B. vom Brocke, "Hochschul- und Wissenschaftspolitik in Preußen und im Deutschen Kaiserreich 1882-1907: das 'System Althoff'," in *Bildungspolitik in Preußen zur Zeit des Kaiserreichs*, ed. P. Baumgart (Stuttgart, 1980), 80ff.
26. K.-H. Manegold, *Universität, Technische Hochschule und Industrie. Ein Beitrag zur Emanzipation der Technik im 19. Jahrhundert* (Berlin, 1970); R. vom Bruch,

This, then, was the complex reality of autonomy in the Humboldtian university. Things became even more complicated during the transition to the postclassical university of the last three decades. One major move, the break-up of the huge old faculties in favor of departments, was recommended by the *Wissenschaftsrat* in 1968, but executed by state law.[27] Another major move, advocated mainly by assistants and students, was likewise put into practice by federal and state law: the rise of the *Gruppenuniversität* as an institution that is codetermined by four estates and based on principles of representative democracy. As is well known, this dramatic shift away from the old *Ordinarienuniversität* (university of full professors) did not substitute for, but only supplemented older principles of self-government. Meanwhile, autonomous university action has to find its way within a web of corporate, hierarchical, bureaucratic, and democratic elements that work together and limit the range of activity.[28] Under these conditions it is at least understandable that state governments, after having pushed through the great transformation of the university, also felt justified in resorting to minute regulation when coping with the ever-rising demands of teaching. Only recently, a certain disenchantment as to the beneficial results of this type of regulation from above has set in. Is it time, then, for a revival of more extensive autonomy within the universities?

The pertinent discussion of the last years makes unmistakably clear that more autonomy is only available if it goes together with more capability for action, planning, decision making, and execution. A crucial area for such action has already been mentioned: the redistribution of funds according to selected developmental options, i.e., a policy that implies not only winners but also losers. The open question is whether the present German university is able and willing to develop the instruments necessary for such active self-government. "Professionalization" has become the keyword in this respect, sometimes phrased as "strengthening of executive structures."

"Universitätsreform als soziale Bewegung. Zur Nicht-Ordinarienfrage im späten deutschen Kaiserreich," *Geschichte und Gesellschaft* 10 (1984): 72-91.

27. Wissenschaftsrat, *Empfehlungen zur Struktur und Verwaltungsorganisation der Universitäten* (Bonn, 1968).

28. Cf. D. Müller-Böling, "Qualitätssicherung in Hochschulen. Grundlage einer wissenschaftsbasierten Gesellschaft," *Wissenschaftsmanagement* 1 (1995): 65-70.

"Strong executive structures" are apparently less controversial if the rector or president of a university, together with his collegiate board, is meant. The Rectors' Conference is willing to entrust rectorates and presidencies with discretionary powers over an adequate free share in the annual budget for promoting initiatives.[29] The *Wissenschaftsrat* goes one step further and recommends that the top management be allowed to confiscate and reallocate vacant positions.[30] This sort of capability (and willingness) may become crucial in the future, if the demographic turnover within the professoriate is taken into account, because it is very unrealistic that departmental decisions to abandon a vacant position will ever take place voluntarily. Consequently, the newly introduced model of a "strong chairman of the department" runs into much more controversy, for it is at the departmental level where the old corporate loyalties are still strongest and determine the notion that a chairman should be *primus inter pares*.

Remarkably enough, not only the *Wissenschaftsrat*, but even the Rectors' Conference recommend a partial retreat from this model in favor of some sort of semi-professional management.[31] German rectors were ready to admit in 1988 that "the relatively weak position of the chairman, caused by the collegiate tradition, is a particularly grave characteristic distinguishing German departments from foreign ones."[32] On the other hand, at a conference in 1994 on universities and research institutes in the former German Democratic Republic, the president of the *Deutsche Forschungsgemeinschaft* wondered, "how a strong chairman may be implemented within a system that can neither bear a strong chairman nor need him."[33]

29. Westdeutsche Rektorenkonferenz, *Zukunft der Hochschulen* (note 4), 71.
30. Wissenschaftsrat, *10 Thesen* (note 20), 61.
31. Westdeutsche Rektorenkonferenz, *Zukunft der Hochschulen* (note 4), 69f.; Wissenschaftsrat, *10 Thesen* (note 20), 60f.; cf. *Autonomie und Verantwortung – Hochschulreform unter schwierigen Bedingungen. Bericht der Hochschulstrukturkommission des Landes Hessen*, ed. Hessisches Ministerium für Wissenschaft und Kunst (Frankfurt/New York, 1995), 347ff.
32. Westdeutsche Rektorenkonferenz, *Zukunft der Hochschulen* (note 4), 69.
33. *Wissenschaftliches Symposium zur Situation der Universitäten und außeruniversitären Forschungseinrichtungen in den neuen Ländern*, eds. G. Berg et al. (Halle/Saale, 1994), 204.

It may very well be that we are confronting here the Achilles heel of university reform in present-day Germany. On the one hand, sociological analysis is able to demonstrate how intra-university redistribution is structurally blocked on the level of departments by all sorts of defensive solidarities (e.g., collegiality, status equality, parity, etc.).[34] On the other hand, it is proposed that universities be institutions of higher learning and research, that also *promote research* according to the rules of evaluation and performance.[35] If this is so, the implication is that there are not only winners but also losers. Will this become part of the new idea of the German university? Are we prepared to give up the fiction that all universities are equal in quality?[36] Doubts are hard to suppress as long as the rectors unite in stating that "it must be the goal of science policy to guarantee the high standard of *all* universities and to promote excellence as well."[37]

Conclusion

University reform discourse in Germany – West and East – is still prone to refer to the *Mythos Humboldt*. If this is not going to be merely a handy device for conservative defense, ongoing functions have to be distinguished from institutional forms of limited historical validity in a changing environment. A productive adaptation of the "idea of the university" as inspired by Humboldt demands the search for functional equivalents. This approach has been applied in the present essay to the three areas of teaching, research, and administration. The results may be summarized briefly:

1. In *teaching*, the old "unity of teaching and research" can only be preserved as a constituent of graduate studies. Basic stud-

34. Schimank, "Probleme" (note 22), 63ff.; cf. U. Schimank, *Hochschulforschung im Schatten der Lehre* (Frankfurt/New York, 1995), 222ff.
35. J. Lange, "Strategische Planung. Grundlage künftiger Hochschulentwicklung," *Wissenschaftsmanagement* 1 (1995), 73.
36. D. Müller-Böling, "Hochschulen als Vorstellungsstereotypen. Von der Gelehrtenrepublik zum Dienstleistungsunternehmen" (Gütersloh, 1994, unpublished).
37. Westdeutsche Rektorenkonferenz, *Zukunft der Hochschulen* (note 4), 73.

ies aiming at qualification for professional life, on the other hand, have to be designed quite differently: less linkage to disciplinary specialization, and more orientation to professional fields. The open question is, how far should and will the organization of basic studies approach the model of school instruction?

2. *Research* remains an indispensable function of the university, but it is endangered and can only be upheld at a very high level of quality, if some degree of specialization and profile formation takes place among and within universities. The open question is, how much difference and inequality within the university system will be accepted or may come about? As an aside it should be noted that the "unity of teaching and research" at the graduate level would not be limited by research specialization in a nation-wide system.

3. *Administration* is a crucial issue for the reform of teaching and research. The question is, what instruments are appropriate in order to justify a revival of university autonomy? In particular, both the willingness and the ability to redistribute positions and funds seem to be wanted. The open question is, whether some professionalization of management can and will go far enough without losing acceptance.

Open questions will not find general answers but only individual ones. Results will depend on personalities, good fortune, timing, etc. Success or failure will increase the measure of differentiation within the university system. Maybe such an outcome is of high value in and of itself, if we would become accustomed to a university world that is – and ought to be – much more dominated by difference and inequality than we are so far ready to accept.

Comment

INTERPRETING HUMBOLDT
FOR THE TWENTY-FIRST CENTURY

Daniel Fallon

Let me begin by praising the paper by Professor Lundgreen, which I find to be persuasive historical, social, and economic analysis. I want to organize my commentary around just two principal issues: the unity of teaching and research, and the adaptation to the contemporary world.

The Unity of Teaching and Research

As Professor Lundgreen points out in his paper, we can find no documentary evidence that Humboldt himself ever used the phrase, "the unity of teaching and research" *(die Einheit von Lehre und Forschung)*. As always with Humboldt, we must interpret his behavior as a minister and a citizen, and we must read his writings carefully in order to assess what ideas he held high for the development of the German people. Much of our assessment of Humboldt comes from a written fragment of what may have been intended as a larger document. Entitled "On the Internal and External Organization of the Higher Scholarly Establishments in Berlin,"[1] the piece was not published until after its fortunate discovery by the historian Bruno Gephardt in a file drawer in the Prussian ministry late in the nineteenth century. In it, Humboldt maintains, "It is further characteristic of higher education that it treats scholarship as a not quite

1. W. von Humboldt, "Über die innere und äußere Organisation der höheren wissenschaftlichen Anstalten in Berlin," in *Gelegentliche Gedanken über Universitäten*, ed. E. Müller (Leipzig, 1990).

solved problem and, therefore, always remains engaged in research; whereas secondary education teaches and learns only about completed and proven conclusions."[2] He then goes on to point out that in higher education, "the relationship between teacher and pupil therefore becomes something fundamentally different than it was before. The former is not there for the latter; both are there for the sake of scholarship."[3] These statements are the clearest we have from Humboldt himself of his advocacy for the unity of teaching and research at the university.

In Germany, as Professor Lundgreen has so clearly shown, the concept of the unity of teaching and research is often taken to mean that students must do research with the professor, using more or less the same standards as the professor applies to his or her own research. This principle seems to be in accordance with the assertions of Humboldt, as just quoted, and it seems further to imply a clear distinction, a formal boundary, between secondary education and higher education. This leads Professor Lundgreen to conclude, as I believe most German scholars do, that there are two clear forms of teaching, one for the university requiring the unity of teaching and research, and one for some lower level, that is of a different, didactic, type. I am not persuaded, however, that this is a valid conclusion. Instead, I believe that human activity easily develops along a continuum. Therefore, there are levels of involvement of teaching and research, in which students can benefit from steadily increasing research involvement as they progress through their studies. We need not posit a binary condition, in which so-called "undergraduate teaching" is considered not to benefit from research and "graduate education" is exclusively the province of joint research engagement by professor and student. Furthermore, I believe that Humboldt understood the workings of this continuum.

Toward the end of the fragmentary essay already described, Humboldt explains the role of the secondary school teacher. "The high school should not be arranged to anticipate instruction at the university, as if the university were just a similar complementary institution," Humboldt argues. "Rather, the transition from high

2. Ibid., 274.
3. Ibid.

school to university is a developmental stage in youth, for which the high school succeeds when the young pupil is so perfectly prepared that he can be physically, ethically, and intellectually turned over to freedom and independence. The student should be freed from requirements, not to pursue leisure or practical matters, but so that he carries within him a burning desire to lift himself into the domain of scholarship, which has to this point only been shown to him from a distance."[4] It seems clear to me from these obervations, and also from the very design he himself created of a system of licensing only university-trained teachers for the high schools, that Humboldt understood the continuum by which research and teaching always at some important level inform each other. For Humboldt, therefore, the unity of teaching and research does not always require that every student learn how to do research as the professor does it. Instead, the only essential requirement is that the professor be an active researcher.

Even in the consideration of the most basic forms of teaching, Humboldt made clear how valuable it was for the teacher to have the mentality of a researcher. "As soon as one stops to search actually for scholarship," he wrote, "or allows oneself to believe that scholarship is not created from the very depths of the soul, but instead can be routinely assembled in an extensive array, then everything is irretrievably and forever lost. It is lost for scholarship, whose nature evaporates when this continues for too long, such that even language is left behind like an empty casing; and it is lost for the state. For only scholarship, which comes from the inner soul and can be planted there, forms character; and for the state, just as for humanity in general, it is not knowledge and conversation that matter, but character and behavior."[5] Although these ideas were written in the context of the relationship of university research to teaching, the principles are expressed universally. It is clear, therefore, that they must also apply to teaching at the pre-university level. In other words, the unity of teaching and research is not a categorical phenomenon limited just to one kind of instruction, but rather a general set of principles that can and should apply to all teaching.

4. Ibid., 278.
5. Ibid., 276.

It seems to me that we might be able to agree on two principles. First, the unity of teaching and research is good and worth protecting. Second, research can inform teaching in many settings so that the unity of teaching and research need not be limited to a conception of teaching in which the student becomes a researcher working at the same level as the professor. I believe that both principles are consistent with Humboldt's ideas, and they allow us to consider a more differentiated undergraduate curriculum in Germany without necessarily abandoning the ideal of the unity of teaching and research. So I concur with Professor Lundgreen that advanced graduate education at the level of the doctoral degree (*Promotion*), and even of the second qualifying thesis (*Habilitation*), requires the unity of teaching and research as traditionally understood in Germany. But I go further than Professor Lundgreen in asserting that many forms of what might be called undergraduate education can coexist at the university without abandoning the ideal of the unity of teaching and research at such "lower" levels.

Adaptation to the Contemporary World

Humboldt was an extraordinary genius who conceived an institution worth preserving. To maintain the essential purpose of Humboldt's university in the contemporary world requires, of course, that we understand how our world today differs from the world that Humboldt knew. Two principles are essential to this understanding: the nature of state and society in Germany; and the relentless advance of mass higher education.

State and Society in Germany. Professor Lundgreen mentions that Humboldt considered giving the University of Berlin some measure of financial independence. Indeed, Humboldt advocated this radical step strongly and recommended to King Frederick William III that a large tract of land owned by the king be granted to the university to serve as an endowment. This recommendation was, in fact, provisionally approved during Humboldt's tenure as minister. Upon his departure, however, it was quietly set aside by Humboldt's successor, Schuckmann, who reinforced the king's uncertainty over

so bold a step, believing that the financial strength of an endowment might give the University too much independence from the
state. Humboldt's intention was to strengthen the University's mission by providing it with some assured assets. It was not, as Professor Lundgreen points out, to free it from state control.

Humboldt's vision of the relationship between the university
and the state was governed, as were so many of his ideas, by an
Aristotelian conception that had been tempered by the contemporary energy of the era of enlightenment, the *Aufklärung*. He did
not see any real separation of the state from the institutions within
it. For Humboldt, all human endeavors were related organically to
an evolving and perfectible state. Thus, a principal purpose of the
university was to produce learned and wise leaders for the state,
some of whom would become ministers. These broadly and deeply
educated ministers would then apply the wisdom they had cultivated to the judicious management of the state's institutions,
including the university. In this conception of an endlessly improving society, wise ministers would make wise appointments of excellent faculty, who, in turn, would educate new generations of even
wiser ministers, who would, in turn, further improve the university.
Unfortunately, matters did not develop in quite this way. Human
frailty, in the form of political convenience, seemed rather easily to
adapt itself to university education.

In its most well-developed form, in the late nineteenth century,
the relationship between the state and the university in Prussia was
characterized largely by the dominant personality of Friedrich
Althoff, the state official responsible for higher education. The
University of Berlin and other universities were strong and leading
institutions under Althoff, but not all would agree that his stew-
ardship was englightened and wise. Max Weber, for example,
excused Althoff as a decent person who was forced to do indecent
administration by a system corrupted through state power and control.[6] The notorious cases of this era were, for example, the "Lex
Arons," in which a tenured appointment was removed retroac-

---

6. *Max Weber on Universities: The Power of the State and the Dignity of the Academic Calling in Imperial Germany*, ed. E. Shils (Chicago, IL, 1974), 26-27. See
also R. vom Bruch, "A Slow Farewell from Humboldt? Stages in the History of
German Universities, 1810-1945," in this volume.

tively by the state because the professor was alleged to have expressed unwelcome political views, and the Bernhardt Affair, in which a mediocre professor was awarded a permanent appointment to the faculty of the University of Berlin as an apparent political reward to the professor, in the absence of any consultation with the faculty of the university.

I agree with Ralf Dahrendorf's analysis of recent German history, which asserts that Germany was unable to develop truly functional modern institutions in the nineteenth and much of the twentieth century because, like Humboldt, most Germans did not distinguish between state and society. Both were the same. In a conclusion to a very lengthy argument, Dahrendorf summarizes succinctly, "Germany's curse is not that she did not become a nation, but that she did not become a society."[7] Dahrendorf asserts that modern democracy requires differentiation between state and society, such that the people can address and manage the normal conflict that is produced within society and thus use democratic institutions to change continuously the state's relationship to society. When Dahrendorf wrote his analysis in the early 1960s, the questions he raised were still unanswered for Germany. Since then, in my view, Germany has indeed become a democratic society with modern governmental institutions. It is these new circumstances that are now governing the debate in Germany about the power of administrative control by the ministry relative to that by the university. I believe this is a healthy and productive debate, and that it will in due course produce reforms that are functionally positive and yet retain many of the structural features that have characterized the administration of universities in Germany since 1810.

It is no surprise that, as Professor Lundgreen points out, the state ministries have been able in recent years to accomplish more than twice the amount of reallocation of university faculty resources than have the universities themselves. This is surely because the ministries are more responsive to public needs and thus participate aggressively in shaping public policy. Yet, the actions of the ministries have been taken in a context of respect for the professional authority of the faculties of the universities, and following negotia-

7. R. Dahrendorf, *Society and Democracy in Germany* (Garden City, NY, 1969), 202.

tion and consultation. The fact that universities are now discussing such concepts as "the strong department chair," or considering the prospect of more forceful forms of university administration, is an indication that universities are responding to the pressure exerted by the ministries. If the universities themselves are able to develop procedures that protect their essential mission while responding effectively to public needs, they stand a good change of assuming substantial control over the dynamic changes that are now taking place. This kind of public challenge and counter-challenge exposes conflict, and resolves it by producing change endorsed by some measure of public opinion. It is the essence of institutional adaptation in a democratic society. Humboldt did not anticipate the state and society of the twentieth century, but he did propose an administration that accorded respect to each party, the ministry and the university, in proportion to its legitimate interests. It is possible to develop an administrative structure today that is true to Humboldt's balanced vision. It will be a solution that reflects the modern reality of a state responsive to the society that determines its direction, and a university that protects its core values, not by insulating itself from society, but rather by finding ways to interpret its core values to meet the public interest.

The Advance of Mass Higher Education. We should not conclude our analysis of the German University of the present without describing the single most important sociological development affecting higher education in the advanced economies of the world. That is mass higher education. In Germany today, as Professor Lundgreen notes, more than 30 percent of the population is now participating in some form of higher education. In the United States, the proportion has crossed the boundary of 50 percent. An advanced economy that produces mass higher education changes all of the basic presumptions about the role and mission of institutions within the higher education sector. To begin with, if most of the population will receive some form of higher education, then the foremost purpose of higher education can no longer be to educate "leaders," since by definition not everyone can be a leader. Instead, the foremost purpose of higher education will be to prepare citizens to participate in a sophisticated economy that demands mastery of knowledge and information.

Not all citizens should be prepared in the same way nor at the same level, but all must be prepared. Such an analysis leads directly to the conclusion that there must be many different kinds of institutions in the higher education sector. Some can be grouped into classes with certain roles and missions. This has, of course, begun in Germany, with, for example, the increasing differentiation of *Fachhochschulen* from universities, the broadening mission of pedagogical schools, and the development of occupational schools *(Berufsakademien)*. More will inevitably develop. The special task of the German university in this context is not very different from the task facing the research university in the United States. It is to find the special role and mission that will characterize a particular kind of university.

In the United States, there are about 3,500 institutions that can be characterized as higher education institutions, including about 1,400 two-year community colleges and 125 research universities. Because research universities are the most expensive types of institution, they will have to struggle to maintain their support, whether public or private. Many observers in the United States today believe, and I am one of those, that the United States can afford only about sixty to eighty research universitites, and that in the coming decades many universities now characterized as research universities will be reclassified as less expensive but still important institutions such as comprehensive universities. For those that remain as research universities, the particular concentration of talent and facilities that makes them so expensive will justify their maintaining the traditional role of preparing leaders in the new economy. Although these research universities will be defined in an essential way by their preparation of graduate students, and the award of the Ph.D. degree, they will also be educating large numbers of the most talented undergraduates, and preparing them for entry-level positions in the new economy. I suspect that a similar outcome is in store for the traditional "Humboldtian" universities in Germany.

And so, in the end, I agree completely with the fundamental conclusions of my colleague, Professor Lundgreen, that the future of higher education in Germany lies in a much more differentiated structure than what we have seen in the past. There will be many different types of higher education institutions serving many German citizens in productive ways. The traditional "Humboldtian" universities will adapt to mass higher education by accommodating the most talented of these students, but not requiring that all do independent research. Many will leave the university, as they now do, after completion of the equivalent of a first degree (usually a *Diplom*), but they will be well prepared for advanced work in an advanced economy. Some will continue with their studies to become academic scholars in their own right, or to pursue professional study in medicine, engineering, law, or other professions. Among those a certain number will continue the time-honored traditions associated with what Humboldt called "the burning desire to lift themselves into the domain of scholarship."

Only a small number of very expensive "Humboldtian" German universities will be needed, and only these will be supported. As in the nineteenth century, and indeed as has been true since the very beginnings of universities in Bologna, Paris, Prague, and Heidelberg, these German universities will compete with each other for good students, for good faculty, and for resources from the public. They will be competing with the strength of their intellects. Having adapted to a modern democratic world of managed conflict and competition, they will nonetheless be true to the genius of Wilhelm von Humboldt, father of the modern university idea. In his fragmentary essay Humboldt wrote, "If, in the final analysis, only one principle dominates the higher scholarly establishments: to search for scholarship in its own right, then there will be no need to worry individually about anything else."[8]

8. Humboldt, "Über die innere und äußere Organisation," 277.

Session Five

DISCUSSION

RAINER KÜNZEL: Why did the rectors convert to the new position in 1992? I would like to comment on that because I was part of this process of conversion. I became vice-president of the Rectors' Conference in 1990, and was on the standing committee that drew up this new paper on the development of higher education in Germany in 1992. I think in our system, the German system, you have to be aware of the fact that the rectors and presidents are elected, and they are usually in a very difficult position to develop new ideas and put them into the open without having the support of the faculty members of their own institutions. The professional organizations of the faculty members like the Faculty Associations *(Fakultätentage)*, for instance, are still far behind the thinking of the rectors and presidents. So it was a second attempt, I would say, to press ahead with these new ideas, and we are still working on that. As you know, the Rectors' Conference is now discussing a paper on financing higher education in Germany which will bring up many new ideas and will cause a lot of turmoil. There is another paper in preparation, which will discuss the question of the relationship between the universities and the state, the question of autonomy and the prerequisites for a really autonomous university. So I think that it is not that simple for the rectors to really change the system, because they have to convince all of those people, especially the faculty members who are still thinking along different lines.

The second point I wanted to make is that I do not believe that this phrase "unity of research and teaching" was really meant to mean in the universities of today that students should be involved in research, but that the teaching personnel should also be doing research because only through research could they be up-to-date teachers, who do not teach outdated material. In that sense, I think we have to preserve this principle. But I totally agree with what you said, that this is the real idea behind the phrase. Actually it was the idea of the protagonists of the university reform in the 1960s to draw students into the process of research by organizing instruction in the form of projects. This is kind of strange to think about, because it is really not a result of a student revolt and not the result of something that the old professors wanted.

KONRAD JARAUSCH: I totally agree with your description and also find your recommendations very convincing. I just wanted to think one step further about their possible implementation. My limited understanding of the German system is that there are tremendous resistances to change in corporate politics, in the bureaucracy, in the limitations of funding and so on. Part of the problem in the last decade has been the disappearance of the political will to do anything. My question is, where is this new will going to come from, or what strategies can one think of in order to move this again?

In two parts of your presentation, you indicated strategies. In the case of emphasizing particular research fields *(Profilierung)*, you said that that is quite possible if there is external funding for it. Thus the funds are added on to the university budget, and everybody can agree because you don't take anything away from anybody. On the administrative level, this is due to a combination of administrative pressure from the ministries and real internal difficulties within the institution which will require some stronger definitions of executive roles. I see some possibility is there. But Burton Clark once talked about the university as a bottom heavy institution, and I think that this is a brilliant phrase. It simply means that professors are the ones whose interests are essential in this. My feeling here is just, to say something very cynical, that unless you can find a way to make it in the self-interest of the majority of the German full professors you will never change anything.

MITCHELL ASH: Daniel Fallon, I found the prediction at the end of your talk quite provocative indeed, that in the end there will only be a limited number of very expensive Humboldtian universities that will be needed or supported. I think that goes further even than anyone in Germany has proposed yet. But the question that I have relates to the question Konrad Jarausch was asking to Peter Lundgreen about the practicality of this. What I am thinking about is the tension between this prediction of yours and the realities on the ground, where universities are economic factors of regional extent. Precisely the multicentric German system is organized in such a way that the more logical outcome is what Peter Lundgreen diagnosed, which is the raising of status of lower-level institutions rather than the implicit lowering of status of existing institutions by limiting the number of top status institutions.

DANIEL FALLON: I am working largely from a model that most of you will recognize is a model of American higher education, and I also recognize the dangers of extending this model to Germany. On the other hand, I see that Germany in fact has incorporated itself well into the European community, that Germany has become part of the Western world generally, and that the factors that influence higher education in the United States are likely also to influence Germany eventually. In the United States, I think that the big phenomenon between, let's say, World War II and about now, has been precisely the expansion of institutions in which each institution has been able to promote itself to the next level in some way. There has been a pressure upwards which Professor Lundgreen references in his paper. This occurs during a period of expansion of the franchise. We went from something like 15 percent of the cohort to 50 percent of the cohort during that period of time. And during that period of time it became possible for each institution because of the expanding opportunities to attempt to become the best institution it could afford to become. Now, what has happened is that in this period of time, as the franchise has been extended, the tremendous cost of higher education has become increasingly burdensome and yet we are at a point at which more and more people are going to need to have higher education.

Now that we have crossed this important boundary of 50 percent, which brings us into functional mass higher education, for the next forty years I see an exact reversal of this trend. That is, during the last forty years, what we have seen has been a blurring of role and mission of institutions. The next forty years is going to see a very sharpened differentiation of role and mission as institutions become more expensive. I think that that is inevitable and is a direct consequence of economic factors.

In the United States, for example, it is true nationally that if you go back one generation, just twenty years, you find that the proportion of a state university's budget that came from legislatively appropriated tax dollars was about 80 percent. Today, on average, it is less than 30 percent, and in some cases, the University of Virginia is a good example, it is down to 12 percent. This did not happen over twenty years because the people withdrew their support of higher education. That is not the reason in my view. The reason is that universities became more expensive than the people could afford. That has resulted in a tremendous shift in public policy in the United States, in which the cost of a university education is being shifted from the general public back to the consumer, and higher education is being seen as a consumer good. These are relentless economic factors, and when you look at those, you then have to ask yourself what it means to be a research university.

The research university is driven by the Ph.D. degree. The Ph.D. degree is the most expensive degree within the entire sector. It is almost the only degree in the university where you pay the student rather than the student paying you, at least in the American setting. Not only that, but you often have to have one-on-one instruction, and in addition you have to build wind tunnels and buy super computers and do other kinds of things. In order to justify that expense in this much more competitive economy, you will have to be able to justify the enterprise itself. That will put relentless pressure on institutions to in fact reduce their scope while at the same time serving more students. And that means increasing student-faculty ratios, reducing expensive research and all of the rest. So we will see, I think, more educational institutions, more students being served, but in fact fewer expensive research universities.

Research universities serve an important social and national goal. They will be supported, but the United States does not need one hundred sixty of them. The United States needs considerably less than that. I think that, if you calculate it against the gross national product, we need about sixty, and I think the logic is inevitable that we will be reduced to that number. I certainly think that in Germany the same is going to be true. You cannot go on forever and ever imagining that the elite university is going to be serving all of the people. At some point, there will come a place where people will say, we are only going to build one big thing and it is going to go to Munich or it is going to go to Heidelberg. There will be a differentiation that is based upon economic needs.

PETER LUNDGREEN: To Rainer Künzel, of course, when I chose the Rectors' Conference as a major source for my lecture, I was aware in the beginning that it would be unfair to blame the Rectors' Conference for being conservative. As a historian and as a sociologist, I know as well as you do that typically rectors of a university, being elected, are representative of the thinking within the universities. They cannot be much more open minded and future oriented than their faculties are. So there is a built-in institutional inertia in bodies like Rectors' Conferences. On the other side, the Science Council has it much easier, because it is a body, as you know, consisting of both people from the universities, state governments, and the federal government. So it is a completely different type of body which is much more prone to thinking about drastic reforms. That is nothing to be astonished about.

What I am astonished about is that the Rectors' Conference in 1992 voted unanimously in favor of this famous recommendation. This is really hard to believe, because if you go four years backward to another famous recommendation of this conference in 1988, it was said, "It must be the goal of science policy to guarantee the high standard of all universities and to promote excellence." Thus, all universities are equal, and some are more equal in terms of getting additional funding. Nowadays, if you take the very recent papers written by such outstanding people as your president, Hans-Uwe Ericksen, Detlef Möller-Böling, and others, they say, for instance, that universities should be institutions of higher learning and research, but also of promoting research according to the rules of evaluation and performance. Now, if this means anything, the indication is there cannot only be winners but also losers. We have not yet become accustomed to this basic idea. We cannot accept that there must be losers both among universities and within universities as soon as you try to redistribute existing funds. This is the thrust of my paper.

RAINER KÜNZEL: Basically I agree. But I think we have not decided yet whether we cannot limit the variance of quality of the institutions by having excellence within the individual institution and mediocrity at the same time. In some subject areas, you could have excellence and in others you are just medium or even less than that. But if we need to have wide differentiation and quality in the entire institution, that is something we have to debate about. Can we find mechanisms that will limit the difference between the best and the poorest institutions? I think we can.

MITCHELL ASH: I find it intriguing to hear this discussion, because it presupposes the concept of quality which Konrad Jarausch introduced into the discussion in the last session. It also implicitly suggests that you can talk about universities as wholes as having quality, as being good or bad. I think most people who teach in state universities in the United States know that this is a very questionable presupposition. Almost all large state universities have some excellent institutions in them and some mediocre departments. This is a fact that most German participants in the debate simply do not even discuss, much less deal with.

Chapter Six

POLITICAL CONTROL
AND FUNDING

The Future of State Support

∽∾

Rainer Künzel

I

Ever since the first German universities were founded in the Middle Ages, their close relationship with the state has had a decisive influence. At the outset, however, their function was by no means to cultivate the arts and sciences as they saw fit, but to train civil servants and – after the Reformation – to promote the religious creeds of their respective rulers. Living at the expense of the state, the universities had to serve its ends. In the early modern administrative state, they formed part of the administrative machinery in each province and were watched over by a tight system of state supervision and control.

It was not until the advent of the Enlightenment and Liberalism that the universities were granted the privilege of engaging in the free cultivation of the arts and sciences. Kant inveighed against the "higher vocational schools"; Wilhelm von Humboldt insisted that universities should not have to serve the state first by training its officials, but by promoting the free development of personality through education and science.[1]

Though the universities subsequently acquired extensive intel-lectual autonomy in the nineteenth and twentieth centuries, that did nothing to change their economic dependence on the state. Consequently, the prevailing philosphy of the state remained cen-tral to the definition of the university's role and function in society. In the wake of the development of parliamentary mass democracy in the Weimar Republic and again after 1945, the notion of edu-cation and science as a public good was reflected in government funding of the entire educational system. The deformation of the social function of education under National Socialism corre-sponded to the deformation of the relationship between the state and society under the policy of *Gleichschaltung*, or forced confor-mity, in every domain of life, which spelled the end of the univer-sities' autonomy and of their separation from the state on the one hand and society on the other.

Germany's postwar democracy, however, provided a clear-cut definition of the social task of universities as public corporations, a definition expressed in law in terms of organizational objectives: to cultivate, free from government interference and control, the arts and sciences in research, teaching, and study with a view to acquir-ing new knowledge, providing high quality general and vocational education and inculcating democratic values.

The *Länder*, or states, of the Federal Republic of Germany are endowed with cultural sovereignty: they are fully responsible for the entire domain of education. In keeping with this principle, the Federal government for a long time exerted no influence at all on the development of higher education. Policies that had to be coor-dinated nationwide were worked out at the level of the Standing Conference of Ministers of Education and Cultural Affairs of the *Länder*. As the financial requirements of the expanding academic sector began to grow beyond the means of the *Länder*, the federal government gradually took a hand in the funding and organization of higher education and research, thus diluting the stringent prin-ciple of cultural federalism. In 1969 the German constitution was

---

1. W. Zeh, *Finanzverfassung und Autonomie der Hochschule* (Berlin, 1973), 15.

extended to institute joint tasks of the federal government and the *Länder*, particularly in the field of education and science. Since that time the federal government bears 50 percent of the cost of building and enlarging institutions of higher education. In addition, it is involved in educational planning and in funding academic and scientific research facilities and projects of supraregional importance, and it is a colegislator of the basic (national) law of higher education *(Hochschulrahmengesetz)*.[2]

Net expenditure on higher education totaled DM 26.1 ($ 18.6) billion in 1993. The federal government contributed about DM 2.5 ($ 1.8) billion thereof, or a little under 10 percent.[3] Roughly two-thirds of the federal contribution was spent on building projects and research equipment and one third on special higher education programs that were launched in a joint effort by the federal government and the *Länder* to alleviate the tremendous strain on institutions of higher education resulting from the rapid growth of student numbers. In addition, the Federal government raises about two-thirds of the DM 2 ($ 1.4) billion in training assistance funds and finances two-thirds of the expenses of the Deutsche Forschungsgemeinschaft (German Research Society), which amount to DM 2.5 ($ 1.8) billion annually.[4] Because of increasing financial difficulties, however, the joint task involving the building of universities has not received adequate funding from the federal government for years, leaving the *Länder* unable to expand and modernize the facilities to the extent desired and necessary. At present, the federal government is also withdrawing gradually from the funding of the special higher education programs.

II

The idea of education and science as a public good implies free access, in principle, to institutions of higher education and that

2. H. Peisert and G. Framhein, *Das Hochschulsystem in Deutschland* (Bonn, 1994), 5.
3. Statistisches Bundesamt, Fachserie 11, Reihe 4.5 Finanzen der Hochschulen 1993 (Wiesbaden, 1995), 19, 24.
4. Ministerium für Bildung, Wissenschaft, Forschung und Technologie, Grund- und Strukturdaten 1994/95 (Bonn, 1995), 274.

funding ought to be provided predominantly by the government. It assumes that, above and beyond the personal benefits, higher education of individuals benefits society as a whole, so that government spending on education using taxpayers' money is comparable to spending, for example, on internal security and legal protection, on infrastructure, social security, or on the reduction of regional disparities in socioeconomic conditions. In other words, the personal benefit to the individual of higher education basically goes hand in hand with, or is complemented by, a benefit to society, which finds expression in the favorable effects on productivity attributable to the generally increased innovative power of society, to improvements in its members' ability to participate in the democratic process, and to their social and communication skills as well as their critical acumen.

The predominantly tax revenue-based funding of university research accords with its primary focus on basic research and the essentially public nature of that research. In keeping with this conception, the main objective of university research is to acquire knowledge, safeguard the independence and originality of university teaching, and train the next generation of young researchers. One manifestation of the independence of teaching and research is the special position of professors as public servants who are free from outside interference in the subject matter of their pursuits.

The notion of education as a private good, on the other hand, is predicated on the assumption that the positive external effects of a high level of education are of marginal importance compared with the personal benefits. Hence, according to this view, institutions of higher education operate as service enterprises in the training and research market: students and those commissioning research are customers in the market for the best training or research services they can get for their money. In this schema, the only purpose of government subsidies and nonprofit foundations is to make sure that society's educational resources are utilized to the greatest possible extent and that research is not confined to problems of short-term economic utility.

As we see in the United States, organizing the system of postsecondary education along free-market lines gives rise to an extremely varied and qualitatively disparate range of educational, research, and other university services in which a specific package of services can be found to match virtually any combination of aptitude, interest, and financial means. Competition for customers tends to generate a glut of educational services, which, in turn, forces service providers to maximize their customer orientation.[5] The German system, in contrast, is based on the notion of equal educational opportunity for everyone whose general qualification for higher education has been formally certified by school-leaving examinations. Consequently, all establishments of higher education offer, as a rule, free tuition of (nominally) equal quality. Given the constitutional freedom of occupational choice in Germany, it is the government's duty to ensure that, in the long term, institutions of higher education can admit as many students as wish to study any particular subject.

III

In point of fact, however, the number of admissions is limited in certain fields (e.g., medicine, pharmacology, biology, psychology, etc.) and there are more or less pronounced disparities in the quality of education at the various institutions of higher education. Certainly, attempts are made at considerable expense to maintain equivalence in terms of comparable formal requirements in the various courses of study: basic regulations governing courses and examinations are laid down jointly by the Länder, but the goal of maintaining homogeneous quality at all institutions of higher education has not been attained for a number of reasons:

1. The funding of institutions of higher education does not adhere to objective and transparent criteria, resulting in marked disparities in terms of staffing and available teaching aids, equipment, and space.
2. There is as yet no effective quality control of teaching; likewise, in research only individual research projects are assessed – and only if externally funded – not the institutions themselves.

5. A. Rosigkeit, Reformdefizite der deutschen Hochschule (Frankfurt, Berlin, Bern, 1995), 90 ff.

3. Wide-ranging regional discrepancies between the supply of and demand for places in higher education put varying degrees of pressure on the departments to provide high quality courses of study and in some cases cause marked disparities in the level of student aptitude.

More important than the failure to sustain the fiction of qualitatively homogeneous education is the problematic idea that not only equal, but also high, quality standards can be maintained through a combination of educational planning and financial control by the government. To realize this idea, the *Länder* and the Federal government have developed an elaborate system of bureaucratic ex ante control:

1. German institutions of higher education are, as a rule, corporate bodies under public law and, at the same time, institutions of the state in the sense of subordinate authorities.
2. State accreditation of institutions of postsecondary education extends not only to the academic degrees they confer, but also to their curriculum planning, internal organization, and accountability. State accreditation is of vital importance because it amounts to a presumption of state-guaranteed quality. Even study and examination regulations are subject to ministerial approval.
3. Though nominated by the schools themselves, professors, chancellors, registrars, and rectors or presidents are appointed by the responsible ministers.
4. Student admissions are subject to state regulations and judicial scrutiny.
5. The state decides the number and kind of academic and nonacademic staff; even the remuneration is determined from case to case by the ministries of higher education or finance, or, if fixed according to the standard negotiated wage rates, it is subject to review by ministries or audit offices of the state.
6. The external detailed control of institutions of higher education by means of staff budgets is supplemented by detailed stipulations as to the use of earmarked funds. Budgetary law

is the most conspicuous expression of the dependency of institutions of higher education. Rather than drawing up a budget on their own, they can only submit a proposed plan for their section of the respective budget of the ministry of higher education, which in turn is part of the state budget. The funds then allocated must be used for the purposes foreseen in the budget. This is monitored by the audit office on behalf of parliament. The audit is not confined to formal checks on compliance with budget law, but covers the "how" and "why" of each measure taken in implementing the budget. The auditors' findings and objections have the power of administrative orders, for they predetermine the future decisions of the school under review. A number of ministries even demand that the audits be conducted in advance to obviate subsequent objections.[6]

7. In the joint funding of institutions of higher education by the federal government and the *Länder*, i.e., in the building of educational facilities, financing of expensive items of equipment, and student grants under the Federal Training Assistance Act, extensive decision making and control procedures have been established in conjunction with specific administrative structures. The only exception is grants for research at institutions of higher education: they are the responsibility of the German Research Society, which operates under the supervision of the institutions themselves.

8. Aside from their hold on the budgetary pursestrings, the *Länder* have exerted excessive influence on postsecondary education over the past fifteen years by setting up central funds of their own to be managed by their respective ministries of higher education. The following figures serve to illustrate the degree to which the ministries impose their science and education policy priorities on the schools through staff appointments and allocation of funds in individual cases: in 1970, 271 academic posts were budgeted for in the central staffing pools of the West German *Länder*; in 1994, the figure was

---

6. D. Müller-Böling, "Qualitätssicherung in Hochschulen – Grundlage einer wissensbasierten Gesellschaft," *Wissenschaftsmanagement* no. 2 (1995), 66.

3,999, including 2,030 professorships, or 10 percent of all the professorial posts in the country.[7]

IV

The discretionary ex ante control of institutions of higher education by the ministerial bureaucracy has exacerbated the problems that have arisen over the past two decades due to the chronic underfunding of institutions of higher education. Across-the-board funding cutbacks and a stop on the restaffing of vacant posts, delays in the allocation of budget funds, and the prohibition of the formation of reserves have given rise to uncertainty in planning, a loss of quality, and wasteful spending.

That is why institutions of higher education have long been demanding greater autonomy of decision making as well as changes in budget law, including:

* extensive substitutability of the various budget items;
* option to carry forward unused funds to the next budget year;
* the right to accumulate and manage their own capital;
* more flexibility in the management of staffing schedules;
* audits by the audit office to be supplemented, or even by and large replaced, by internal controlling, modern methods of accounting, and public accountability.[8]

In addition, the institutions of higher education demand that their funding be based on competitive and quality-related criteria. To ensure that scarce resources be used economically, costs and benefits need to be transparent. Hence, the "incrementalistic" method of funding, still widespread today, whereby the institutions must apply to the maintaining body for the required funds with reference to "historical expenses" must be supplanted by a funding procedure based on real costs, performance, and quality criteria. Institutions of higher education should have to compete for the

7. Wissenschaftsrat, *Personalstellen der Hochschulen 1994* (Köln, 1995), 218.
8. W. Blümel, I. Bender and T. Behrens, *Flexibilität der Hochschulhaushalte* (Speyer, 1993), 8.

central staffing and funding pools at the ministries, which should be awarded – albeit on an appreciably smaller scale – with educational and structural considerations in mind. Additional revenue that institutions receive from contract research, academic and scientific services, continuing education, or realization of assets must be at their disposal for use in carrying out their principal tasks.

V

The deterioration in financial status experienced over the past decade has also prompted efforts on the part of most *Länder* governments to delegate to the institutions not only the responsibility, but also a greater share of the requisite decision-making powers.

In Berlin the appropriations for institutions of higher education are posted in the state budget as a block grant. This grant is managed by the presidents of the institutions in concert with a special board of trustees responsible for institutions of higher education. Since 1993, unbudgeted expenditures and budget overruns have been permitted to cover current material and staff costs as well as investment projects, as has the budgetary substitutability of staff and material expenses. However, the formation of reserves is still not allowed. The selective formation of reserves for medium-term objectives is possible at the Technische Universität Hamburg-Harburg, on the other hand, which since 1991 has also been working with a block budget.

North Rhine-Westphalia has been testing the merits of increased budget flexibility since 1992 in a pilot scheme that has in the meantime been extended to every institution of higher education in the state. Not only does it provide for the budgetary substitutability of material and staff funds and for the use of staff funds to finance equipment, but it also allows the use of savings for the limited (5 percent) creation of limited-tenure posts. Most additional earnings are left to the institutions, although reserves can only be formed on a scale of up to one percent of total funds available.

Lower Saxony has gone furthest in flexible budgeting for institutions of higher education. While its arrangements are generally similar to those in North Rhine-Westphalia, two universities and one *Fachhochschule* were transformed in 1995 into state-owned enterprises for an initial period of ten years. Commercial accounting has supplanted governmental accounting there. The state subsidy is broken down into allotments for current purposes, for building maintenance, and for expenditures on equipment. The arrangement provides for extensive budgetary substitutability of all appropriations; they can even be brought forward to the following budget year. The schools keep their entire revenue. What is more, they have set up controlling systems of their own and manage their cash transactions themselves in collaboration with a bank. The state treasury is merely responsible for the allocation of subsidies and the safekeeping of reserves and provisions.

Other *Länder* are not planning any such pilot schemes, but have of late been allowing institutions of higher education greater leeway in the area of budgeting. Without exception, the institutions as well as the *Länder* have been giving favorable accounts of their experiences with the more flexible arrangements. In the long run, however, it does not look as if permitting the flexible employment of budget funds will be enough. Indeed, institutions of higher education want full decision-making powers over matters of staff, real investment, and current funds.[9]

VI

The latest reforms in the German system of higher education have been introduced primarily for more effective management of scarce resources and with a view to shifting the onus for the functional shortcomings of the overcrowded and underfunded schools from the government onto the institutions of higher education.

Yet, however skeptical one may be about the politicians' motives, there can be no doubt about the important opportunities afforded for the development of the tertiary education system. Economy of operation is only part of the picture. If attaining excellence in research and development and providing high quality, academically sound education for a growing segment of the population are

9. K. Neuvians, M. Jensen, "Globalhaushalte für Hochschulen – Ein Vergleich Dänemark/Deutschland," *Wissenschaftsmanagement*, no. 1 (1995), 14ff.

regarded as key target variables, further reforms will be needed. They must amplify the elements of competition in the field of quality, whilst avoiding the downside of hard-line market orientation by means of planning and control. In its educational planning, the government must seek to provide a wide range of educational opportunities with equal standards of quality, while keen quality competition in every educational domain should ensure the highest possible average degree of excellence with limited variance.

The principal means of quality control is regular external and internal assessment of teaching and research, which, if it is to meet with any degree of acceptance, should be conducted by the institutions themselves. Procedures along these lines are being tested in various *Länder*.[10]

Changes in admission policy could also contribute a great deal to quality assurance. One oft-mooted demand is that at least some of the students be admitted on the basis of an entrance examination or a subject-related weighting of the grades on their school-leaving examinations. Instead of a special admission procedure, a probationary year could be introduced at each school with intensive counseling and varied testing methods. What is more, demand-related components could be integrated into the supply-oriented control system if the demand for places to study (with or without tuition fees) would be allowed to influence the allocation of funds to the respective departments.

Generally speaking, the internal distribution of funds among institutions of higher education ought to follow the criteria of external funding.[11] Added incentives could encourage greater individual commitment. This purpose would be served by breaking down salaries into a basic salary and a function and performance-linked bonus, but also by limiting the duration of material and staff appropriations to research institutes and individual faculty members or by awarding grants for research and teaching under competitive conditions. Nonacademic personnel should be included in this performance and workload-based system of remuneration.

---

10. Hochschulrektorenkonferenz, Europäische Pilotprojekte für die Qualitätsbewertung im Bereich der Hochschulen (Bonn, 1995): 78 ff.

11. H.-U. Erichsen, "Qualitätssicherung in Forschung, Lehre und Management," *Wissenschaftsmanagement*, no. 2 (1995), 61ff.

Professionalizing the governing bodies of institutions of higher education, especially their leading executive managers, is of vital importance to the reform process and to its success in the long run. But this demand is at odds with the traditional corporate principle of cooperation between colleagues at German universities. What is more, it violates the principles of the group university and extensive codetermination. So it will have to be implemented in a way unlike the approach in the United States. It is conceivable, for example, that the independence of the president or the executive committee guaranteed by the delegation of decision making powers and responsibilities for a limited period of time could be reinforced by implementing an external board of trustees, which, on the basis of an electoral vote of the members of the institution, would have the final say on appointments to the top management positions. On the other hand, substantially enhanced decision-making powers and independence of the governing bodies have to be coupled with a requirement to consult with internal and external control boards and to disclose to those concerned the reasons for and consequences of the decisions reached. Leadership is impossible without transparency and communication; only leadership can guarantee acceptance and lay the foundations for the development of corporate identity in the sense of collective responsibility.

For a long time the definition of *universitas*, the community of teachers and students, had been so biased at German universities toward the interests of the tenured full professors that the other members of the higher education institutions had to revolt in the 1960s to exact sufficient attention to their needs. Now problems of inefficiency and dwindling funds call for modernization strategies that will strike a new balance between individual freedom and institutional responsibility. Toward that end we still have a long way to go.

Comment

POLITICAL CONTROL AND
FUNDING IN AMERICAN UNIVERSITIES

C. Peter Magrath

Let me first make one introductory comment about myself. I am speaking from the perspective of a person who has worked within large, complex research-intensive universities and has served as president at three of them, particularly in Missouri and Minnesota. Now I serve as the chief executive officer for an association with a horrible acronym, the National Association of State Universities and Land-Grant Colleges, or NASULGC. We represent about 190 public four-year universities, and we primarily, though not exclusively, represent the research-intensive universities in the public sector of the United States.

I would like to begin my presentation by going into some description of how American universities are funded. Here we need to distinguish between the so-called private universities and the public universities. Funding for the private universities comes from tuition, from sales and services, and from grants and contracts, particularly federal grants and contracts for the great, distinguished private universities, such as Johns Hopkins, MIT, Tulane, etc. In some cases these universities also receive some increments of direct state dollar support. This is not a major factor, but it can be important. For the public universities, revenue sources are tuition, which has been rising enormously in recent years, sales and services, grants and contracts, especially for the research-intensive universities, and state appropriations. Clearly, as these listings indicate, the differences in funding sources between the major public and private research universities are not great. In many respects, they are quite similar.

It is important to keep in mind, however, that 84 percent of enrollments in American higher education are in public sector universities, even though we have about an equivalent number of private colleges and universities and public universities. There are a total of about two hundred universities, private and public, that would call themselves research universities; a smaller number would be regarded as among the leading research universities. All public and private universities, especially research universities, depend on public, especially federal support. However – and this is not very different from the situation in Germany in terms of the federal government – only about 6 percent of funding for American higher education comes out of federal appropriations. Though these funds are not a high percentage of total university revenues, they are very important for us in terms of research and scientific support from the National Institutes of Health, the National Science Foundation, and other agencies. They are also very important for us, both in the private and public sectors, in terms of student aid or assistance. Since tuition is so much a part of how we generate our support, student aid, of which much, indeed the majority, comes from the federal government, is enormously important. Even as we are meeting here, there are battles going on with regard to student aid support in which all of us, both in the public and private sector, are enormously engaged.

Now "industry" is a word that academics do not like to use in referring to themselves, but we can speak of an industry at least in terms of volume of expenditures; thus, the total higher education industry in the United States expends about $175 billion. Federal research dollars, depending on how we count this, amount to about $13 billion, which tend to flow to the major research universities, public and private. Student aid totals about $24 billion. State appropriations are a very important part, but a declining part of the total. For the last year that I have data, 1994, state appropriations were about $46 billion. That is actually a decrease of $4 billion between 1990 and 1994 in real dollars.

However, the major difference in my judgment between the public and private universities in the United States has very little to do with how they are funded. The major difference between the public and the private universities is the boards of trustees or the governing boards; this is an issue of control, of academic freedom, of discretion for the university, of autonomy. Do state dollars, by which I mean public dollars, mean bad political control that violates academic freedom, freedom of inquiry, and freedom to teach? In my judgment, based on the historic record of accomplishments of American universities, the answer is no. I do not believe that the source of funding, per se, is a major factor in political control of a kind that I assume we all abhor. There are exceptions. And, yes, of course, as is clearly true in Germany and virtually every country that I am familiar with, much of our research activity is directed or supported by public funding authorities. Much of our research support, whether in medicine, agriculture, or anything we might want to consider, is directed to certain outcomes and results, even though we fortunately do receive, thanks to the National Science Foundation particularly, a considerable amount of support for what we like to call basic research. Though an enormous amount of our research is either directly or indirectly influenced to try to accomplish certain things, it is not narrowly dictated in ways that I think on the historic record interfere with the freedom of the professor, with legal academic freedom. I am not speaking here of the tenure system, which is coming under increasing questioning in the United States. We have a whole set of traditions, and also of legal protections, that do protect us from the wrong kinds of interference.

In any case, the amount of public funding for universities, particularly funding from the states, is declining. One statistic from a recent study of state budget shares will show you where the appropriations are going in our states. This compares 1990 with 1994. Medicaid, which provides basic health care support for low-income people in the United States, has increased – and that is why this is a big issue politically in Washington now – from 9 percent to just under 13 percent of appropriations at the state level. Funding for corrections or prisons is increasing dramatically, going up on the average almost 0.7 percent, which is a lot of money. As a matter of fact, I have suggested to some of my friends in public universities that they rename their universities as correctional institutions to get more money. And they laugh, but then they say it's a good idea. Elementary and secondary education, which is also fundamentally supported at the state and local level, although federal support is of some importance, is holding its own at about 36 percent of state level appropriations. But higher education has declined from about 14 percent to 12.5 percent from 1990 to 1994. If we went back and looked at data for the last twenty years in the United States, you would see a consistent downward trend in terms of state appropriations for the public universities. This has also affected the private universities, because Hopkins used to receive some support from the state of Maryland, the University of Pennsylvania received support from its state, and so on. So this decline in the share of state level funding is a factor that affects all research universities.

At best, most of the public universities, in particular research universities such as the University of Minnesota, Ohio State, or the University of California, are receiving one-third of their dollars from the states. In many cases, it is twenty percent or even lower. In fact, one of the major issues that are being quietly debated within public higher education is this: to what extent do public universities privatize or become as private as possible in various ways? I want to come back to that in a moment.

A third point that I think is obvious – and I think this is true for German as well as American universities, indeed for public universities in any society – is that public universities, and I would argue the private universities as well, do serve and must serve in a large, broad sense the public needs of their societies. They are, after all, part of society, regardless of how they receive their funding and their support. That is, of course, particularly true for state universities. But I think that this sense of societal obligation affects virtually all universities. I also want to add that in my judgment in the United States, generally speaking, political leaders, to the extent that they pay attention to higher education at all, do value our universities, in spite of some of the issues that we are facing. Much of the business and corporate leadership enormously values the research and public universities also. In fact, in some of the budget battles that are going on now, some of our strongest allies are the leaders of some of the largest American corporations, who understand the importance of universities, research, and the education of students at all levels to their interests. These business leaders do not understand our strange ways and our peculiarities, but we have dialog with them.

When we turn to the issue of political control, three problems arise. I have alluded to one of them already, but I want to mention it again. It is the governance problem, particularly the boards of regents or trustees, who exercise enormous influence and control over our universities. They have a great deal to say as to who is appointed as president, and they have a great deal to say as to how the institution operates. Generally speaking, in our public universities, trustees want at times to control, manage, and involve themselves internally in ways that essentially do not occur at an MIT or at a Cornell or at Johns Hopkins. Presidential leadership, which is fairly powerful in American colleges and universities, is enormously threatened by an increasing tendency to have boards of trustees that are dominated or influenced by what I can only bluntly call political hacks, for whom the most important thing that ever happens in their lives is that they are on the board of trustees of the University of Michigan or Michigan State or whatever. This is not a trivial problem; I can get very specific about problems in Michigan, in Colorado. There are even those who feel that the quality of the regents in the University of California is not what it used to be. This is a very major problem that underlies a considerable amount of the turnover among American public university presidents. I think this, even more than funding, is the problem that concerns a lot of us.

Secondly, as is true obviously with the German universities, we have great problems of fiscal stress. We are, however, better off in my judgment than we complain about and we do an awful lot of complaining in the United States. As I have repeatedly told my friends and colleagues, I have tried the whining approach and pleading poverty. If it worked, I would recommend it. In Germany, France, the United States, it does not work. We will not win if we whine. That does not mean we cannot speak factually and calmly about our difficulties. But if we whine, we will not win and we will lose the support that we have from our business allies and friends. The good side is that the demand for higher education services is enormously high. This can be demonstrated in any number of ways. People do want college educations for themselves. Older people want college educations. Demand for research services, for medical breakthroughs, all of that remains extraordinarily high. But we are in a totally new fiscal environment in the United States today.

I am one of those who liked the Cold War. It was a simple world. We knew, or thought we knew, who was good and who was bad.

The Cold War provided a tremendous amount of financial support in the United States for higher education. Our first student aid programs at the federal level, back in the late 1950s and early 1960s, were approved under the heading, "National Defense Education Act." When you are in a war, you fight the enemy and you invest resources for defense. We did that and it affected American higher education enormously in terms of research support and also in terms of expanding our higher education system. Well, clearly, the Cold War is gone, and none of us really mourns it. But the whole framework of justification that was an important reason for the support that we received in the United States is no longer there. That is why we make enormous arguments now, and I think fairly valid ones, about economic competitiveness and the need for highly trained, educated men and women in a knowledge society. Corresponding to this is a change in reform agenda in the United States that is confronting many of our universities.

In this context I want to go back to the comment I made earlier about privatization, which is an important issue in the United States. Now, some of our universities, such as the University of Virginia or the University of Michigan, and I think also to a large extent UCLA, will always be public universities in name. But they have decided that, given the fiscal pressures and the circumstances that they face, they would rather accept what they think is inevitable declining state support and ask for greater freedom from state budgetary and other controls, in return for which they will have greater discretion in using their funds while living with very attenuated state appropriations. The University of Virginia, for example, does not receive much more than 10 percent of its funds from state support. For other public universities, the percentage is higher. On the average for the research type universities, the level varies between 25 and 35 percent. But the trend line is very clear. On the other hand, some of the other public research universities, such as Minnesota, Ohio State, and Indiana University, are concluding that they want to stay as public as possible. That doesn't mean that they will not try to raise more and more private funds; they do a lot of that already. But they are going to try to limit their tuition increases as much as possible, and continue to hope that they can attract the maximum amount of public support that is possible.

I have just spent a little time in Indiana, which is an eight-campus system, although most of us would think of Bloomington as Indiana University. There the entire university system and its president, Miles Brand, have committed themselves to what their new president calls "America's New Public University." In the charter that is being proposed for the years ahead, they have three points that they make rhetorically, but there is some real meaning, I think, behind the rhetoric. Let me explain by taking each of the words in the title, "America's New Public University," in turn.

Their argument, first, is that the history and character of Indiana University are American, because it is grounded in traditions of American universities as learning communities in which knowledge is discovered and conveyed in order to enlarge the culture and enlighten the citizens of a democracy. The word "Public" denotes a reaffirming of obligations to Indiana citizens and to the university's role as a port of entry to a high quality of life for a widely diverse population; access, respect, and opportunity for all are among the chief commitments enunciated here. Under the word "University," the Indiana statement reads: "We are a university not only because of the curricula of each of our campuses enables students to study in one of several disciplines and professions and to make connections among them, but also because we are a single institution, geographically distributed." This will be the hardest thing of all for them to do, to create a single university composed of campuses with complementary missions.

One final point and then a conclusion. The debate in the United States – and I think this applies as well to public and private universities – also has to do with a question raised by Rainer Künzel for the German universities: Is higher education more a public or more a personal good? After all, the private universities are also in public service, at least so I am told. I have a daughter who goes to New York University, a private institution, and I can tell you that the tuition there is about $18,000 to $20,000 a year. But the bills that I receive say, "A private university in public service," as the university's slogan. I happen to agree that our private universities perform public purposes; they simply operate in somewhat different ways. Traditionally, we have always believed that higher education is both a public and a private good, but we have in recent years subtly and not so subtly shifted the emphasis enormously, both for public universities and also for private universities, to regarding higher education increasingly as a private gain and a private benefit.

Let me give you one major example. Roughly two-thirds of the student assistance that comes out of the federal government here in Washington, D.C., is in the form of loans to students to pay higher tuition. One-third is in the form of direct grants; but that percentage has been declining steadily in the last twenty years, and I do not believe that that trend will be reversed. Now, if I have to borrow to pay for my education, and I have to repay that from my private funds, the message to me is that the education that I am receiving is really intended primarily to benefit me, though I am getting some help and low-cost loans for the short term. As a result, there is an enormous amount of loan indebtedness on the part of American college students, whether they are in private colleges or public ones. That is not in my judgment going to change.

Because I agree with Dr. Künzel's concluding remarks, I will repeat them: "Now, problems of inefficiency and dwindling funds call for modernization strategies that will strike a new balance between individual freedom and institutional responsibility. Toward that end, we still have a long way to go."

Session Six

DISCUSSION

JACKSON JANES: This is a question to Rainer Künzel. You talked about the fact that the German federal government is pulling back from funding. In an average figure, can you say that the funding from the state governments for state universities in all of the *Länder* is 80 percent or 90 percent?

RAINER KÜNZEL: Ninety percent.

GUNTER PFISTER: I would like to ask the following question of Dr. Künzel. Listening to you and hearing about the constraints and hierarchies involved, I would like you to tell us a little bit more about how you are maintaining autonomy.

RAINER KÜNZEL: Maintaining? Well, we don't have autonomy at the present time. I tried to point out to you that there is no such thing as autonomy in the university nor in the system of state administration. We are striving for more autonomy. We feel that this form of external bureaucratic control does not lead to an efficient way of operating the system, and that it also does not strengthen responsibility within the system. So what we need is more competition and more autonomy in decision making.

HANS-JOACHIM MEYER: I would only like to make one remark. Rectors and presidents of universities are not appointed by the minister. They are elected by the universities, and this election theoretically is confirmed by the minister. But I don't know of any single example that the election of the rector or president of the German university was not confirmed by the minister.

RAINER KÜNZEL: It was probably before your time, not in the last few years.

RICHARD PETTIT: I work with the Fulbright Senior Scholar Program. Yesterday Konrad Jarausch gave us a very concise overview of what has been going on in higher education in Western Germany from 1945 to 1989. He mentioned that West Germany has experimented with private institutions in higher education. I know a little bit about these experiments; Rainer Künzel indicated that they have failed. Have they failed utterly, definitely, forever?

ERIK WILLENZ: Professors Magrath and Künzel have inspired me to address a few questions, and maybe some small rejoinders, to Professor Magrath's account of our American educational system. I'm not sure I heard him right, but when he elucidated the financial resources of our universities, in particular on the private side, he may have omitted one important factor which I think is critical to the philosophy of education. That is the endowments, the incomes from which are absolutely essential. And the battle of endowments determines, in my worm's eye view, the independence and autonomy of many of the private universities, although the Harvard-sized institutions have rarely been charged with great curtailment of academic freedoms. But I do remember in my days at the University of Chicago – this goes back a long way – when a famous and renowned professor of international relations was fired by Robert Hutchins, who was then the president, because a major endower threatened to withdraw his funds from the school. This goes back a long time, but I could replicate that with other accounts.

Secondly, I am not sure that I feel that the character of the funding here is in any way comparable with that in Germany, because the access to education here is much more limited, even though – and I fully agree with you here – what has happened in the last forty years is considerably enhanced accessibility, encouraged in part by the National Defense Education Acts. Here I think a great deal of mischief was conducted by expanding universities in ways that were not supportable unless we extrapolated the Cold War into the indefinite future. Well, it was the indefinite future for us living through it. Nevertheless, I think it was a mistake. And this brings me to a point Professor Künzel made. He pointed out that one of the reforms – and I may have misunderstood him – was competition as the watchword for the future. But this must not reach the extremes of the market system and should be somehow reined in by planning and coordination. This seems to me a contradiction in terms. I hope you do not pursue this to a great extent, because there is going to be a painful reawakening if you push this. If a university is to fulfill its purpose, competition is the worst possible watchword to follow, because excellence does not necessarily come out of competition.

PETER QUINT: I would like to focus attention on the relationship between the state budgets in a public university in America and the budgets in a German university. Now, in what sense is there more or less autonomy for the American university or the German university? It seems to me that when you go and present a budget to the state legislature, you have to account for your funds, you have to say where the money is going, and so on. Yet we would feel, I think, that there is some autonomy within the state university in America to have new programs, make changes, and so on. One obvious source of autonomy or flexibility is one Professor Künzel talked about, reserve funds. But I remember the reserve fund at the University of Minnesota – I think this was after your time, Peter; I don't want to raise any horrible memories. But the reserve fund was called a slush fund by the state legislature. And it turned out that the provost bought himself a $10,000 desk from it. Well, for years, in the state of Minnesota, every farmer in the backwoods said, that's a $10,000 desk for so and so. So building up a reserve would be a nice thing, but you do have to account for your funds. I think the University of Virginia segregates the private funds from the public ones.

Now, if you charge tuition, that is an obvious source of funds. But the state legislature reduces its public support as your tuition goes up. So I think you would want to have a situation like I remember at Columbia. There, David Truman, the provost, once closed down the biology department because he thought it was old fashioned, though he claimed that he admired very greatly the people running it. He brought in a group he did not like so much, but they were modern biologists. The point here is that he made that decision. The trustees were not involved. How do you get in a German system or an American state legislative system the capacity to make a difficult decision like that within a public framework?

PETER MAGRATH: Could I comment on this, because I think you raise excellent questions. One I neglected, although it was in my notes. Yes, endowments and private fundraising are extraordinarily important to private and public universities, and Hutchens was president at Chicago a long time. There are still personnel issues that come up similar to the examples cited, but I do not think it is a front-and-center issue, although we can certainly find cases to talk about. With regard to reserve funds, these are okay if they are not hidden reserves. If we are open and clear in communication – and I think this applies for private sector as well as public sector universities in any country – we will be all right. I could speak at length about the Minnesota situation, but I won't, except to say that what was wrong was not that there were reserve funds. It is that they were hidden, and only three people knew about them, none of whom was on the governing board of regents, much less the legislature, at a time when the university was, as we always are, under fiscal stress.

I think one of the great mistakes that we have sometimes made – and this has been more of a public university problem – is to play games with state legislators and state bureaucrats and state officials. I am all for playing games if you can win a game, but this is not a game that we can win. I think being open and forthcoming about what one has can build enormous credibility. I will give you one vignette as an example that is personal and may be self-serving. When I was at the University of Minnesota we were at one point going through a really serious budgetary reduction because the state had a fiscal problem of major proportions. This was about 1980 or 1981. I am talking about a cut in real dollars, not merely a reduction in the requested funding increase. I went to the two key legislators and said, listen. If we are cut in this budget by $30 million, we can deal with it. It will be hard, but this is what we can do. If we are cut $31 million, I will go to the governing board and ask for financial exigency. And I said, you've just got to believe me. Don't say, well, if you can take a $30 million reduction, why can't you take $31 million or $32 million. I said, $30 million is the breaking point. And they believed me, because I had, I think, been open and candid with them. I think that's eventually money in the bank for us in the public or private sector.

MITCHELL ASH: This is more of a comment than a question, but I think it will help focus the relationship between these two contributions. Listening to Peter Magrath talk, I was impressed with the basic structural similarities in the situations of the German and American university systems that I hadn't expected to hear brought out in that form. So I kept asking myself, if there are that many similarities, can't we go beyond describing them and ask, what can the two systems learn from each other? In the Cold War era, this question was always formulated asymmetrically: What can Germany, meaning West Germany, learn from the United States? After the end of the Cold War, I think now is an appropriate time to try and make that question a little more symmetrical and to think of a more general way of formulating it. Let me offer just one thesis as a brief answer to that question.

Mixed financing is apparently the true guarantor of autonomy in higher education, at least in the United States. I am not just talking about freedom of speech, but about institutional autonomy. The problem at present, it seems to me, is that we have a Scylla and Charybdis situation. On the one hand, American public institutions, and German ones as well, to some extent, want to get out from under the political ax of the state. One way of doing that is getting alternative sources of funding, no matter where the source may be. In the American system, it is often the federal research pot, which is going to get smaller, so that is not going to be as available as it was. Private sources are another. But that is the Charybdis – commercialization, the consumer orientation that I hear is also being regarded as a danger in Germany.

So it is clear that what needs to be steered is a middle course. The problem is, what sorts of middle courses are available. I find it interesting that the universities Peter Magrath named, Minnesota, Ohio State, Indiana, are precisely those state universities that have had relatively little success in raising independent endowments. That makes it understandable that they are going to hew the line more toward more public funding or a more public orientation. But this is always a relative thing. So it seems to me that the more effective strategy is going to be to think in every case of ways of reminding the states that there is a public obligation to support the universities. But the most effective way of doing that is finding other sources of money.

RAINER KÜNZEL: I would first like to say something about the attempts in Germany to run universities or institutions of higher education on a private basis. In the beginning, it seemed that in one case, the University of Witten-Herdecke was successful because they had a relatively stable financial basis. There were large companies that were financing the institution. But it was a very small university that offered courses in a very limited spectrum, like medicine and economics, areas where it was easier to get funding and where there was a lot of pressure of demand on the public institutions. There were a lot of students applying for these courses at the public institutions, so they could get excellent students and could really live in an exceptional situation.

Two years ago or so, the companies withdrew their money. So that university is now partly and to a growing extent being financed by the state. That is in a sense the failure, because all of the time the president of the university had pointed his finger at the public institutions and told them that if they wanted autonomy, they should see to it that they get the money from other sources, but not from the state. Yes, they did charge tuition, but it was a kind of tuition framework where the needy students were accepted and could get the appropriate funding from elsewhere. The other institutions that try to stay private are either church run or concentrate on just one subject, like business management. The latter are not universities, but *Fachhochschulen*. So that's all of the experience we have with privately funded universities. I would say on the whole that they have failed.

The second question is, to what extent does competition bring us anywhere? Well, we are competing. We are competing for excellent students, we are competing for excellent academic staff and so on and so forth. We are competing for money, of course. But the problem is that we don't control the way this competition operates. We don't have the freedom to really decide on the measures to be taken in order to be successful in this competitive environment. I think that what we have to have is a mixture of competition and planning. On the state level, we need to decide on the structure of the entire system. We need to decide on what kind of opportunities for study there will be in the entire state. Then we have to see to it that different levels or different kinds of study opportunities or educational opportunities will develop excellence in the course of a mixture of competition and quality assessment. What we need is quality assessment on an internal and external basis with external peer groups. So I think that what we need, in addition to the supply-oriented or input-oriented control systems, are some elements of output-oriented and demand-driven control mechanisms.

The last point would be the question of how we talk about tuition fees at the moment. I will not go into that at length, but the main question is, what can we do so that if we start raising tuition fees, the public money is not cut accordingly? The idea that we have brought up recently is that we will try to negotiate with the state that for each dollar of tuition fees, we get so many dollars of public money, so that we use tuition fees as seed money to get public money. If we can come up with a formula that really serves the financial needs of the universities, that might work.

Chapter Seven

WHOM DO GERMAN UNIVERSITIES NOW SERVE?

German Universities in Transition

⬠

Evelies Mayer

In the early 1960s, when I was a student of sociology at the University of Frankfurt, Ludwig von Friedeburg taught a seminar on "University and Society." More than one hundred students listened to a message not previously heard: von Friedeburg pointed out that, with the changing orientation of parents and their children toward high school education, the universities had to make a shift from elite to mass education in order to meet the needs of their future students. Some years later von Friedeburg became minister of education in the state of Hesse. In 1970, during his tenure, legislation on higher education was passed, eliminating the hierarchical structures of the *Ordinarienuniversität* (university of full professors) and paving the way for more vocationally oriented study programs. Thereafter, the number of students at Hessian institutions of higher education increased from some 40,000 in 1970 to almost 165,000 in 1994.[1] Currently, the trend toward a quantitative expansion of

---

1. H. Wolf, "Wissenschaft und Forschung," in *Hessen: Gesellschaft und Politik*, eds. B. Heidenreich and K. Schacht (Stuttgart, Berlin, Cologne, 1995), 190f.

the student population has been delayed, but only temporarily. Demographic changes will precipitate an increase in numbers of entering students again. Presently, 1.9 million students are enrolled in German institutions of higher education.

I will concentrate on governmental failures to support adequately the transformation of the German university into a system of mass higher education by failing to grant sufficient financial support or to contribute reform concepts. I will briefly outline the Hessian concept of university reform in order to show some of the difficulties institutions of higher education and the state governments face in their endeavor to reshape higher education. By referring to my experience with the Hessian system of higher education and by presenting some empirical data, I will answer the question, whom do German universities serve today? I will conclude by summarizing an outlook for the future of the German research university.

In Hesse, as in other states, the period of active reforms in the early 1970s put forward demands for open access to the traditionally elitist institutions of higher education, for more democratic decision-making processes within these institutions, and for new and more vocationally oriented modes of teaching. This active reform period was not only fueled by the demands of students and younger academics for more participation in universities' affairs, it was also nourished by widely shared political considerations, such as the conviction that a country can successfully compete on the world market only by generating highly qualified manpower, and that in democratic societies access to postsecondary education is a civil right. These arguments had a highly persuasive power in the initial phase of reform. But the period of active reform came to an end before the detailed reform measures prescribed first by state laws and later by the *Hochschulrahmengesetz* of 1976 (Federal Framework Law of Higher Education) took root in the universities. The main outcome of this reform period was a more highly differentiated structure of higher education characterized by the emergence of more practical and very successful operating *Fachhochschulen*, which provided a counterweight to the universities, and the development of a dense network of nationwide coordination of educational planning.

Ministers of higher education on the state and federal levels have since failed to promote further the process of reform. In 1977, instead of getting off the ground a broad initiative for restructuring the higher education system, the heads of the state and federal governments reacted to the explosion in student numbers by setting up the following agreement: Institutions of higher education would be granted additional financial support for a limited period of "demographically based" increase in student population. At the same time, these institutions had to accept an "overload" of students. This so-called *Öffnungsbeschluß* was based on a fundamental historical error: an overestimation of demographic development and a failure to recognize the changing patterns of societal orientation toward higher education. It was the beginning of a series of omissions that finally led to the present bankruptcy of higher education policy in Germany. In a recent newspaper interview Dieter Simon, the former head of the German Science Council, summed up his experience with reforms in higher education as follows: "At high speed higher education policy of the federal and state governments is reduced to the catchwords 'provide open access, maintain open access, and look the other way.' One could also call it bankruptcy."[2] Even the "education summit" *(Bildungsgipfel)*, a 1993 meeting to which Chancellor Kohl invited the representatives of states and science policy organizations, did not lead to further reform initiatives. The meeting turned out to be an abyss into which the hopes for substantial reform and adequate financial support for institutions of higher education sank. The failure of the meeting is further proof of the well known fact that governments have their own priorities, and those had shifted in Germany since the mid-1970s to areas of political interest other than education.

Today, the rhetoric of economic necessity to "invest in the intellectual potential" of the young generation survives in speeches of government and party officials. Higher education policy itself, however, is dictated by ministers of finance but barely pushed forward by their colleagues responsible for higher education and research. Strangled by current budget cuts and even, in some states, forced to reduce personnel, university administration and faculty are grudgingly implementing the innovative strategies that had recently been put into effect. The tragedy of higher education

2. D. Simon, "Eine Nation, die Bankrott machen will," *Die Tageszeitung*, 26 September 1995.

policy in Germany is that, from the beginning of the debate on mass higher education, the obligation of state agencies to reforming higher education was merely half-hearted. During the years when student enrollment was increasing, governments on the federal and state levels claimed to be committed to transforming the higher education system from an elite to a mass system. In reality, they did not initiate profound changes in financing and administering the research universities. If creative structural changes had been implemented in the early 1970s, the twin goals of providing mass higher education and maintaining the mission of the research university could have been more successfully combined. Unfortunately, for several reasons this did not happen.

First, the commitment of state authorities to substantial reforms within the higher education system was at no time very strong, even during the active period of reform. Second, there was never a shortage of reform ideas. Even though science and higher education organizations were competing to prove they were taking action by presenting one reform proposal after another, the suggestions for change seldom affected deeply the science and higher education policies of the federal government or even the state governments, which control the institutions of higher education. In general, in the political arena, the most effective means of demonstrating political action is to make a law. So, a series of state laws for higher education and the Federal Framework Law of Higher Education marked the period of active reforms in the early 1970s. Unfortunately, laws alone do not change reality, especially not in organizations as complex as institutions of higher education. Here, laws have to be implemented in a very subtle and thoughtful way to effect the intended changes. This means, in most cases, that the process of implementing a new law can only be accomplished by a joint venture between the state government and institutions of higher education, a policy pattern quite unheard of by German state officials.

Third, by contrast, during the past decade the prevailing pattern of the relationship between governments and state-funded institutions of higher education was mutual accusation. The universities, for example, were publicly held responsible for the fact that their students took too long to complete their degrees, whereas academics blamed external conditions or lack of personnel and financial resources for the length of time to degree. This pattern of mutual accusation diverted energies that could have been directed toward implementing reform. On the other hand, the permanent calling to account of each others' faults might also be seen as a sign that the commitment to modernize the conventional institutional framework of higher education had no firm base either in government authorities or in the institutions of higher education. Under these circumstances the rapid expansion of the German system of higher education during the last quarter century was not accompanied by profound structural and curricular changes, changes that could have bridged the widening gap between rapidly rising student numbers and public support for expenditure on higher education. Consequently, the conditions for teaching and research deteriorated considerably.

Higher Education Reform in Hesse

I have just described the situation I encountered when I took office as minister of science and culture in Hesse some years ago. At that time I knew from my experience teaching at a university that a strong commitment to restructuring the system of higher education, and especially to restructuring the research university, was overdue. I knew that, historically, the state of Hesse had demonstrated a broad commitment to education for everybody, from kindergarten on. I knew that institutions of higher education had to open up to a more diverse student body and to new societal interests and needs, especially those of the rural areas. And I knew that research activities in Hesse were mainly concentrated in the universities and not in research institutions outside the university, as was and is the case in most other states. Finally, I knew that specific structural changes in the Hessian economy, for example in the chemical or biotechnology industries, were heavily dependent upon maintaining the continued quality of teaching and research in the university. But I also knew that initially, the political parties that formed the Hessian government had no strong political will to invest more money in higher learning and were particularly unwilling to invest in research activities inside and outside the university.

It was clear to me that in order to bring about the necessary changes, I had to take a new approach. Instead of resorting to the customary instrument of cost-effective but time-consuming change, in other words formulating new law, I chose instead to implement first a number of substantial reform measures:[3]

- Maintaining open access to institutions of higher education by expanding the infrastructure of the more experiential and vocationally oriented *Fachhochschulen*.
- Revising and modernizing university curricula in all fields of study along the federal framework regulations.
- Setting up central committees for a systemwide evaluation of curricula in various fields of study.
- Establishing a program for innovation in teaching.
- Introducing a procedure whereby departments reported regularly to the president on the effectiveness of teaching and examinations.
- Shifting responsibility for decision-making processes from the ministry to the universities.
- Installing a committee of highly distinguished external experts (*Hochschulstrukturkommsion*) to evaluate the Hessian system of higher education and research as a basis for further innovation.

These measures were accompanied by a moderate increase of academic and nonacademic staff and a substantial growth in the capital budget for construction.

To bring about these initiatives for change, I relied on a process of reform based on persuasion instead of coercion. My implementation strategy was not to tower over the institutions of higher education or to treat them as subdivisions of the ministry, but rather to involve faculty, students, and staff in this comprehensive process of restructuring: I wanted them to participate in the various strategies of reform. This process gained momentum when the Hessian universities realized that the ministry shared their concept of the research university and was trying to balance

3. Hessisches Ministerium für Wissenschaft und Kunst, ed., *Der Hessische Weg: Aktualisierte Materialien zur Studienstrukturreform* (Wiesbaden, 1994).

the need to provide an excellent education with the research mission of the university.

Let me illustrate this process. When I installed the evaluation committee, which consisted of external experts from various scientific backgrounds, presidents of the universities, and rectors of the *Fachhochschulen,* faculty and students alike protested impetuously. The committee was accused of being an appendage of the state government whose mission it was to expand the ministry's influence on teaching and research activities within universities and to scrutinize institutions of higher education in order to provide recommendations for budget cuts in the future.

Alerted by the public discussion on breaking up what was considered to be a structural and functional muddle in higher education and questioning the Humboldtian idea of unity of teaching and research as an appropriate frame of reference for mass higher education, faculty and students alike demanded more control of the evaluation process and requested that members of Hessian institutions of higher education represent them on the committee. The protests against the committee reminded me of the good old days of the 1960s students' rebellion, but with the difference that not Marx but Humboldt was quoted to emphasize the quest for autonomy in the governance of the universities' inner affairs and to support suspicious resistance to any signs of political intrusion. It took a while for the committee to convince its critics that the evaluation was aimed at renewal from inside the university and thus would strengthen rather than weaken the institutions' autonomy. Once presidents, rectors, faculty, and students understood that the universities and *Fachhochschulen* were benefiting from the committee's work, they participated constructively in the evaluation process.

The review of the Hessian higher education system aimed not only to provide quantitative data for future governmental strategies for restructuring teaching and research, but also to provide the opportunity for intense dialogue with different groups and departments in the universities and Fachhochschulen. As a result, the committee's recommendations were based on comprehensive self-evaluations by each institution and ultimately responded to the different cultures in disciplines and fields of study and research.

Consequently, the evaluation process was a first step toward initiating a self-generating and self-determined process of renewal to be carried out on an ongoing basis within the institutions of higher education.

After the committee's report, *Autonomy and Responsibility: Reform of Higher Education in Times of Trouble*, was published in 1995, it was widely discussed by faculty and students in the institutions and in joint sessions with the ministry.[4] But presently these debates are overshadowed by the disastrous financial situation of the state of Hesse. The committee's reform proposals had already taken into account financial restrictions, but to a lesser extent. Hopefully, a broader discussion of the committee's full range of recommendations will continue and, despite the severe cutbacks in personnel and financial support, will lead to a far-sighted conceptual framework, to activities for curricular reform, and to changes in the decision-making processes within the institutions of higher education and in their relations to the ministry.

Whom Do German Universities Now Serve?

To answer this question, let us look at surveys of German students and academics. How do students and academics view their universities? Of course there are always complaints about poor working and learning conditions, but when it comes to the respective professional interests, faculty and students alike love the university. Faculty love the university because it affords them the opportunity to do research. Students love the university because university study still seems to guarantee future status and job security.

According to four representative surveys of the professoriate conducted between 1976 and 1992, university faculty are coping with growing pressures due to the increase in numbers of students by holding on to their primary professional interest in research.[5]

4. Hessisches Ministerium für Wissenschaft und Kunst, ed., *Autonomie und Verantwortung. Hochschulreform unter schwierigen Bedingungen. Bericht der Hochschulstrukturkommission des Landes Hessen* (Frankfurt a.M., 1995).
5. U. Teichler, Quality and Quantity of Staff in Higher Education. *Higher Education Policy* 7, No. 2 (1994): 19-23; here, 21f.

They manage to devote the same amount of time to conducting research now as they did during the last twenty years: in 1976 professors spent 23 percent of their time doing research; in 1992, they engaged in research 29 percent of the time. Obviously, professors themselves preserved time for research activities despite the growing demands of mass education. The crucial questions are, therefore, is there a decline in the quality of teaching, and how well are the growing numbers of students being served when professors do not extend their work time to accommodate their teaching responsibilities?

The survey findings revealed a typical pattern: faculty protected their research time, not at the expense of teaching but by reducing the amount of time spent preparing for classes and counseling individual students. So it is not surprising at all that in a comparative study of the academic profession in thirteen countries, German professors show the highest rate of positive response to their professional work.[6] Apparently, German universities are still serving the professoriate's primary interest in research by granting far-reaching freedom to allocate worktime beyond the prescribed teaching load.

Students, in spite of their complaints about poor teaching services, packed classrooms, and professors whom they hardly ever meet personally, are also being served. Students consider higher education the admission ticket to their chosen professions or their future occupational career paths. Especially in times of high and growing unemployment, the system of higher education provides a meaningful alternative to unemployment after graduation from high school or vocational training. Statistics also show that the unemployment rate among academics is still the lowest among occupational strata. Furthermore, in Germany, one still can observe strong links between levels of education and status, and income and position in the workforce. So it is not surprising that, given

6. E. L. Boyer, P. G. Altbach, M. J. Whitelaw, eds., *The Academic Profession: An International Perspective* (Princeton, NJ, 1994); J. Enders and U. Teichler, *Berufsbild der Lehrenden und Forschenden: Ergebnisse einer Befragung des wissenschaftlichen Personals an westdeutschen Hochschulen* (Bonn, 1995); idem., eds., *Der Hochschullehrerberuf: Aktuelle Studien und ihre hochschulpolitische Diskussion* (Neuwied, Kriftel, Bonn, 1995).

these realities, the German system of higher education still serves students' needs in an important way.

In addition, results of annual representative polls of entering students started in 1983 verify the fact that the system of higher education has the built-in flexibility to provide an immense variety of educational opportunities.[7] The 1994 findings show that 86 percent of entering students could choose a field of study related to their personal interests. This is the largest proportion of students studying in their field of choice since 1983. The 1994 survey also found that most students are entering study programs for which they have an intrinsic inclination, although according to the findings, students easily combine this intrinsic inclination with extrinsic motives such as professional orientations and a desire for social status. Moreover, at the outset of university studies, most students are optimistic about stepping into their desired profession or workplace. Furthermore, the majority of entering students select institutions closest to home without looking at the quality of education they get there. For more and more high school graduates it becomes more and more attractive to enter the practically oriented *Fachhochschulen*, even if these are more overcrowded than universities. Thirty-five percent of entering students had already graduated from a track in the system of vocational training and education.

To sum up these and other more detailed findings, despite the apparent deficiencies in most institutions and fields of study, students are deeply convinced that higher education and the career paths they anticipate following are closely related. Given this perception, institutions of higher education are still attracting high school graduates as well as serving students who have already graduated from the vocational training system. Universities are supporting the interests of both groups of students by helping them either pursue their respective fields of study or aim toward a predictable occupational career.

Universities are serving students' needs in yet another way. If one looks at the various ways in which students combine education, work, and study and how they construct individual career

---

7. K. Lewin, U. Heublein, and D. Sommer, "Studienbeginn im Wintersemester 1994/95: Fachhochschulstudium immer attraktiver fur Abiturienten," *HIS* (*Hochschul-Informations-System*) – *Kurzinformationen*, A 10/95 (1995).

paths by alternating between phases of study and work, one becomes aware of the changing roles of students. This "new type of student" is no longer totally devoted to sitting in on classes, preparing examinations, and enjoying the pleasures of a student's life.[8] He or she is pragmatic enough to cope with packed classrooms, book hunting, and the often chaotic structures of study programs. But this is only one aspect of the new student's life. These students tend to separate study and coursework, which they see as an important training ground, from their life outside the institution, and they use their academic knowledge to contribute to various social, cultural, and political activities in their neighborhoods.

Students are the ones who link the institutions of higher education to society in a new way. Stimulated by the changing lifestyle of their students, institutions of higher education are beginning to fulfill new functions as centers of economic, social, and cultural development in the regions in which they are located. *Fachhochschulen* are adapting to their new role as cultural and economic centers more easily than universities. But also the universities give a new impetus to the regions and, in turn, are getting back inspiration for teaching, learning, and for new research topics. So both institutions, *Fachhochschulen* and universities, show an astonishing flexibility when diversifying their functions to fit the needs of their region.

We can conclude from the survey findings that both groups, faculty and students, in German universities are more or less content with the opportunities their institutions are offering them to pursue their personal career goals. Even as institutions of mass higher education without an adequate teaching structure, universities are still providing the "freedom" for faculty to conduct research and are also allowing most students the "freedom" to study very individually according to their chosen subject, their career considerations, their needs of combining work and study, and their lifestyle, which is not totally bound to the university as a learning center but devoted to social activities in their communities, too. In recent years universities made every effort to accomplish the

---

8. K. O. Hondrich, "Totenglocke im Elfenbeinturm. Über den wandel der Hochschulen und den Studentenneuen Typs," *Der Spiegel*, 48:6 (February 7, 1994): 34-37.

difficult task of serving the needs of a growing, heterogeneous student body by creating an incredible variety of more or less structured new study programs and a wide range of special programs in continuing education. Moreover, by offering special courses, seminars, and events, universities are developing a new role fostering the cultural and economic needs of communities and regions in which they are located.

As long as German universities are adapting to organizational deficiencies and financial constraints and also contributing to the professional and personal interests of faculty and students, there will be complaints but no persistent resistance to reinforced financial restrictions and political interference. But one can expect a further decline of the already weak involvement of faculty and students in any reform activities. Both groups will concentrate on pursuing their individual interests rather than identifying themselves with the future of their institution.

The Future of the Research University

The future prospects of German universities are uncertain. Financial support is lacking; there is an intensifying struggle over scarce public resources and the efforts to create policies for change, which might enable the system of higher education to cope with high student numbers and with new demands in teaching and research in a wider frame of reference while combining those tasks with a new understanding of the universities role in society, are invisible to the public. The challenge to prepare the research universities adequately for their future is twofold: first, reforms are hard to bring about in institutions with long and well estimated traditions. Second, it is even harder to introduce change in a fiscal climate that subjects higher education to heretofore nonexistent financial stress.

State officials preparing Chancellor Kohl's education summit in 1993 agreed on statistics that proved that the German system of higher education was grossly underfinanced. In order to restore the 1977 level of public financial support for higher education (the year of the *Öffnungsbeschluß*), one would have to increase state funding by one-third. That means that the current budget for expenditure and for investments would have to be increased by DM 9 billion per year, and federal and state governments would have to share the cost. But it is unlikely that there will be a chance to reverse the present trend of declining public financial support. According to Science Council statistics, public expenditures for higher education dropped from 1.32 percent in 1975 to 0.93 percent of the GNP in 1992.[9]

The current crisis of state finances will affect the system of higher education more seriously than politicians might imagine. Stagnating or reduced financial support for universities over a period of time will lead to widening the gap between standards of modernity and the existing infrastucture in laboratories and libraries. In the long run, the quality of teaching and research will suffer. Continuous financial restrictions will also reduce the willingness of universities to join in reform activities on a broader scale. Consequently, reform activities that were started in the early 1990s in response to the increasing public criticism of the universities' educational performance will lose momentum.

Unfortunately, on the whole, activities for change face setbacks in a time when there are more favorable conditions for reform. Recently, student numbers have been decreasing in the old states and are only rising moderately in the new states. This trend is projected to last until the year 2003.[10] During this period, faculty and administrators are in some way relieved in coping with too many students and could divert energies to curricular and structural changes. But ministers of finance are apparently using the declining student numbers as the best excuse for further budget cuts and personnel reduction. In this way they suppress the already limited innovative energies of universities to develop procedures that support and protect their future teaching and research mission by responding constructively to the needs of mass education and to the needs of the future knowledge production.

Almost twenty years after the *Öffnungsbeschluß* there is a widely shared notion of what is wrong with the German higher education

9. J. Lange, Entwicklung und künftige Perspektive der Hochschulen. *Beitrage zur Hochschulentwicklung*, No. 3 (1994): 335-57.
10. Bundesministerium fur Bildung, Wissenschaft, Forschung und Technologie, *Grund- und Strukturdaten 1994/1995* (Bonn, 1994).

system. There is also no debate over whether renewal is required. Universities must undergo major changes in defining their mission and structure in order to avoid becoming institutions of the past. They must answer challenging questions: What will higher education be about in the twenty-first century? How will the university maintain the ability to generate and pass on the creative and innovative power of scientific knowledge?

Reform proposals exist in abundance, and many universities have begun to lay the groundwork for change. But, just as in 1977, political decisions about substantial reform are being postponed. Present strategies for overcoming the crises of state finances appear to be leading to a second major historical error in higher education policy. In cutting budgets and personnel, the beginning of a successful restructuring of the higher education systems in general as well as many small initiatives for reform will be delayed or will come to a halt.

If there are no social forces to stop this short-sighted fiscal policy, the ability of universities to live up to their research mission together with their teaching obligations will be critically weakened. Universities will be throttled by the ministers of finance as long as there are signs of alleged financial abundance. Why pay for basic research when one views research as a personal hobby and a privilege of professors? Why pay for costly research facilities in the universities when research in science and medicine is so successfully conducted in the laboratories of the Max Planck Society, as the latest Nobel prize winners prove? Why pay for a variety of study programs at universities, when *Fachhochschulen* and *Berufsakademien* as highly specialized industrial liaison institutions for advanced vocational training can offer less costly alternatives at the expense of additional financial support for universities? The willingness of ministers of higher education to acquiesce when it comes to balancing the budget, and their heartbreaking efforts to demonstrate political action by symbolic measures of reform instead of presenting an outspoken resistance to the trend of disconnecting fiscal policies from the process of restructuring higher education, will lead to further financial and organizational restrictions.

Among the consequences of negligently by-passed comprehensive reform policies for higher education will be:

1. Dismantling or significantly weakening the research infrastructure of universities and their capacity to compete for dwindling outside funding. (Between 1980 and 1990 outside funding of research activities rose in real terms by 43.5 percent, whereas state funding for research only went up by 3 percent in real terms.)
2. Emphasizing the teaching functions of universities at the expense of research activities, so that universities will function primarily as *Höhere Berufsbildungsanstalten* (advanced institutions of professional and vocational training).
3. Emergence of less costly institutions of higher vocational education, the latest example of which is the *Berufsakademie*.

In the long run, universities will not win the battle to maintain their research mission in more than a symbolic way without substantial and additional financial support from the federal government and the states. The *Länder* will not win the battle to maintain their political responsibility for developing the higher education system if they do not take a stance on a reform that will preserve the wide range of research capacities in universities. Some *Länder*, such as Bavaria, are taking firm steps in this direction. They are aiming at a more productive balance between teaching and research and are strengthening at the same time the important economic, cultural, and social role of institutions in the different regions. I hope other *Länder* will follow.

There is another hope: *Mythos Humboldt* lit a fire under American universities some one hundred years ago. Why should *Mythos Humboldt* not be a driving force for the renewal of German research universities in the twenty-first century? Only such a renewal will enable institutions of higher education to hold on in principle to the idea of the university Humboldt outlined for his time: by developing procedures of renewal that protect their essential teaching and research missions while striving for quality in both areas, universities might serve as a constituent part of civil society, serving the personal interests of faculty and students and meeting public needs as well.

Comment

GERMAN AND AMERICAN UNIVERSITIES IN THE AGE OF CALCULATION

Steven Muller

Universities in different countries have many things in common, but in the case of German and American universities such shared characteristics should not blind us to major differences. A German university is owned and operated by a *Land* government acting within a framework established by the federal government. An American university may be public or private, but even a public American university is not operated directly by government. German universities are in effect state agencies, whose professors are civil servants and whose budgets are largely furnished by and supervised by the state. American universities, both public and private, are organized as corporations, and are therefore governed by a corporate board of trustees, or regents. As individual corporations, American universities have much greater individual autonomy – including fiscal autonomy – than their German counterparts. If they are public universities their professors will be paid by state funds, but paid as university employees, not as civil servants.

The American corporate form of university governance is sufficiently different from German practice to warrant additional comment. For instance, the board of trustees, or regents, may, in the case of public universities, be appointed by the state governor, or even publicly elected along political party lines, but its function is *not* to represent state government, but rather to represent the public interest. Neither private nor public American universities function as parts of government. Both function as either private or public corporations, operating in the public interest, and the public interest is represented by their governing boards. Under the law, university governing boards function much like the boards of American business corporations. The latter represent the interests of the stockholders who own the company. The former represent the public – not government – because the public owns the university if the institution is public, or awards essential tax exemptions if the university is a private corporation operating in the public interest on a not-for-profit basis.

The autonomy of American universities is reinforced by the fact that all of American education is under the jurisdiction of the states, because education is not specified as one of the activities assigned to the federal government by the United States Constitution. In Germany, responsibility for higher education is shared between *Länder* and *Bund* governments, within a framework created by federal legislation. In the United States, the federal government lacks jurisdiction or authority over education, including higher education, and there is no national policy nor national legislation for higher education. Thus the Department of Education in the American federal government has no authority over education at any level, because such authority is vested in state and local government. The federal department can conduct studies, monitor compliance with constitutional guarantees such as equal treatment under the laws, award scholarships and other grants, but it may neither regulate nor direct. American universities are chartered by states, not the federal government, and their performance is evaluated either by their own mechanisms of accreditation or by agencies of the states, not the federal government.

In brief, this describes the foundation for the diverse and competitive character of American higher education, so different from the more orderly and centrally regulated German counterpart system. American colleges and universities compete in a free market for students (who of course pay tuition charges for the instruction they receive) and faculty. They resemble one another to the extent that the market rewards similarities, and differ to the extent that the market rewards differences. Each institution is free to experiment in almost any way it chooses that its own governing board will permit. If the experiment fails it will cease, and it may damage the institution that made the attempt, but no one else. If it succeeds, it will rapidly be imitated and may even lead to a new norm. The primary virtue of the situation is extreme flexibility; the primary defect is lack of organization, supervision, and parity.

The German situation presents almost the complete opposite: organization, supervision, and parity are its cardinal virtues, and its primary defect is lack of flexibility. Some Americans might even argue that the lack of tuition charges by German universities is a second major defect, because in highly developed and commercialized societies value and cost are so closely related that anything free may also appear as worthless. By the same token, some Germans might argue that high cost to students is an additional primary defect of American higher education, because it is unfair and socially discriminatory. This is not the occasion to debate either of these arguments, but they do illustrate the divergences between universities in the United States and Germany.

These divergences are relevant when one considers the need of universities everywhere to adapt rapidly and comprehensively to the impact on higher education of the new knowledge technology. The university, which began as an institution of traditional belief, evolved two centuries ago into the university of reason; then was transformed only within the last half-century into the university of discovery; and is now being reshaped by the new electronic knowledge technology into the university of calculation. This new technology in all its forms challenges the status quo throughout society, but particularly in universities, whose central purpose as institutions is to acquire, develop, teach, and disseminate knowledge. In the United States, individual colleges and universities have already begun to experiment with responses to this challenge. Successes will be imitated, and failures will not be repeated. Over time, a composite overall pattern of response will become viable and will at some point – one hopes – arrive at a new general level of relative stability, at least for a time.

In Germany, the tendency to postpone change until the best solution for everyone has reached the point of comprehensive adoption is likely to complicate matters. Cries for major reforms have already been issuing from and around German universities for years, so far with only modest results. Perhaps this can be cited as evidence that German universities have not wasted their time and effort on relative trivia and will therefore in great position to make the grand and comprehensive changes that are now required. More likely, however, the prevailing paralysis of the existing German university system may continue indefinitely, not because the need for change is denied, but because of lack of agreement on the best course for all concerned to follow, under central direction. This is of course overstated. There innovations within and among German universities, and some *Länder* have been more willing and able than others to encourage and authorize reform. Nevertheless, it does appear that the limited autonomy of the individual German university inhibits experimentation and flexibility, and that the effort to achieve a central and comprehensive response to a rapid series of radical challenges may prove to be counterproductive.

The purpose of these comments is to suggest that greater institutional autonomy for German universities, and freer competition among them, would serve better to assist urgently needed change than the prevailing situation. However, it is emphatically *not* my purpose to suggest that German higher education should look to American universities as a model. American universities do demonstrate some of the advantages – and disadvantages – of high levels of institutional autonomy, but their autonomy is deeply rooted in idiosyncratic patterns of governance and operation. These idiosyncrasies defy imitation, and in particular run counter to German tradition and practice. When Daniel Coit Gilman shaped the new Johns Hopkins University in the 1870s, in the image of Wilhelm von Humboldt's vision of higher education, he successfully formed a new institution in the United States, but he did not replicate the University of Berlin. If Germany were to find it useful, or even necessary, to bestow greater autonomy and flexibility on its universities, a German way of achieving this objective would have to be found and put into practice. American experience can only indicate some of the effects of greater autonomy and lessened central direction. But the particular way in which American universities attained and practice their individual autonomy cannot be imitated. Just as the Basic Law established the same fundamental features of political democracy as the French or American constitutions but created a distinctive German model, so only a distinctively German model of more autonomous and diverse German universities could successfully evolve from the stagnation of the present.

DISCUSSION

IRMGARD WAGNER: I just recently read the latest series in *Die Zeit* about the new generation of optimists at German universities. I do not know whether you got your data from the same inquiry. What strikes me in the first installment of that series more than anything else is the permanent repetition of the term *Massenuniversität*. You all have referred to that, too, mass university. At the same time as the claim is made, the German universities still should be research universities. When I hear that German professors admit that they spend only less than 30 percent of their time for research activities, I'm transfixed.

One of the things in the article is that those interviewed appeared to accept the mass university: "the elite studies abroad anyhow." What seems to be happening, and I think what Dr. Muller said would confirm that, is that in the 1990s after unification, the GDR model seems to have been transferred onto West Germany or the Western universities, where the universities simply are there to train professionals, whereas research is conducted at research institutions. It seems to me that the way that German universities have developed in the 1990s has led more and more to that split. So what are we? The mass university or the research university? I don't know how they're going to solve that problem.

MITCHELL ASH: I was actually going to respond more to Steven Muller, but just to take that last statement briefly, I referred to that issue at the end of my talk. I am astounded to hear you say that the GDR model has been transferred to the West. I will leave it to the speakers to respond more specifically, but I think it is probably more precise to say that conservative modernizing reforms that had begun already in the West have been introduced also in the East. In a certain sense, there is an affinity there with the priority of practical training that had already existed in the East. But precisely the East German structures that had prioritized practical training are the ones that were eliminated and then replaced by West German versions with similar priorities. I think that would be a more precise description of what happened.

Let me just respond very briefly to Steven Muller's comments about whether the two systems are more alike or not. Of course, I take the point that there is a fundamental difference in self-governance and a fundamental difference in the understanding of the role of the state in the German and the American systems. I think it is absolutely correct to emphasize that. But I think that we should not take that difference as a describer of everything that is going on.

What I was pointing out when I was expressing my impression from the first talk about similarities was not the legal essence of the two systems or their political connection to the state or the lack thereof, but institutional realities that seem to be getting more and more similar. Let me just briefly make one or two points about that. When Steven Muller says, correctly, that what Germans see when they come to America is chaos because of the great variety of structures in the American system, I would say that that is what American students see, too, when they come to American universities. It's a jungle out there and getting through it, especially in the large public research universities, is in many respects the real behavioral lesson that American students learn that is maybe more important than all of the cognitive content in our instruction. Learning how to deal with large, complex institutions is an important thing for people who want to be successful in a large, complex society like this one. How to deal with large institutions is what people who want to be successful in a large, complex society like Germany also need to learn. I think there is a similarity there in institutional realities, despite the differences in legal and governmental aspects.

I have one other point related to this. When Steven Muller said that it was incomprehensible to many Americans that German students do not finish on time, whereas American students are so eager to do so, I think we need to remind ourselves that more recent data from the United States indicate that American students do not seem so eager as they once were to finish on time. Time to degree is lengthening in the United States, especially in public universities, for a wide variety of reasons. But one of the most important ones is another similarity between the institutional and social realities of life in the American and German systems. In Germany, as we heard, and also in America, students spend a lot of time working – probably as much time working as they do studying. Real life for them is not necessarily in the classroom, just as it isn't in Germany either. I think there are a lot of similarities there that need to be taken account of.

Last, but not least, Steven Muller points rightly to the difficulty of making anything change in such a system with the *Gruppenuniversität* and all of its complex problems. I referred yesterday to a suggestion I heard that I think also points to the similarities between the two systems. It's true enough that the *Gruppenuniversität* and a lot of the awfulness of committee work is legally mandated in Germany, whereas it is not in the United States. That is a fundamental difference. Nonetheless, in the American universities, as in German universities, something is true that is true of all large social institutions. There are groups within such institutions that have interests. And the conflicts amongst the groups with those different interests are fought out in committees that are supposed to achieve consensus, but that is a very long and complicated process in the American universities as it is also in German universities. I think Steven Muller has exaggerated the speed with which change can happen from the presidential level at American public institutions, as opposed to smaller private ones. There are just as many difficulties here as there because of the complexity of life in large institutions.

EDWARD LARKEY: I have a couple of comments to make as a graduate of the University of Marburg in the 1970s. I think university reform, or let's say the reform of higher education in Germany, has taken place more outside than inside the university. By that, I mean it has been driven not so much by educational principles as it is by the demands of the employment market. If we see what happened to the teachers' surplus of the 1970s, they went into retraining programs and have gone into professions for which no university programs then existed, such as the media. Thus niches were created that led to people going into new professions.

This seems to be complemented by what's going on in the East since unification. Some of the people from the Academy of Sciences and other researchers who became unemployed as a result of unification are also becoming either self-employed or employed outside of the traditional university curricula. At least among the people I know who are doing this, it is a very feudalistic kind of dependency that they are engaged in, very short-term employment, with projects funded only temporarily. So it's very difficult to engage in any kind of long-range planning of your own career.

I would be interested in finding out how much of what is done in this informal sector is research that comes back into the university by way of curricular changes using books that these people produce. Perhaps this is also a case of extra-university reform that the universities are utilizing in some way, shape, or form. I think there are very important things, very deep structural changes, that are going on there that the university would also need to take into consideration.

FRANK TROMMLER: Steven Muller, I believed you as long as you described the differences of the German and American universities. However, the deeper you got into the explanation of what is there and what is coming, especially through technology, the less I believed you about the coming differences of German and American universities. I think that what you described as the coming transformation of the American university will probably destroy the real asset of the American university, namely the idea of community. That means the community that is represented in college life, and in the close relation of teachers and students. The identification with the university with this place of learning is not there so much in Germany and in other European countries, as in the United States. However, if universities now become information and learning agencies, more or less plugged into larger networks, the question is, why are we still maintaining colleges? I have one simple explanation. Most parents would say, to keep the children out of my hair for four years. And that is most important – getting young people away from home, but still not yet fully into the profession. This is something that has to be calculated if one goes into planning and installing these learning and information agencies. I think the difference in the lifestyle of students in Frankfurt and in other German universities from America is not so great here, because these students in Europe will also use these universities as information and learning agencies. So at this moment, I would just challenge the assumption that the situation is different in this field.

EVELIES MAYER: I would like to respond to all of the questions, not just to one. First of all: the combination of mass and research university exists in American universities also. The need to combine professional training and high-level research does not lead to a contradiction, but rather embodies a challenge – the challenge of housing a variety of different kinds of institutions performing different tasks, and of dealing with their needs in a flexible manner.

I do not think that the GDR model has been brought to the West, but rather that ours has been forced onto them. The more interesting question, which we have not been able to discuss here, is how much we have influenced one another in this process.

On the question of time to completion, I must correct a certain oversimplification. Time to degree is now dropping, not rising, and studies have shown that there is a certain linkage here to reform measures. Recent studies in North Rhine-Westphalia and in Hesse have shown, for example, that the average time to degree is now lower in North Rhine-Westphalia than in Hesse.

On life within and around the university, I want to emphasize that many intellectual and academic activities, including research activities, involving cooperation among students and middle-level research staff, take place outside the universities. I am referring to discussion groups and policy groups, for example on environmental questions or engagement in cultural work. Here my impression from extensive travels as minister is that feedback comes back from these activities into the universities. I cannot claim that problems are always resolved within the universities, but rather that an exchange of inner- and extra-university groups takes place, which leads to solutions; a very fruitful exchange of ideas is taking place.

This brings me back to the question of whether the reform discussion is too much directed to the past and not the future. I do not look to the past, but I do continue to believe in the idea of reform. It is very important to me to say in this connection that we should not forget the students. I have pleasant memories of sometimes hard discussions with students during our reform survey project, and that many of the most interesting proposals came from students. I also remember the numerous computer letters from students; when I studied them closely, I became more aware of future developments that we of the older generation could never have realized.

If I were still in office, I would have created a small extension law instead of reformulating our higher education law. This would have included an experimentation clause, a further paragraph allowing more experimentation within individual universities, stengthing of possibilites for greater administrative autonomy, and lastly a provision for student participation.

RAINER KÜNZEL: I would like to add three bits of information that I think are important to understand what has been going on in Germany. The first is that I think on the whole the German university system has been quite successful under the conditions that we've had in the past twenty years. If you are aware of the fact that, as was already mentioned, public spending on higher education as a percentage of GNP has dropped from 1.32 percent to 0.89 percent during the last fifteen years, at the same time when the number of students rose by 70 percent, and if you know at the same time that in the United States, public spending on higher education and research as a percentage of GNP is 3 percent, then you know what the differences are in financing higher education institutions. To give you another figure, per capita public spending on higher education in Germany shows Germany at the bottom of the ranking list among the OECD countries. Only Greece, Turkey, and Spain are doing a little worse than Germany. All of the other OECD countries are spending more per capita on higher education and research. This is one piece information that I just wanted to give you.

The other is that we do not distinguish between full-time students and part-time students. On account of that, the average study time of the students must be much longer than it is in a system where you distinguish between full-time students and part-time students, because a growing percentage of our students are really part-time students. They are working, they are having a family, they are having kids. Ten percent of the students are having a family. They are combining studying and working and living, and they are making being a student a way of life, so to speak. Of course, that takes time.

The third point I wanted to make relates to the question of mass versus research university. The mass university has not ceased to be a research university, not in all subject areas. There is excellent research being done. Most universities have areas of excellence. And it's certainly not true that the elite students go abroad to study. We take pride in sending more students abroad, because we think that taking up studies abroad is in itself valuable. Many of our younger research people of course go to the United States, but they are accepted in research programs over here because they have already achieved a great deal before. So I think on the whole it is not quite as bad as it seems to be, although I am one of the critics of our system, as you have heard.

A question at the end. Who do the members of the board of trustees report to? This is important, because I am intrigued by this idea of having a buffer between the state and the university. But who are these people responsible to? That is an important question. Who are the ones that control the board of trustees and see that these people that are responsible for the university are really feeling responsible and are not just being proud of being a board member and adding that to their personal career?

STEVEN MULLER: Let me try to respond to some of these points. First, I want to say something which you have just brought to mind though it is not your question. Having worked in both languages in comparative German-American higher education since 1967, I admire almost all of my colleagues who work in the administration of German universities, because they do almost impossible things under very difficult circumstances and I have nothing but respect for them. I wish their circumstances were better.

Second, I honestly believe that, in talking about the impact of new learning technology on all of education, there is no exaggeration in saying this is here, this is coming; this is not Flash Gordon a long time away. It's here now. But how we adapt to it will differ. For example, Frank Trommler makes an excellent point, which is that in the United States when we talk about universities, people don't understand that very well, either. Universities are institutions which operate at two levels. First there is the collegiate level, what we call the undergraduate level. Almost all universities, except Rockefeller University and maybe one or two others, have an undergraduate or collegiate component. But then they also offer the doctorate, by and large, whereas what we call colleges operate the undergraduate phase and may offer a master's degree, but generally don't offer doctorates.

The American collegiate experience is a residential experience with a tremendous community flavor, which serves three or four vital purposes. First, it removes the students from their homes, which is a relief to them and their parents. Secondly, it keeps them off the labor market, which is very important in this country. Third, it gives them the opportunity to interact with a peer group and to some degree deparochialize, because it used to be that they knew very little outside where they grew up. Now, of course, again through television and all kinds of other media, they are more aware of what's out there, but they don't interact with it. And we're trying this brave experiment also where they meet people very different from themselves, racially, religiously, and so on, which is essential for survival in this country. I don't know whether you all know that two out of five Americans now are no longer caucasian. That will become three out of five about 40 or so years from now, which will mean the majority of Americans will be non-caucasian unless you include Latin Americans and Hispanics as caucasians, which is not part of this calculation.

For that reason, I believe that the collegiate situation will survive, because it serves other purposes than educating people. I know I learned more from my fellow students than from most of my teachers, and I had very good teachers. I think that talking to your fellow students will still be important. I also think, however, that this will take the form of having a group of students at one college, who will be talking electronically with their peers at other colleges. How you adapt to this is not cut and dried. Certainly it can't be all alienation and lack of human communication.

The governance question is a very key question. The regents or trustees of state or community colleges and universities are accountable to the state government in various ways. In Maryland, for example, they are generally appointed by the governor. In many states, they are appointed by the governor but require confirmation by the legislature. In some states, they are elected. It is perfectly true that in that process, you get some people who really are not very useful. It is also true that of course legislatures and the press keep their eye on public institutions. So there is a public accountability, as well. And it's interesting that some of these people serve a long time. In California, I think regents of the University of California are appointed for sixteen years. In Maryland, it is a much shorter time.

For the private institutions, there is another very American phenomenon. These are self-perpetuating boards that are not accountable to anybody. Each university in our country has a body of people called alumni, who have lived on that campus and have spent, they always say, some of the happiest years of their life there and who are solicited for support from the day they enroll, when their parents are solicited, to the day they die. Often, because records are slow, even posthumous letters have gone out trying to raise money from alumni. They care about their institution because if you went to Cornell and something good happens at Cornell, you want to be able to brag about it because you were once there. If something bad happens at Cornell, you don't want to be asked, what's happening at your university. Therefore, the eye of the alumni and donors on the board of trustees is always there. These are not hundreds, but thousands of people who are very interested in what happens at that university. And they get regular reports from the institution which is part of fundraising.

So if you say from a German point of view, to whom are they legally accountable, the answer for a private American institution college or university is nobody. But if you ask, how are they socially accountable, they are socially accountable to the donors and alumni. Now in our country we also all get foundation grants. The foundations always ask you for a list of your trustees, your recent financial statement, your most recent annual report. As a result, the public accountability of American higher education is really quite high, whereas the legal accountability for the private sector is nonexistent. Protecting the quality of trustees is easier to do in the private sector, though it doesn't always happen. It's harder to do in the public sector because that gets politicized. What has prevented the politicization from getting too bad is that the existence of the private sector demonstrates the difference in ways that we screen the legislatures from generally doing their worst.

It is true that there are a lot of problems that German and American universities have in common. I just believe that before we can talk about how we can address them jointly, we had better understand how enormously different we are. There are some things you are spared, because the success of an American college or university presidency in many, many institutions is, first of all, judged by how much money you can raise. If you can raise enough money, you are forgiven many sins. If you are terrific but raise no money, you're gone. Particularly with public institutions, the success of the athletic teams has a great deal to do with the respect of the legislature and the public for the institution, which is absurd. You can criticize anything in Germany, but what is more ludicrous than judging Stanford or Harvard by its football team or its swimming team? And yet for state universities, that's a perennial problem. Such problems will not go away, except that there may be ways in which the cyber world can address them.

Chapter Eight

THE UNIVERSITIES AND CONTEMPORARY GERMAN POLITICAL CULTURE

∽

Hans-Joachim Meyer

The role of the universities in contemporary German political culture can only be discussed in the context of history. Hence, I will take up again some of the themes and issues that have already been dealt with in the course of this conference. But my point of view will be a different one. What I am going to say will quite necessarily reflect what people in politics are thinking about universities. You may regard such views as blatant nonsense, glaring injustice, and stupid prejudices, and quite often I would agree. However, if the present political influence of German universities is examined, such views cannot be ignored. Quite often, they are more important than any explanations we might offer.

German history seems to provide particularly good examples of the intricate relationship between intellectual developments and political life, and of the role of universities in politics. The invitation to the academic disputation of a number of theses put up at the door of a church by a professor at a German university, namely Martin Luther in Wittenberg, was the prelude to one of the most important religious and political revolutions in human history. The intellectual spring of the Renaissance and the Reformation stimulated political as well as academic life, yet the turmoil and the wars that followed, especially the Thirty Years' War, eventually caused the decline of the German universities. Three hundred years later, it was another great event of intellectual and academic history, namely, the foundation of the University of Berlin as a new model for academic teaching and research by Wilhelm von Humboldt, which helped to transform Prussia after her defeat against Napoleon into a modern state and prepared the liberation from Napoleonic rule. However, the wars of liberation brought neither political liberty nor national unity, but were followed by the era of restoration. Although the great expectations had not become reality, they were still alive.

In the decades before the revolution of 1848 the German universities became centers of national aspirations, liberal thinking, and democratic ideas. In the eyes of the governments of the reactionary Holy Alliance, of course, the universities were centers of subversive conspiracy, which they tried to suppress. When in 1848 the first German national parliament met at Frankfurt am Main, many of the deputies were university professors and quite a few had been dismissed from their academic posts in the years before the revolution because of their political ideals. However, noble thoughts do not necessarily lead to effective action. While the deputies drafted a liberal constitution, political power slipped out of their hands and the first German parliament, as one of the deputies sarcastically remarked, turned into a rather dull academy of political science.[1] While German liberals and democrats had failed in their attempt to achieve national unity by setting up a modern and constitutional state, Bismarck, a fierce opponent of the revolution, was successful in his policy of uniting Germany under Prussian leadership. As a result, the influence of liberal and democratic ideals was waning and German universities increasingly combined academic excellence with political conservatism. Particularly in Prussia, the most important of the German states, the universities were pillars of Protestant conservatism and national-

1. Ludwig Simon: "Jetzt sind wir als Staat verloren. Wir sind jetzt höchstens eine Universität, wo, nach meiner Meinung, eine sehr langweilige Politik gelesen wird." Stenographischer Bericht vom 16. Oktober 1848. Quoted in: *Der Vorkampf deutscher Einheit und Freiheit*, ed. T. Klein (Langewiese-Brandt, Ebenhausen-München und Leipzig, 1914), 316.

ist ideology. With few exceptions and minor modifications, this political characterization is also true for the universities at the time of the Weimar Republic. Most professors and most students kept their distance from democracy, and some of them attacked the new political order whenever possible. Thus they helped to pave the way to the dictatorship of the Nazis, whose policy and ideology abolished academic freedom and quite often destroyed academic excellence.[2]

It is difficult to say whether the historical role of German universities before 1945 is of any importance for their present position in contemporary political culture. My impression is that for most Germans there is not much more left than a vague remembrance of former academic greatness and an ill feeling as far as the political responsibility for the past is concerned. This is the consequence of the deep historical break of 1945, which, like an abyss of error and shame, separates contemporary Germany, in both East and West, from a past that inevitably seems to have led up to criminal megalomania and well-deserved catastrophe. In fact, remarkable and important changes have taken place that distinguish present-day German society from what was regarded as typically German. However, what people think or feel is not necessarily identical with what really influences their thinking and their behavior. At least, the inclination to base political decisions and political actions on theoretical, preferably philosophical, grounds and to pursue aims thus defined with zeal and rigor, regardless of what reality may require, is still a prominent feature of German politics.

In any case, it is probably true to say that the present position of German universities in contemporary political culture is predominantly shaped by postwar history, particularly by the late 1960s and the developments that then began. In both parts of Germany, 1968 was the most decisive year in postwar academic life and marked a turning point, although in East Germany the changes brought about at that time had been systematically prepared by those who had been in power since 1945. There have been, to be

2. For a concise treatment of the history of the German university from the time of Wilhelm von Humboldt up to the modern reforms, see D. Fallon, *The German University: A Heroic Ideal in Conflict with the Modern World* (Boulder, CO, 1980).

precise, two separate and contrasting ways of history in East and West Germany for which this year was so important. I do not consider it my task to describe these two historical ways, but rather to characterize and to compare their effects and results as far as they may help to explain the present political role of German universities. These effects, however, are still so different in East and West, in spite of the fundamental changes in East Germany during the last five years, that I am going to deal with West German universities and East German universities separately.

I start with the West German universities because for obvious reasons their contribution to political culture is by far the most important. What I intend to say is of course in many ways determined by the fact that I am an East German. It was through the eyes of West German television reports that I observed what was happening at West German universities in 1968 and in the following years and although most of these reports more or less openly supported the cause of reform, I saw them in a context of East German experience and my initial sympathy with the student movement soon gave way to anger and fury. I was forced to live behind the Wall and could not understand how thousands of young people were obviously ready to abandon the chances of a liberal democracy in favor of a utopia that I, as the result of bitter personal experience, had learned to regard as an illusion and a sham. Later I understood that in spite of revolutionary tendencies and activities that I found appalling, the events of 1968 had really introduced a new phase in the development of West German democracy and helped to strengthen liberal elements in its political order. At this time the universities undoubtedly played a leading role in shaping the intellectual climate in West Germany and, hence, made an important and lasting contribution to the political culture of the 1970s and 1980s.

As far as I can see, this contribution can be defined as follows. First of all, up to the late 1960s society and education in West Germany had continued German tradition, and, accordingly, had been strongly elitist – both in structure and in the underlying concepts. The beginnings of the students' protest had their basis in the demand for a broader access to the educational opportunities, which, in turn, were regarded as the first steps upwards on the social ladder. Fundamental educational reform, particularly the reform of secondary and tertiary education, had not only the aim to open doors that so far had practically been closed to many young people and to offer them a possibility of advancement, but, since in this way the general degree of social mobility was increased, educational policy was also regarded as a means of achieving social change. It was this anti-elitist concept of education and its explicit social consequences that gave the reform movement its mass basis. Claims have been formulated and expectations have been awakened that until now make it difficult in West Germany to argue in favor of standards and excellence.

The anti-elitist trend was strongly coupled with anti-authoritarian concepts of education and society. In spite of the experiences of Nazi dictatorship and the growing acceptance of Western democray in the Federal Republic, the traditionally strong role of authority in Germany, both in education and in society, had so far not really been questioned. The two father figures of the Federal Republic, Konrad Adenauer, the Chancellor and leader of the Christian Democrats, and Kurt Schumacher, the chairman of the Social Democratic Party and leader of the opposition, had both been strong personalities without any hesitation to use power and leadership for what they had regarded as necessary and justified. The claim to authority and the acceptance of authority were basic elements of German life. Now, there was an increasing tendency to put any claim to authority on trial with the clear aim to demolish it – a trend that was, of course, eagerly taken up by the young generation. Furthermore, as personal authority is usually based on a position in the political hierarchy or in social or academic structures, this trend was coupled with an increasing emphasis on individual rights and liberties versus the demands and expectations of society and tradition. Eventually, this development would result in a change of the delicate balance between individual rights and general duties that had been achieved in the constitution of 1949. The principle of liberal democracy was soon no longer regarded as a political ideal of common action but became a justification of expanding the scope for the individual pursuit of personal happiness and self-fulfillment.

The new anti-authoritarian tendency went together with a highly critical approach to German history. Although the political parties in the Federal Republic, with the exception of a tiny minority, had been unanimous in condemning the crimes of Hitler and the Nazis, particularly the murderous persecution of the Jews, and although it was generally recognized that Germany alone had to accept the responsibility for the Second World War, there was a widespread tendency to forget the past and, instead, to concentrate on the task of reconstruction and of securing economic success. A popular view was that in some mysterious way an uneducated man named Hitler and a small clique of clowns and criminals had got hold of Germany. Now, however, everything was again in order and West Germany, that was soon to become identified with Germany, had a good chance to become the good boy of the Western world.

In the mid-1960s, however, after an economic miracle had been achieved and a democratic order had been established, an increasing number of people, particularly of the young generation, demanded a critical examination of how the Nazi dictatorship and their crimes had been possible. This tendency got an additional impetus when it was discovered that the authority of quite a few professors and politicians could be easily undermined by having a closer look at what they had written and what they had done between 1933 and 1945. Meanwhile, more than two decades had passed since the catastrophe of 1945 – time enough for the young people to know nothing from personal experience, and this enabled them to pursue their tactics with the righteousness of ignorance that is so easily tempted to pose as innocence. This proved to be extremely successful because in fact many of the older generation had, for some reason or other, if only at some time, supported or cooperated with the Nazis. And who else than those who had been in prisons, concentration camps, or in exile, could have the nerve to maintain that they were innocent?

Since these tactics was so extremely successful, the temptation became soon irresistible to extend this kind of debate to the problem of German division and to the concept of German nation. Had not national unity provided the basis for German aggressiveness? Was German division not the justified punishment for the crimes of the Nazis and the best guarantee for peace in Europe? In fact, such questions were used as killer arguments in the political debate, not only about how to see the past, but increasingly when dealing with political opponents, particularly when they were not of a left persuasion. For some people it became even fashionable to think of themselves no longer as Germans. In the late 1960s and in the early 1970s there had also been a strong wave of anti-americanism that went far beyond the criticism of the American involvement in Vietnam. To a certain extent, it acted, at that time, as a kind of countertrend and for some of the students and young intellectuals formed a bridge to their revolutionary illusions that turned Mao, Ho Chi Minh, and Che Guevarra into attractive heroes for the well-off children of a truly affluent society. Seen over the distance of more than twenty years, this was only an episode and most of the demonstrators and would-be revolution-aries returned to the comforts of a liberal and highly individualized society and to the advantages of Western democracy.[3]

I venture to suggest that the old Federal Republic, which in 1989, shortly before the fundamental changes in Eastern Europe began, celebrated the fortieth anniversary of its constitution, the *Grundgesetz*, was in many respects deeply influenced by the devel-opments at West German universities since 1968. This was my impression in the years before 1989 when I had no chance to go there and see for myself, and it has been confirmed by my experi-ences since that time. In fact, I am today more strongly convinced of this than I was seven years ago. It is true: the immediate contact between society and university had soon come to an end.

There were various reasons for the growing estrangement between academia and the public. The overwhelming majority of the people outside the universities were repelled by the revolu-tionary slogans of the demonstrations and quite often also by the behavior of the student activists, by their appearance and their language. Then the drastically increased number of students, a fashionable disdain of standards, and the low effectiveness of study programs and university governance turned the universities into unattractive and undignified mass institutions. I still remember vividly how revolting I found the appearance of university build-ings in West Berlin when I first saw them. Since there seemed to be

---

3. The aspirations of the radical left-wing students are documented, e.g., in *Die 68er*, ed. C. Seibold (Munich, 1988).

no chance for a change, most voters and taxpayers lost the patience to accept the constant complaining of universities that they would need more money. As one of my West German friends once said to me: "This is a kind of system into which you may throw a billion marks, and you wouldn't even hear a bump." Last, but not least, it was the aggressive strategy of student activists, particularly of the extreme left-wing, which drove representatives of the so-called establishment, that is, practically of any important political party or organization out of the universities. By tiny militant minorities the academic institutions were – practically by force – prevented from serving as a stage for politicians and thus from providing a forum for the political debate of the society. Although such events have become less frequent, their effects will be felt for a long time, and such things haven't disappeared at all. In 1991 I had the plea-sure to attend a meeting at the Free University of Berlin, which the students quite deliberately turned into a kind of irrational hap-pening. One year later West Germans set up an extremist group in Dresden that started their activities by trying to break up a meet-ing with Willy Brandt. They failed in their attempt, because in Dresden they were totally isolated.

Although as a result of all this, West German universities have been separated from the mainstream of political debate in West German society for quite a long time, the political culture of this society, at least when represented by academics, intellectuals, and journalists, is nevertheless to a large degree the product of the development for which the year 1968 has become the most impor-tant symbol. I would like to specify this in a twofold way – posi-tively and negatively. On the one hand, it was not to a small extent a result of the mental and intellectual changes starting in the late 1960s that the Federal Republic, forty years after her foundation, could proudly consider itself to be not only one of the most pros-perous, economically most successful and politically most stable countries of the Western world, but also as one of the most liberal and democratic as well as one of the least nationalistic countries – certainly the best political order the Germans so far had ever had in their history. On the other hand, it was undoubtedly also the result of 1968 that the West Germans in the same year, that is, when they celebrated the anniversary of their constitution, were blissfully unaware of what the developments in Eastern Europe really meant and, as a necessary consequence, were gloriously unprepared for German unity and for the new historical challenges resulting from the radically changed international situation.

The same factors that had determined the role of the universities in West German political culture up to 1989 also explain their present position. However, the context has dramatically changed. West German universities are still strongholds of liberal individualism and at a time when some people may hope to turn back history and to forget about its lessons, the importance of this should not be underestimated. At the same time, however, liberal individualism today quite often stands for not much more than a mixture of privileges and ideology – a mixture that has become so characteristic of West German society and makes it highly immobile and unwilling to accept the necessity of change and reform. Germany struggles with an enormous range of problems, and practically every aspect of social and political life requires a reassessment to find solutions in the spirit of freedom, democracy, and social justice. But the role of the universities in this debate, I am sorry to say, is almost negligible. I am very grateful to many West German professors who made a great personal effort and provided valuable help in the reform process of the East German universities, but the intellectual or theoretical contribution of the universities to the difficult tasks of national unification, possibly with the exception of university reform, is hardly noticeable. For a larger part of the academic community, particularly in the humanities and in the social sciences, the course of history has refuted their expectations. Reality proved them wrong and they find it difficult to face up to reality. It may sound ridiculous, but sometimes one gets the impression that they feel hurt and offended by what unexpectedly happened.

Furthermore, the great promise of social change through education has lost its appeal. Too many drop-outs and, in addition, thousands of students who are practically no longer studying, if they ever had the real intention to do that, impair the reputation of the universities. At the same time the universities have to grapple with the lowering of standards that too often accompanies the increase in number of those who, according to German tradition, on the basis of the Gymnasium diploma called the *Abitur* have a legal right to be admitted to whatever course they want to study. Last but not least, the attempt to make the universities a model of free discourse and general participation in decision making did not transform the traditional *Ordinarienuniversität* (university of full professors) into an academic democracy. Instead, the so-called *Gruppenuniversität* too often turns out to be a farce, because the majority of the students are not interested in participation, while at the same time the decision-making process is too slow and the management is not effective enough for such a complex organism as a modern university. Hence, neither as a center of intellectual life, nor as a forum of public debate, nor as an example of democratic participation or of effective leadership, are the present-day West German universities really able to exert a decisive influence on contemporary political culture.

For obvious reasons the role played by East German universities in present-day political life is even smaller than that of West German universities. Also for them the year 1968 marked a turning point, though in a totally different direction. It is true that already in the years before 1968 the Soviet authorities and the communist leadership in East Germany had taken important steps to gain influence on academic life. Thus, in 1951 they had introduced the study of Marxism-Leninism as a compulsory subject for all degree courses. And of course communists or their fellow-travelers had quite soon taken up the leading positions of university management and in such politically relevant fields as law and economics. An increasing number of scholars had left East Germany or had been forced to give up their professorial chairs, particularly in the humanities and in the social sciences, including such outstanding figures of the intellectual left as Hans Mayer and Ernst Bloch. But the core of the universities had remained intact and for a long time it would have been possible to overcome the effects of communist penetration comparatively easily.

This was changed drastically by the so-called third university reform of 1968, which abolished the last elements of academic autonomy, made Marxism-Leninism quite officially the basis of any kind of academic teaching and research, and quite explicitly put the university under immediate party control. It would of course be very naive to take the official proclamations of political power and ideological leadership at their face value. By and large the East German universities continued to be places of serious work, and not seldom really excellent teaching and research was done there, but at the same time they were functioning as important institutions for spreading ideology and buttressing the policy of the party leadership. In this respect the East German universities undoubtedly played a significant role in the official political life of the GDR. I hesitate to use the term political culture in this context. The East German universities had definitely been much more integrated into the system of party dictatorship than the Polish or the Hungarian universities. And when I was at the Lomonossov University of Moscow for an academic term, in 1979, I had the impression that even there the grip of the party was not so firm as I was used to, although this may have been due to the difference between German thoroughness and Slavonic liberality. Probably in any dictatorship bureaucratic sloppiness is the biggest chance for the simple individuals who are forced to enjoy the blessings of such a kind of political rule.[4]

In any case, the East German universities did not have any share in preparing the revolutionary change of 1989. On the contrary, their offical representatives were among those who even after the decisive events in October 1989 tried to stem the rising tide of protests and demonstrations and to avoid the total collapse of the stumbling regime. There had, however, been growing unrest within the universities, particularly since it had become obvious that the East German party leadership made the stupid attempt of stabilizing their rule by keeping a critical distance from their Soviet allies and protectors and to their policy of glasnost and perestrojka. Starting in the second half of October 1989 there was an increasing number of activities of students and of nonprofessorial staff members to bring about a change also at the universities. Thus, in November 1989 the communist youth organization at the Humboldt University in East Berlin had to give way to a freely elected student council. This was followed by demands to work out new

---

4. A well-balanced analysis is given in *Bericht der Enquetekommission des Deutschen Bundestages der 12. Wahlperiode "Aufarbeitung von Geschichte und Folgen der SED-Diktatur in Deutschland"* (Drucksache 12/7820), 68-74.

university statutes and to hold elections for the academic bodies. In February 1990 – to give another example – the Technical University of Dresden elected a new rector and a new academic senate. I could go on this way and it may sound like a success story. In reality, however, the development was a highly complex and contradictory one and it comprised a number of partially overlapping trends, that quite often were represented by the same persons.

First of all, there was a widespread demand to introduce equal participation of all university groups, particularly of the students, the assistants, and the professors, in all university bodies. This clearly followed the example set by the events of 1968 in West Germany. At the same time there was a strong effort to return to the traditional structures and forms of academic life that had been abolished in the same year by the East German communists. Interestingly, representatives of the old regime could be found among the supporters of both directions – either to preserve the East German universities as bastions of radical left-wing thought or to use rediscovered academic autonomy as a shelter against change and reform. On the whole, the old forces were on the retreat, though still quite powerful. The champions of a true reform of the East German universities came from the students and, particularly, from the non-professorial academic workers, the so-called *akademischer Mittelbau*, who quite often were openly critical of the professoriate whose composition had of course been influenced by the communist party. The impetus of the university reform movement was, however, seriously impaired when it became clear how deeply the secret police had penetrated the university staff and that also some supporters of the reform seemed to have been among the informers.

Quite apart from developments within the universities, there was a deep public mistrust that the universities themselves would be able and willing to put academic things right. In fact, when in November and December 1990 the newly elected governments of the restored East German *Länder*, on the basis of the Unification Treaty, decided not take over some university departments, for example in law, economics, and philosophy, but to dissolve them and to establish totally new ones, there were passionate protests from the students who regarded this as an intervention into their own affairs and as a violation of academic rights. Outside the universities, however, there was wide support for these decisions. In fact, if at that time the governments had proposed to dissolve all universities and to have a totally new start in academic life, they would have had a comfortable majority. There was a wide gap, indeed, at that time between the universities, on the one hand, and the public, on the other. Let me add that in my view such a radical decision would have been a terrible mistake and I am glad that it was possible to avoid it. In any case it was clear that only a radical reform of the East German universities could bring back public support and respect.[5]

Meanwhile the reform of the East German universities has been successfully completed, academic autonomy has been fully restored, and over the last two years public recognition has slowly, but constantly, returned. There is a growing awareness of how important the universities are for providing a reliable basis for economic recovery. So far, however, public support and respect are almost exclusively based on what the universities can offer as specific products of academic teaching and research, i.e., as specialist competence and new findings and inventions. In particular, this pertains to the natural sciences and to engineering. At the same time, the universities have still a long way to go before they will again be generally recognized as centers of intellectual life. Such a position, however, would be the prerequisite for having a major influence on contemporary political culture. An influence on contemporary political culture would primarily have its basis in the work of the humanities and the social sciences.

The question is: Why is the influence of these academic fields still so weak in East Germany, although most of them have been radically reformed and although East Germany and the united Germany in general are brimming over with burning issues and unsolved problems? In my view, the answer could be this: As a result of the reform the professoriate in the humanities and in the

---

5. H.-J. Meyer, *Die Hochschulen in den neuen Ländern. Eine problemorientierte Bilanz* (Dresden, 1994). A critical approach to the recent history of higher education in East Germany is shown by most contributions in *IV. Hochschulreform*, ed. P. Pasternack (Leipzig, 1993). Cf also the bibliography of books and similar publications in *DDR-Wissenschaftsgeschichte & Umbau von Hochschule und Wissenschaft in Ostdeutschland*, ed. P. Pasternak (Leipzig, 1994).

social sciences now comprises people from West Germany and from East Germany. This mixture could be fruitful and will, as I hope, soon prove to be fruitful. So far, however, West Germans are still trying to understand the part of the country that until 1989 they practically did not know. This has proved to be more difficult than most of them expected. In addition, they have been called from the old Federal Republic to East Germany as carriers of urgently needed competence and experience. Practically all of their time is devoted to the task of passing on their competence. This explains why some of the newly appointed faculties, e.g., in law, still look and behave like foreign aid people in a third world country.

The East Germans, on the other hand, have either been appointed from the so-called *Mittelbau* or have happily survived as professors. For them the years after 1989 have been a combination of euphoria, shock therapy, and a crash course in Western lifestyles. Quite often they are in their present academic positions because in the past they – deliberately or following their interest – avoided general themes but did remarkable work on highly specialized topics. Quite a few of them, although they kept a critical distance from the former regime and accepted a short way to unity, had not really expected to be reduced to the role of newcomers to a complete society, the basic knowledge of which they still haven't quite mastered, yet they loathe being regarded as somebody defending the GDR or being ridiculed as one of these constantly complaining, ungrateful, and weeping *Ossis*. While the former West Germans still lack orientation in East Germany, the East Germans have still to acquire competence and to develop self-confidence before dealing with fundamental issues of Western society. As a consequence, the influence of East German universities on contemporary political culture is very weak.

In many respects, the small impact of universities on public life is a new and unusual situation in German history. This situation is neither in the interest of the academic community nor in that of the public. On the contrary, there is such a vast array of problems and the insight that old models and former kinds of approach are no longer of any use is so widespread, that places of independent thought are urgently needed for thoroughly considering where we are and what has to be done. At such a time an intellectual vacuum is a real danger. Universities are the ideal places to take up fundamental challenges, because they are independent institutions and academic communities at the same time and because they provide the opportunity for interdisciplinary work. What German universities, however, first need is a sober and well-balanced reform to strengthen their capability for effective action and for competition. The prospects for such a reform are not too bad. Some people maintain that German unification had already provided a chance for reform but that, unfortunately, we missed this chance. In my view, this alleged chance is nothing other than a myth. There was not the slightest chance for an all-German university reform in 1990 or 1991, and there is a very easy way to prove this. You only need to ask people what they have in mind when they speak of university reform and you will soon find out that the university reform that is alleged to have been made possible by German unity is nothing but a cover term for a wide variety of highly differentiated and often directly conflicting ideas. And then you should ask how this university reform should have come about and you will detect the good old German absence of any sense of political realism.

I am convinced that the conditions for a realistic university reform in Germany are still ripening. What we probably first need is a better understanding of the new challenges that will arise for our West European societies from the increased competition of the new economies in Eastern Europe and in Southeast Asia. I could also say what we need is more pressure and less complacency. For such a reform the East German universities are well prepared. They know what radical changes mean. This experience could prove their first valuable contribution to contemporary German political culture.

There are three conditions that must be fulfilled if the universities should again make a significant contribution to German political culture. First of all, they must develop a corporate identity to give a new sense to the concept of academic autonomy, which so far has been almost only considered as the administrative frame for pursuing individual academic freedom. Secondly, the universities must develop an effective structure for taking and implementing decisions as well as for developing a profile of their own. Consequently, they must be given extensive rights concerning their budget, recruitment of professors and academic staff, and determining working conditions. Thirdly, the universities need competition – not only in research, but also in teaching. That would require having the right to select their students, or at least a large percentage of them, according to criteria defined by the faculties. Also in the future, this admission should be decided on the basis of *Abitur* examination results, so that the *Abitur* would then be treated as both a necessary qualification and a specific achievement report, but no longer as a legal claim. What we need is competition among the universities to get the best young people and among young people to get to the best universities. Only if universities face the necessity to be effective communities of cultural conflict and cultural consensus and only if they are given the chance to develop into such communities, can they set an example for society and propose convincing concepts for meeting the challenges of the future.

DISCUSSION

JACK SEYMOUR: I would like to comment about the situation in 1968, which you feel had such a profound impact on the German state. There were other things that were going on at the same time that could also have had this impact. I think especially of the election of 1969. There is an argument that can be made that Germany entered into the community of modern nation states for the first time in its history in 1969, because it was in that year that for the first time there was a significant transfer of power from one political party to another through democratic mechanisms. That had never really happened before in Germany. In fact I think my recollection of it is as an outsider watching Germany at the time and reading the magazines was that you could almost sense German citizens holding their breath when the SPD, of all parties, took power. And the world went on, and didn't collapse, and the buildings didn't get burned down. When that happened, people relaxed, and they began to function. From that point forward, Germany became a functioning democratic society. That happened at the same time as the occurrences that were going in the university, but they also had in my view a very profound impact on German public life.

MITCHELL ASH: I, too, have a question primarily directed to the impact of 1968. As I noted the list of things which you were attributing to 1968, and the list got longer and longer, I kept asking myself just what the connections of some of these things were. In particular, I want to focus on one of them. There is surely consensus on the point that the West Germans had become progressively ignorant of Eastern Germany and were therefore unprepared for unification, so my question is not addressed to that. But I wonder about the degree to which this quite obvious fact can be attributed to the universities.

There are two ways of looking at this, it seems to me. On the one hand, one could suggest that university scholars' ignorance of East

Germany was due to illusions that they shared with people who were not in the university. So one has to ask, can we really attribute the widespread ignorance to the universities alone? That's one possible question. A second one is more focused. It relates to the large institutions for *Deutschlandforschung* that were set up in some of West German the universities and did provide a steady stream of research reports. Now, these research reports have since come under very scathing attack, as you know. Many people have accused these scholars of preaching what was called the convergence theory and therefore not fomenting ignorance but misinformation about East Germany. Well, we can't have it both ways. Either the university fomented ignorance or it fomented misinformation.

A third possibility is that these institutes were providing information that was not entirely wrong, but was ignored by the political leadership of the West German state for its own reasons. This is the option of the three that I actually favor. There was a lot of information out there about Eastern Germany which could have been quite helpful, in particular in economic policy, that was simply not used by the German government when the time came to implement postunification policies. This is a separate debate. All I am trying to suggest is that there is a problem with the logic of attributing ignorance of East Germany, which no one denies existed, to the university.

EDWARD LARKEY: Along those lines, I'd like to ask how you set up this model whereby the West Germans need to become acquainted with the East German system. I would submit that if that was going to happen along, let's say, more democratic lines than it has up until now, that it could be facilitated by incorporating more of those who were at the universities before the *Wende* into the university structure afterwards and not just implementing, to put it crassly, a complete takeover of East German universities by West Germans on a wholesale basis. What is happening now is that to a great extent East German social experience is not being funneled into a unified German historical consciousness. I wonder if the university is not a reflection of the way that structure has been implemented through unification. It seems to me that it is, just judging from the kinds of people who were taken over, for example, at the Humboldt University or at the University of Leipzig. The most recent example I know is in the Forschungsschwerpunkt Zeithistorische Studien in Potsdam, where very competent historians from East Germany are not employed any longer because their usefulness has expired and they could then leave. There seem to be a lot of difficulties with incorporating East Germans into the system as it is now developing.

HANS-JOACHIM MEYER: First of all, let me emphasize that I see the importance of the elections of 1969, and I would like to make it quite clear that it was not my intention to give a one-sided presentation. I pointed out the enormous influence on the unfolding of a liberal democracy in West Germany resulting from this, quite apart from the fact that there were trends which I openly loathed and disliked.

With regard to the point Mitchell Ash raised, my point is not ignorance or misinformation. My point is that people developed an outlook, starting in 1968 and the years after this, of intentional uninterest. This is something totally different from ignorance or misinformation. Speaking about being interested in national history or in national unity as having something to do with the attempt to restore German imperialism, to put it bluntly, this is the point. It was possible to analyze data and facts, and of course there might have been some people in research who knew better. Of course I know that the West German government was also not interested. The point is that the outlook which developed out of the anti-elitist trend and then the anti-authoritarian viewpoint is a break with what is regarded as typical German tradition. This was then used as a weapon in the internal political debate, so that already the accusation that people were still pursuing the aim of reaching German unification was a weapon against the political opponent in West Germany. That's the point, not misinformation or ignorance, but being uninterested as a result of a quite definite outlook.

It is difficult to answer your question, Mr. Larkey. You are referring to scholars covered by the *Wissenschaftler-Integrations-Programm* (discussed in Chapter 4), which is a very difficult matter. Let me say a few words in this context. I think it was this morning that again the suspicion was expressed that there was a separation of teaching and research in East German universities, which is simply not true. This is one of those myths which have been deliberately invented and spread by representatives of West German science and by journalists. The representatives of West German science were pursuing, bluntly speaking, I presume, two different kinds of aims. The first aim was to use this claim as a good argument in the fight for distributing money. The second is that it has long been the aim of representatives of the universities to reintegrate, to reincorporate important fields of research into the universities. They had the illusion that the time of German unity would be a good chance to do that. They had this fantastic idea that it would be possible to push all of the potential of the academy institutes back into the East German universities.

This was, as I said, nonsense. First of all, the number of research institutes which had really been transferred in 1968 from East German universities to East German academies of sciences probably could be counted on the fingers of one hand. From the very start, the ministers of the East German *Länder* were warning that this whole program wouldn't work, because at a time when we were forced by fiscal constraints to reduce the size of academic staff of the universities, it was totally impossible to integrate 2,000 scientists into the universities. So this program was doomed to failure. I can't speak about Potsdam, I can only say that we tried to keep as many of the East German colleagues as we could in the universities. Speaking about Saxony, I can only say that roughly 70 percent of the professors of all of the academic institutions come from the so-called new *Länder*, mostly from Saxony, and about 30 percent from West Germany or from abroad. I think this is a fair percentage. Of course, I know that in some fields, particularly in law or economics, the percentage of people coming from West Germany is much higher. If I remember correctly, of the professors of the department of economics at Leipzig University, there are two East German professors, from the amount of I think 16.

You spoke about experience. I would use the term competence, or incompetence. It is difficult to develop competence for a society and for a political order, for a totally different kind of state, when living in a socialist type of state, provided that people were really interested in doing this, which I doubt. There are exceptions; let me give an example. When I think of the dean of the law department at Humboldt University in East Berlin (Rosemarie Will), she certainly proved to be qualified quite apart from the fact that I do not share her political views. Quite certainly she is competent and highly qualified for her field, but these are exceptions.

STEVEN MULLER: I would like to ask you a question on the basis of what you said. The question is very short and simple. I will ask it and then I will say a few words to justify the question. That will give you a chance to think over whether you want to answer it and how. The question is whether German professors should continue to be civil servants of the *Land*. It is interesting that while you said 1945 really was a new beginning with very little reflection back on the past, you also said before you got to that point that in the period after 1948, the politics of the universities became essentially a combination of conservatism – liberal conservatism, I guess – and nationalism.

HANS-JOACHIM MEYER: It was at the turn of the century.

STEVEN MULLER: To the best of my knowledge, you know, that's absolutely right and it makes some sense. Germany having not been a single nation in the past, one can understand why that would be. That would have been different if Germany had been a state for three centuries. What happened afterwards is that during the Weimar period, you said that professors and students were, if anything, opposed to the Republic, and would have preferred a more stable, conservative approach. Then, of course, one wonders what on earth happened to the Humboldt mythos under Hitler. But at the beginning, there was a change in government toward what looked like a more conservative order and the civil servants went along with the government. After they did that, then the whole thing ended.

Now nothing surprising has happened since, because during the period after the economic miracle in West Germany, when there was money, money was spent, the establishment gained a lot of strength. Sixty-eight placed new demands, but interestingly enough, after 1968 in the West, the money was there to make it a less elitist and more comprehensive system, which is good. What happened in the East, of course, was that the state through the party took complete control. You would hardly expect twenty years after the third higher education reform in '68, the universities which were SED creatures would become leaders of the movement to overthrow the government, especially since that new elite had a lot to lose. So that all makes sense.

But all this does raise an interesting question in terms of your solutions, with which I obviously wholeheartedly agree. Developing a corporate identity, developing an effective decision-making process, which must include financial control as well, and living with competition in research and teaching: is all that best done by civil servants as professors?

HANS-JOACHIM MEYER: Before I answer your question, I think it's only fair to say that at present, in Saxony, I am passionately defending this position because there is quite considerable pressure within parliament and within the cabinet to reduce the positions which are reserved for civil servants. That is to say, there is quite a strong group who would have preferred not to make Saxony's professors of Saxony civil servants. Probably, if I hadn't had the support of the prime minister or the minister president in this respect who, as you of course know, is a professor himself, I probably wouldn't have been successful. My argument at present is that it is not possible for an individual in West Germany and quite certainly not for an East German one to change the system. We would lose the competition. We would not get scholars and scientists of standing to Saxony. On the contrary, we would lose our people to other lands, or we would have to have much more money for the individual professor. This is possible, as you know. Most professors of the Max Planck Society are not civil servants, but they are much more expensive. So I'm talking about the present situation. Now, about the future.

If demanding that the universities become truly autonomous institutions necessarily implies that professors can no longer be civil servants, the still unsolved problem in my view is, how to guarantee or how to bridge this tension between civil service standing and personal independence, which in my view is necessary for academic freedom. At least there should be a core in the university of personally independent persons to pursue what they regard as necessary and true, but at the same time, to keep up the demand of showing excellence. As far as I can see, this problem has not yet been solved. Of course, in order to convince people that professors should no longer be civil servants, one needs a convincing model in other respects, including financing.

So to answer your question, as part of the aim to achieve true academic autonomy, it is no longer possible to have professors as civil servants, but we must have a model. We must find a system which will guarantee personal independence of the leading, the responsible academic personnel of the university in order to guarantee academic freedom.

STEVEN MULLER: And Max Planck is not a model?

HANS-JOACHIM MEYER: Yes, but this is an independent society and they solved this problem simply with more money.

STEVEN MULLER: It's not a bad way to solve problems.

HANS-JOACHIM MEYER: Of course. Could I add one word? At present, there is a very interesting debate in Germany, a debate which comes from the *Wissenschaftsrat*, the *Hochschulrektorenkonferenz* and the *Kultusministerkonferenz*, concerning the future structure of medicine, or rather of medical institutions. The question is, what will be the position of the clinic director, the *Chefarzt*, in the future? You know that it will be necessary to separate teaching and research from normal clinical treatment. In order to do this, the financial and legal position of the *Chefarzt*, the clinic director, has to be totally redefined. I think that as a result of this attempt, we could also have some insight into how this could also be done with the other professors, or at least with a majority of them.

RAINER KÜNZEL: I would also like to express my view on this particular question. I understand the fiscal argument, the present-day fiscal argument, because state employees are more expensive than civil servants. So there is a problem. But in principle, I am convinced that professors should not be civil servants. They should be state employees or employees of the university. If it's a completely state-financed university, they are indirectly state employees, but it doesn't really matter. They should be employees, but they should not be paid on the basis of tariffs negotiated between government and trade unions, because that implies so many difficulties that I think it would be an impossible situation. The reason for my position on that question is that Article 33 of the German constitution requires obedience to the principles of civil service law, meaning that civil servants are treated as subordinate persons in a hierarchy of a state bureaucracy. That is in conflict with the freedom of thought and speech, which is essential for the position of a scientist or a professor at the university. In the past, we have had several phases when controversy between professors and state representatives was decided on the basis of Article 33 to the disadvantage of the professors or other civil servants involved in this debate.

MITCHELL ASH: I want to begin by responding to a point made in Edward Larkey's question that we haven't really discussed adequately yet. You were expressing the fear that there would be a lack of East German social experience funneled into the creation of a common German historical consciousness. I think it is very apposite in this setting to reflect on this. I think an appropriate response to your fear needs to take note of two things.

First of all, I think we need to be aware of the danger of confusing the part for the whole. What I mean by that is the number of German history professors who are from Eastern Germany is not really a direct indicator of how much East German social experience is going to be funneled into the creation of a common German historical consciousness. This is not true for German society as a whole, and it is certainly not the case in the universities, either. The figures that were reported in my talk yesterday indicate that more than half and in some universities more than two-thirds of the professoriate as a whole in the new states are from East Germany. They are not historians, this is correct, but they will still be bringing their experiences into common discussions. To what extent they will actually do this in the public arena remains to be seen.

But the second aspect of the answer in response to your fear does focus on the case of the historians themselves. It was quite difficult, and I think their case is quite unique. There is, after all, no shortage of published historical reflection on the GDR. But much of it is coming from the fringes of academia, from journalists and from writers and from people just reporting their own experiences, not so much from historians. There are, however, massive research programs underway in the historical institutes for a history of the GDR. There is a group in Mannheim that keeps a list, and there are about 750 projects on that list. So there is not going to be any shortage of historical reflection on the GDR. There is a hot debate about who should carry out such reflection, and I think there we have to be very cautious about taking a position of the sort that says, only Eastern Germans are qualified to write the history of the GDR. That could be disastrous for German political culture.

HANS-JOACHIM MEYER: And vice versa.

MITCHELL ASH: Yes, the opposite position could be equally disastrous. I think what's required is collaborative work in which perhaps West German historians are going to take a leading role for certain obvious reasons, but the best work will come from projects directed by Western German historians who are reflective about and sensitive to the problem you have raised, and are therefore inclusive in the construction of their research teams. There are such West German historians. Jürgen Kocka, the founding director of the Forschungsschwerpunkt Zeithistorische Studien, is one of them. So I think that your fears, although they have a certain basis, will not be justified in the longer term.

Concluding Remarks

MITCHELL ASH: My summary begins with the point that I made at the end of my talk, and which Minister Meyer also addressed in his talk. What we have been talking about in this conference so far have been largely questions of institutional and structural change – the history and the role of the German universities as institutions. Only at times have we focused upon the question of political culture that was the central topic today. But the real challenge for the future, it seems to me, is to respond to the challenge of unification precisely by endeavoring to create a common German political culture, to overcome this *Mauer im Kopf* – the wall in the head – this image that was created by journalists and has had a powerful impact not only on journalistic discussion but on people's thinking about these issues. The East German universities are a logical place to begin trying to find ways of symbolically representing the overcoming of that divide. I think there are people trying to do that.

A second challenge is the one that Steven Muller so eloquently put to us just a short time ago, the challenge of the technological culture of the future. This is a challenge that is addressed not to the new Germany, of course, but to the whole postindustrial world. The Germans have been, however, quite remarkably slow in responding to it. Whether that is necessarily a bad thing is an interesting question that we haven't really discussed. German industrialization happened very rapidly, but it didn't happen first. There are certain advantages to waiting and seeing what other countries make in the way of mistakes and then organizing it better. Now, whether that's what the Germans are really going to do remains to be seen.

FRANK TROMMLER: The history of using the United States in German debates to get momentum going is a long one. This tendency was certainly stronger in the 1960s and 1970s, when many West Germans went to the United States and saw some models that they could follow, not just in the university area but in industry and business as well. Very often, even if the Germans talked to each other, if it took place on American soil, it already had the aura of a momentum brought back to Germany. This is something that one should see as a very fruitful history. It is a very important part of the development of a free democratic society in the Federal Republic, now including the new states. Perhaps this could even be applied to this conference. It will not be the great jump start for reform, but at least it should be seen as a dialogue that should go on, and that become fruitful through deeper reflection on these issues in the future.

SELECTED BIBLIOGRAPHY

General Readings on German Universities

Becker, W., Bode, C., and Klofat, R., eds. *Universitäten in Deutschland – Universities in Germany*. 1995.

Handbuch der deutschen Bildungsgeschichte, 5 vols., C. Berg, A Buck, and C. Führ, eds. Munich, 1989-1994.

Daxner, M. *Ist die Uni noch zu retten? Zehn Vorschläge und eine Vision*. Reinbek bei Hamburg, 1996.

Fallon, D. *The German University: A. Heroic Ideal in Conflict with the Modern World*. Boulder, CO, 1980.

Glotz, P. *Im Kern verottet? Fünf vor zwölf an Deutschlands Universitäten*. Stuttgart, 1996.

Goldschmidt, D. *Die gesellschaftliche Herausforderung der Universität. Historische Analysen, internationale Vergleiche, globale Perspektiven.* Weinheim, 1991.

Jarausch, K. *Deutsche Studenten 1800-1970*. Frankfurt a.M., 1984.

Mittelstraß, J. *Die unzeitgemäße Universität*. Frankfurt a.M., 1994.

Ritter, G. A. *Großforschung und Staat in Deutschland*. Munich, 1992.

Schriewer, J., Keiner, E., and Charle, C., eds. *Sozialer Raum und akademische Kulturen. Studien zur europäischen Hochschul- und Wissenschaftsgeschichte im 19. und 20. Jahrhundert*. Frankfurt a.M., 1993.

Strobel, K., ed. *Die deutsche Universität im 20. Jahrhundert*. Greifswald, 1994.

Suggested Readings for Chapter 1:
A Slow Farewell to Humboldt?
Stages in the History of German Universities, 1810-1945

Bollenbeck, G. *Bildung und Kultur. Glanz und Elend eines deutschen Deutungsmusters*, 2nd ed. Frankfurt a.M., 1994.

vom Bruch, R. *Wissenschaft, Politik und öffentliche Meinung. Gelehrten-politik im Wilhelminischen Deutschland (1890-1914)*. Husum, 1980.

vom Bruch, R. *Autonomie der Universität – Gelegentliche Bemerkungen zu einem Grundproblem deutscher Universitätsgeschichte* (Beiträge zur Geschichte der Humboldt Universität zu Berlin, no. 31). Berlin, 1993.

vom Bruch, R., Graf, F. W., and Hübinger, G., eds. *Kultur und Kulturwissenschaften um 1900. Krise der Moderne und Glaube an die Wissenschaft*. Stuttgart, 1989.

vom Bruch, R. and Müller, R. A., eds. *Formen außerstaatlicher Wissenschaftsförderung im 19. und 20. Jahrhundert. Deutschland im europäischen Vergleich*. Stuttgart, 1990.

Harwood, J. *Styles of Scientific Thought. The German Genetic Community 1900-1933*. Chicago and London, 1993.

Jarausch, K. *Students, Society and Politics in Imperial Germany. The Rise of Academic Illiberalism*. Princeton, 1982.

Jeismann, K.-E., ed. *Bildung, Staat, Gesellschaft im 19. Jahrhundert. Mobilisierung und Disziplinierung*. Stuttgart, 1989.

Johnson, J. A. *The Kaiser's Chemists. Science and Modernization in Imperial Germany*. Chapel Hill and London, 1990.

Kampe, N. *Studenten und "Judenfrage" im Deutschen Kaiserreich. Die Entstehung einer akademischen Trägerschicht des Antisemitismus*. Göttingen, 1988.

McClelland, C. E. *State, Society, and University in Germany 1700-1914*. Cambridge, 1980.

Menze, C. *Die Bildungsreform Wilhelm von Humboldts*. Hanover, 1975.

Müller, R. A. *Geschichte der Universität von der mittelalterlichen Universitas zur deutschen Hochschule*. Munich, 1990.

Paulsen, F. *Die Geschichte des gelehrten Unterrichts auf den deutschen Schulen und Universitäten vom Ausgang des Mittelalters bis zur Gegenwart*, 2 vols. Berlin, 1920.

Ringer, F. K. *The Decline of the German Mandarins: The German Academic Community 1890-1933*. Cambridge, MA, 1969; German ed., *Die Gelehrten. Der Niedergang der deutschen Mandarine 1890-1933*. Stuttgart, 1983.

Schmeiser, M. *Akademischer Hasard. Das Berufsschicksal des Professors und das Schicksal der deutschen Universität 1870-1920*. Stuttgart, 1994.

Schubring, G., ed. `*Einsamkeit und Freiheit' neu besichtigt. Universitätsreformen und Disziplinenbildung in Preußen als Modell für Wissenschaftspolitik im Europa des 19. Jahrhunderts*. Stuttgart, 1991.

Suggested Readings for Chapter 2:
The Humboldt Syndrome
West German Universities 1945-1989

Allerbeck, K. *Soziologie radikaler Studentenbewegungen.* Munich, 1973.

Anrich, E. *Die Idee der deutschen Universität. Die fünf Grundschriften aus der Zeit ihrer Neugründung.* Darmstadt, 1956.

Ash, M. G. "Verordnete Umbrüche – konstruierte Kontinuitäten. Zur Entnazifizierung von Wissenschaftlern und Wissenschaften nach 1945." *Zeitschrift für Geschichtswissenschaft* 43 (1995): 903-23.

Dahrendorf, R. *Bildung ist Bürgerrecht.* Hamburg, 1965.

Hufner, K., Naumann, J., Kohler, H., and Pfeffer, G. *Hochkonjunktur und Flaute. Bildungspolitik in der Bundesrepublik Deutschland 1967-1980.* Stuttgart, 1986.

Oehler, C. *Hochschulentwicklung in der Bundesrepublik Deutschland seit 1945.* Frankfurt a.M., 1989.

Peisert, H. and Framheim, G. *Higher Education in the Federal Republic of Germany.* Bonn, 1990.

Picht, G. *Die deutsche Bildungskatastrophe.* Olten, 1964.

Rudolph, H. and Husemann, R. *Hochschulpolitik zwischen Expansion und Restriktion. Ein Vergleich der Entwicklung in der Bundesrepublik Deutschland und der Deutschen Demokratischen Republik.* Frankfurt a.M., 1984.

Schelsky, H. *Einsamkeit und Freiheit. Idee und Gestalt der deutschen Universität und ihrer Reformen.* Reinbek, 1963.

Tent, J. F. *Mission on the Rhine. Reeducation and Denazification in American-Occupied Germany.* Chicago, 1982.

Titze, H. *Der Akademikerzyklus. Historische Untersuchungen über die Wiederkehr von Überfüllung und Mangel in akademischen Karrieren.* Göttingen, 1990.

Suggested Readings for Chapter 3:
Humboldt Coopted
East German Universities, 1945-1989

Anweiler, O., et al. *Vergleich von Bildung und Erziehung in der Bundesrepublik Deutschland und in der Deutschen Demokratischen Republik.* Cologne, 1990.

Giles, G. "The Structure of Higher Education in the German Democratic Republic." *Yale Higher Education Program Working Papers,* YHEP-12. New Haven, 1976.

Glaessner, G.-J. and Rudolph, I. *Macht durch Wissen. Zum Zusammenhang von Bildungspolitik, Bildungssystem und Kaderqualifizierung in der DDR. Eine politische-soziologische Untersuchung.* Opladen, 1978.

Jessen, R. "Professoren im Sozialismus. Aspekte des Strukturwandels der Hochschullehrerschaft in der Ulbricht-Ära." In *Sozialgeschichte der DDR,* eds. H. Kaelble, J. Kocka, H. Zwar. Stuttgart, 1994.

Lonnendonker, S. *Freie Universität Berlin: Gründung einer politischen Universität.* Berlin, 1988.

Macrakis, K. and Hoffmann, D., eds. *Science under Socialism: East Germany in Comparative Perspective.* Cambridge, MA, in press.

Müller, M. and Müller, E. E. "... *stürmt die Festung Wissenschaft!" Die Sowjetisierung der Mitteldeutschen universitäten nach 1945.* Berlin, 1953.

Rexin, M. "Die Entwicklung der Wissenschaftspolitik in der DDR." In *Wissenschaft und Gesellschaft in der DDR,* ed. R. Thomas. Munich, 1971.

Richert, E. "*Sozialistische Universität": Die Hochschulpolitik der SED.* Berlin, 1967.

Schmidt, G. "Aspekte der Hochschulpolitik in der DDR." In *Das Profil der DDR in der sozialistischen Staatengemeinschaft,* eds. I. Spittmann and G. Helwig. Cologne, 1987.

Stallmann, H. *Hochschulzugang in der SBZ/DDR 1945-1959.* Bonn-St. Augustin, 1980.

Tent, J. F. *The Free University of Berlin: A Political History.* Bloomington, 1988.

Suggested Readings for Chapter 4:
Unification in German Higher Education
"Renewal" or the Importation of Crisis?

Berg, G. and Hartwich, H.-H., eds. *Martin-Luther-Universität. Von der Gründung bis zur Neugestaltung nach zwei Diktaturen.* Opladen, 1994.

Berliner Hochschulstrukturplan. Berlin, 1993.

Buck-Bechler, G. and Jahn, H., eds. *Hochschulerneuerung in den neuen Bundesländern. Bilanz nach vier Jahren.* Weinheim, 1994.

Habermas, J. *Die Normalität einer Berliner Republik.* Frankfurt a.M., 1995.

Kocka, J. *Vereinigungskrise. Zur Geschiche der Gegenwart.* Göttingen, 1995.

Küpper, M. *Die Humboldt-Universität. Einheitsschmerzen zwischen Abwicklung und Selbstreform.* Berlin, 1993.

Markovits, I. *Die Abwicklung. Ein Tagebuch zum Ende der DDR-Justiz*. Munich, 1993; English ed., *Imperfect Justice. An East-West German Diary*. New York, 1995.

Mayntz, R., ed. *Aufbruch und Reform von oben. Ostdeutsche Universitäten im Transformationsprozeß*. Frankfurt a.M., 1994.

Muszynski, B., ed. *Wissenschaftstransfer in Deutschland. Erfahrungen und Perspektiven*. Opladen, 1993.

Pasternack, P., ed. *IV. Hochschulreform. Wissenschaft und Hochschulen in Ostdeutschland 1989/90. Eine Retrospektive*. Leipzig, 1993.

Politische Kultur im vereinigten Deutschland. Der Streit um Heinrich Fink, Rektor der Humboldt-Universität zu Berlin. *Utopie kreativ*, Dokumentation. Berlin, January 1992.

Schramm, H., ed. *Hochschule im Umbruch. Zwischenbilanz Ost*. Berlin, 1993.

Schluchter, W., *Neubeginn durch Anpassung? Studien zum ostdeutschen Uebergang*. Frankfurt am Main, 1996.

Weissbuch 2. Unfrieden in Deutschland. Wissenschaft und Kultur im Beitrittsgebiet. Berlin, 1993.

Zur Situation der Universitäten und außeruniversitären Forschungsein-richtungen in den neuen Ländern. *Nova Akta Leopoldina*, Neue Folge, Nummer 290, Band 71 (1994).

Suggested Readings for Chapter 5:
Mythos Humboldt Today
Teaching, Research, and Administration

Hochschulrektorenkonferenz. *Konzept zur Entwicklung der Hochschulen in Deutschland*. Bonn, 1992.

Jauss, H. R. and Nesselhauf, H., eds. *Gebremste Reform. Ein Kapitel deutscher Hochschulgeschichte. Universität Konstanz 1966-1976*. Konstanz, 1977.

Lundgreen, P., ed. *Reformuniversität Bielefeld 1969-1994. Zwischen Defensive und Innovation*. Bielefeld, 1994.

Mikat, P. and Schelsky, H., eds. *Grundzüge einer neuen Universität. Zur Planung einer Hochschulgründung in Ostwestfalen*. Gütersloh, 1966.

Schimank, U. *Hochschulforschung im Schatten der Lehre*. Frankfurt a.M. and New York, 1995.

Westdeutsche Rektorenkonferenz. *Die Zukunft der Hochschulen. Über-legungen für eine zukunftsorientierte Hochschulpolitik*. Bonn, 1988.

Wissenschaftsrat. *Empfehlungen zum Ausbau der wissenschaftlichen Einrichtungen. Teil I: Wissenschaftliche Hochschulen*. Bonn, 1960.

Wissenschaftsrat. *Anregungen zur Gestalt neuer Hochschulen*. Bonn, 1962.

Wissenschaftsrat. *Empfehlungen zur Neuordnung des Studiums an den wissenschaftlichen Hochschulen*. Bonn, 1966.

Wissenschaftsrat. *Empfehlungen zur Struktur des Studiums*. Bonn, 1986.

Wissenschaftsrat. *Zehn Thesen zur Hochschulpolitik*. Bonn, 1993.

Readings for Chapter 6:
Political Control and Funding
The Future of State Sponsorship

Alewell, K. *Autonomie mit Augenmaß*. Göttingen, 1993.

Beckmeier, C. and Neusel, A. *Leitungsstrategien und Selbstverständnis von Hochschulpräsidenten und -rektoren*. Kassel, 1994.

Bertelsmann Stiftung, ed. *Evolution im Hochschulbereich*. Gütersloh, 1990.

Blümel, W. and Bender, I., eds. *Flexibilität der Hochschulhaushalte* (Speyerer Forschungsberichte 130). Speyer, 1993.

Blümel, W. and Bender, I., eds. *Flexibilität der Hochschulhaushalte* (Speyerer Forschungsberichte 131). Speyer, 1994.

Daxner, M. *Globalhaushalt – Mythos und Realität. Beiträge zur Hochschulforschung 2*. Munich, 1993.

Erichsen, H.-U. "Qualitätssicherung in Forschung, Lehre und Management." *Wissenschaftsmanagement*, no. 2 (1995): 61-64.

Fittschen, D., "Probleme der Hochschulleitung als Folge diffuser Aufgabenstellung." *Verwaltungsarchiv* 85, no. 3 (1994): 317-79.

Frackmann, E. "Finanzierung, Qualitätssicherung und Controling. Alternative Koordinationsmechanismen und Informationssysteme im Hochschulbereich." *Bildungsforschung und Bildungspraxis*, Sondernummer 1995.

Hanau, P. "Haushaltsrecht der Universitaten aus der Sicht der Wissenschaftler." *Mitteilungen des Deutschen Hochschullehrerverbandes*, no. 6 (1992): 361-64.

Hochschulrektorenkonferenz. *Arbeitsbericht 1993*. Bonn, 1994.

Hochschulrektorenkonferenz. *Arbeitsbericht 1994*. Bonn, 1995.

Hochschulrektorenkonferenz. Mehr Autonomie für die Hochschulen. Dokumente zur Hochschulreform 77. Bonn, 1992.

Hochschulrektorenkonferenz. *Stellungnahmen, Empfehlungen, Beschlüsse 1960-1989*, 4 vols. Bonn, 1991.

Hödl, E. and Range, V. *Finanzautonomie an der Hochschule. Zwischen Effizienz und Effektivität*. Wuppertal, 1993.

Karpen, U. and Knemeyer, F.-L. *Verfassungsprobleme des Hochschulwesens*. Paderborn, 1976.

Ministerium für Wissenschaft und Forschung des Landes Nordrhein-Westfalen. *Der Modellversuch: Hochschule und Finanzautonomie.* Düsseldorf, 1994.

Müller-Böling, D. "Qualitätsmanagement in Hochschulen." In 6. *Deutscher Bibliothekskongress. 84. Bibliothekartag, Dortmund 1994,* ed. H. Lohse. Frankfurt a.M., 1994, 75-83.

Neuvians, K. and Jensen, M. K. "Globalhaushalte für Hochschulen – Ein Vergleich Dänemark/Deutschland." *Wissenschaftsmanagement,* no. 1 (1995): 14-20.

Peisert, H. and Framhein, G. *Das Hochschulsystem in Deutschland.* Bonn, 1994.

Rosigkeit, A. *Reformdefizite der deutschen Hochschule.* Frankfurt a.M., 1993.

Volle, K. "Mehr Autonomie für die Hochschulen." *Wissenschaftsrecht* 28, No. 3 (1995): 187-210.

Zeh, W. *Finanzverfassung und Autonomie der Hochschule.* Berlin, 1973.

Suggested Readings for Chapter 7:

Whom Do German Universities Now Serve?

Boyer, E. L., Altbach, P. G., and Whitelaw, M. J. *The Academic Profession: An International Perspective.* Princeton, NJ, 1994.

Bundesministerium für Bildung, Wissenschaft, Forschung und Technologie. *Grund- und Strukturdaten 1994/1995.* Bonn, 1994.

Enders, J. and Teichler, U. *Berufsbild der Lehrenden und Forschenden. Ergebnisse einer Befragung des wissenschaftlichen Personals an westdeutschen Hochschulen.* Bonn, 1995.

Enders, J. and Teichler, U., eds. *Der Hochschullehrerberuf. Aktuelle Studien und ihre hochschulpolitische Diskussion.* Neuwied, Kriftel, Berlin, 1995.

Hessisches Ministerium für Wissenschaft und Kunst, ed. *Der Hessische Weg. Aktualisierte Materialien zur Studienstrukturreform.* Wiesbaden, 1994.

Hessisches Ministerium für Wissenschaft und Kunst, ed. *Autonomie und Verantwortung – Hochschulreform unter schwierigen Bedingungen.* Frankfurt a.M., New York, 1995.

Lange, J. "Entwicklung und künftige Perspektiven der Hochschulen." *Beiträge zur Hochschulentwicklung,* no. 3 (1994): 335-57.

Teichler, U. "Quality and Quantity of Staff in Higher Education." *Higher Education Policy,* 7 (1994): 19-23.

Suggested Readings for Chapter 8:
The Universities and Contemporary German Political Culture

Negt, O. *Achtundsechzig. Politische Intellektuelle und die Macht.* Göttingen, 1995.

Niedermayer, O., and von Beyme, K., eds. *Politische Kultur in Ost- und Westdeutschland.* Berlin, 1994.

Seibold, C., ed. *Die 68er.* Munich, 1988.

Thielbeer, H. *Universität und Politik in der deutschen Revolution von 1848.* Bonn, 1983.

List of Contributors
and Discussants

Contributors

Mitchell G. Ash is Professor of History at The University of Iowa.

Gunnar Berg, formerly Rector of the Martin Luther University, Halle-Wittenberg, is Professor of Physics at the same institution.

Rüdiger vom Bruch is Professor of History and History of Science at the Humboldt University Berlin.

John Connelly is Assistant Professor of History at the University of California at Berkeley.

Daniel Fallon, formerly Vice President for Academic Affairs and Provost of the University of Maryland, College Park, is Professor of Psychology and Public Policy at the same institution.

Konrad Jarausch is Lurcy Professor of History at the University of North Carolina-Chapel Hill.

Rainer Künzel is President of the University of Osnabrück and Vice President of the German Conference of University Rectors (Hochschulrektorenkonferenz).

Peter Lundgreen is Professor of History and Prorector at the University of Bielefeld.

C. Peter Magrath is President of the National Association of State Universities and Land-Grant Colleges, Washington, D.C.

Evelies Mayer, formerly Minister of Science and Culture, State of Hesse, is a Fellow at the Center for Studies in Higher Education, University of California at Berkeley.

Hans-Joachim Meyer is State Minister for Science and Art, Free State of Saxony.

Steven Muller, President Emeritus, The Johns Hopkins University, is Professor at the School of Advanced International Studies and Co-Chairman of the American Institute for Contemporary German Studies, The Johns Hopkins University.

Discussants

Dr. Clifford Adelman
Senior Research Analyst, United States Department of Education

Mr. Gregory Henschel
Education Research & Improvement, United States Department of Education

Dr. Jackson Janes
Executive Director, American Institute for Contemporary German Studies

Prof. Edward Larkey
Department of German, University of Maryland, Baltimore County

Prof. Kathryn M. Olesko
Department of History and Center for German and European Studies, Georgetown University

Dr. Richard Pettit
Fulbright Scholar Program, Center for International Exchange of Scholars

Prof. Guenter Pfister
Department of Germanic & Slavic Language & Literature, University of Maryland

Prof. Peter E. Quint
University of Maryland School of Law

Prof. Jeremiah Riemer
IRC Coordinator, American Institute of Contemporary German Studies

Mr. Jack Seymour
Director, McCloy Program on European Cooperation, The Atlantic Council of the United States

Mr. Bruce L.R. Smith
Senior Research Staff, The Brookings Institution

Prof. Frank Trommler
Department of German, University of Pennsylvania

Prof. Irmgard Wagner
Department of Foreign Language and Literature, George Mason University

Dr. Erik Willenz
Professor Emeritus

Index and Glossary